The USSR
The Politics of Oligarchy

About the Book and Author

In this text, Dr. Hammer presents an analytical model of the Soviet political system and its process of political decisionmaking, based on the theory of "bureaucratic pluralism." He interprets the Soviet regime as a product of three different influences: the Tsarist tradition of nondemocratic rule, the revolutionary movement that overthrew Tsarism, and the Stalinism of 1924–1953. Since the death of Stalin, the Soviet regime has slowly evolved from a personal dictatorship into an oligarchical system. According to the author, this transformation has permitted the great Soviet bureaucracies, such as the military high command and the economic managers, to increase their power and influence over policymaking and to pursue their own interests in addition to those of the regime. From this perspective, the role of party leaders in the Politburo appears to be that of political brokers among conflicting interests, allocating resources among the various bureaucracies.

This second edition has been completely revised and updated to reflect the realities of the Soviet system through the 27th Party Congress, which met in February 1986. Dr. Hammer applies the model of bureaucratic pluralism in the areas of public policy and economic planning, illustrating the theme that the evolution of a powerful bureaucratic organization has prevented the achievement of the original Leninist vision. He discusses specific features of the Soviet society that deviate from original principles (often based on dissident sources from within the USSR) and examines the role of party leaders in this ideological transition. Finally, he analyzes the rise of Gorbachev to power and the first steps taken under his leadership, such as the anti-alcohol campaign and efforts at economic reform. Because Dr. Hammer's analysis is particularly valuable for understanding the Gorbachev regime and the future of the Soviet system, this text is essential reading for all students of Soviet politics.

Darrell P. Hammer is professor of political science at Indiana University. He was formerly a senior scholar at the Russian Institute of Columbia University and an exchange scholar in the USSR Academy of Sciences.

SECOND EDITION, FULLY REVISED AND UPDATED

The USSR
The Politics of Oligarchy

Darrell P. Hammer

Westview Press / Boulder and London

To Louise, Rebekah, and Owen

Copyright © 1986 by Westview Press, Inc.

Published in 1986 in the United States of America by Westview Press, Inc.; Frederick A. Praeger, Publisher; 5500 Central Avenue, Boulder, Colorado 80301

First published in 1974 by Holt, Rinehart & Winston

Library of Congress Cataloging-in-Publication Data
Hammer, Darrell P.
  The USSR: the politics of oligarchy.
  Includes index.
  1. Soviet Union—Politics and government—1953–
2. Oligarchy. I. Title. II. Title: The U.S.S.R.
JN6511.H24 1986   320.947   85-22645
ISBN 0-8133-0051-7
ISBN 0-8133-0052-5 (pbk.)

Printed and bound in the United States of America

 The paper used in this publication meets the minimum requirements of the American National Standard for Permanence of Paper for Printed Library Materials Z39.48–1984.

10   9   8   7   6   5   4   3   2

Contents

List of Figures and Tables xi
Preface xiii

1 Vision and Reality in Soviet Politics 1

Visionary Marxism and Pragmatic Leninism 2
Authoritarian Politics 6
The Bureaucratic Model 8
References 12

2 Twentieth-Century Russia 13

Russian Empire 13
The Revolution 18
Soviet Russia Under Lenin 20
Soviet Union Under Stalin 26
After Stalin 35
References 36

3 The Collective Society 37

Social Stratification 38
Dimensions of Social Cleavage 39
Sovietization of the Village 46
Political Socialization 48
Citizen, Party, and State 53
References 56

4 Soviet Political Ideology and Doctrine 58

Ideology Versus Doctrine 58
Russian Tradition 60

Russian Socialism... 61
Marxism in Russia 63
Leninism.. 64
Trotskyism 67
Stalinism... 68
Dissidence and Dissent...................................... 69
Soviet Ideology Today....................................... 72
References.. 75

5   The Communist Party 77

Party Composition... 77
CPSU Organization 80
National Party Organization 84
The Apparatus.. 88
Territorial Apparatus 96
Party Officials 98
References... 100

6   The All-Union Government 102

The Supreme Soviet 102
Council of Ministers 110
Party and Bureaucracy 117
References... 119

7   Government and Administration in the Provinces 121

Nationalities Policy 122
Federal System in Practice................................. 125
Regional and Local Government 135
Regional Power Structure................................... 138
Future of Soviet Federalism................................ 139
References... 141

8   From Brezhnev to Gorbachev 143

Succession Process... 144
Rise of Gorbachev 150
Beginning of Transition 152
Andropov and Chernenko 154
Gorbachev as General Secretary............................. 158
References... 162

9 Law Enforcement and Human Rights 163

Security Police... 164
Law and Courts 167
The Procuracy.. 169
The MVD... 171
CPSU and Law Enforcement.......................... 172
Soviet Criminal Law 173
Fight with Corruption................................ 175
Individual Rights 177
References... 180

10 The Industrial and Military Bureaucracies 183

Interest Groups and Bureaucracy 183
Bureaucratic Economy................................ 186
The Military and the Political System 194
The Scientific Establishment 199
References... 202

11 Public Policy and the Welfare State 205

Social Services 207
The Demographic Problem 214
Coping with Alcohol Abuse 216
Managing Soviet Culture 218
References... 223

12 Bureaucratic Pluralism................................ 225

Totalitarianism Versus Pluralism...................... 227
Pluralist Approach 228
Argument Against Pluralism........................... 231
Conflicts of Interest 232
Party and Bureaucracy 233
Policy Process 235
Conclusion 238
References... 238

Afterword 241

Index 249

Figures and Tables

Figures

5.1   CPSU apparatus in a union republic 97
6.1   Dual subordination in the Soviet administrative
      system... 115
11.1 USSR Ministry of Culture.............................. 220

Tables

1.1   Political leaders in the USSR 3
3.1   Evaluation of occupations by Soviet citizens 56
5.1   CPSU under Khrushchev and Brezhnev:
      Social composition....................................... 78
5.2   CPSU under Khrushchev and Brezhnev:
      Nationalities 78
5.3   Education of CPSU members 79
5.4   CPSU members by age group 79
6.1   Foreign affairs committees of the Supreme
      Soviet 106
7.1   Major nationalities: A statistical profile 129
7.2   Nationalities in the union republics 130
7.3   CPSU membership by nationality 132
8.1   Soviet leadership in January 1982........................ 149
8.2   Political standing of Soviet leadership in
      1984 and 1985 158
8.3   Soviet leadership in November 1985 160
10.1 Soviet economic growth................................ 188
11.1 Comparative figures for population growth............... 215
A.1   Soviet leadership in March 1986 246

Preface

This book is a political analysis of the Soviet Union, completely revised and updated from the first edition that appeared in 1974. Although the contemporary situation is emphasized, I have provided background on the Tsarist system, the revolutionary movement, and the Stalinist era, essential to an understanding of the Soviet political system today. Indeed, Stalinism is one of the major issues of contemporary Soviet life, and it cannot be ignored by Western analysts as it has been by Soviet writers. The reader will find the main thesis of this book set out in Chapter 1: Lenin embarked on a visionary program that could not possibly have been carried out; as a realist, he saw the impossibility of the task early in the history of the USSR, and the contradiction between the original vision (in whose name the Communist party still holds power) and the reality of Soviet politics still has not been resolved.

The analysis falls into four parts. Chapters 1 through 4 are an examination of historical, cultural, and social background of the Soviet political system. In Chapters 5 through 7 the Soviet institutions are depicted—the Communist party, the national government, and the regional and republic systems. Chapter 8 discusses the intriguing topic of elite politics—the politics of succession by which Soviet leaders are chosen. The leaders, and General Secretary Mikhail Gorbachev in particular, are not the central figures in this book: The center of the analysis is the historical tradition and the institutional framework that tradition produced. Beginning in Chapter 9, policy issues and the institutions that manage public policy are examined.

I owe thanks to many people who helped in the development of this new edition but most particularly to the hundreds of students at Indiana University, Bloomington, who have patiently shared in my efforts to understand the Soviet political system. My thanks go also to the International Research and Exchanges Board, under whose auspices I spent several months in the Soviet Union getting reacquainted with the country. Although many have contributed to the pages that follow, the responsibility for both the factual material and the interpretation is, of course, mine alone.

In this study reference is made to the constitution of the USSR and to the statute (*ustav*), or rules, of the Communist party. An English translation of the constitution of 1977, along with a detailed commentary, can be found in Robert Sharlet's 1978 book. All citations from the constitution refer to the 1977 document, unless the earlier (1936) constitution is specifically mentioned. All references to the Party Statute are from the version published in 1985 and ratified by the 27th Party Congress in 1986. The constitutions of the fifteen republics that make up the USSR can be found in F.J.M. Feldbrugge's work (1979). For the text of the 1936 constitution, see the translation by H. J. Berman and J. B. Quigley (1969). The latter volume contains a number of other basic documents, including the Party Statute that was replaced in 1986. Biographical information about Soviet leaders given in this book is taken from standard Soviet sources: the directories of Supreme Soviet deputies, and the yearbooks of the Soviet encyclopedia.

In addition to the official Soviet sources used, this study is also based on unofficial sources, usually referred to as *samizdat*. The term is used for various kinds of underground writings circulating in the USSR that have not been published because of lack of clearance by the Soviet censorship agency. The typical samizdat document is typed and retyped by the readers and circulates in the form of smudged carbon copies. Much samizdat literature is written by political dissidents. Some of Aleksandr Solzhenitsyn's writing, for example, originally circulated in samizdat form because the censor would not approve it for publication. However, samizdat also includes documents that do not originate with dissidents. For example, some secret Soviet documents have circulated in this way, and eventually reached the West. One such document, a confidential report on the prospects for Soviet economic reform written by respected economist Tatiana Zaslavskaia, is available in the West even though it has never been published in the USSR. The Zaslavskaia report is discussed in Chapter 10.

Samizdat documents have been systematically collected by the Samizdat Archive in Munich and are regularly published there. The Samizdat Archive assigns a number (AS no.) to each document, and some samizdat material in this book is cited by that number.

Darrell P. Hammer

REFERENCES

Berman, Harold J., and John B. Quigley, trans. and eds. 1969. *Basic Laws on the Structure of the Soviet State*. Cambridge: Harvard University Press.
Draft Party Statutes (with changes). 1985. *Pravda*, Nov. 2. [*Current Digest of the Soviet Press,* Dec. 4, pp. 17–32.]

Feldbrugge, F.J.M. 1979. *The Constitutions of the USSR and the Union Republics: Analysis, Texts, Reports*. Alphen, Netherlands: Sijthoff & Noordhoff.

Resolutions and Decisions of the CPSU. 1977–1982. 5 vols. Toronto: University of Toronto Press.

Sharlet, Robert. 1978. *The New Soviet Constitution of 1977: Analysis and Text*. Brunswick, Ohio: King's Court Press.

1
Vision and Reality in Soviet Politics

In 1920, Vladimir Lenin wrote a brief description of the Soviet political system for the benefit of foreigners. Following Marxist theory, Lenin called the Soviet regime a "dictatorship of the proletariat," that is, a dictatorship of the working class over the rest of society. He pointed out the dual nature of the Soviet system: on the one hand, the system of representative councils (soviets), elected by the working class and the peasants; on the other hand, the Communist party, elected by no one and dominating the soviets.

According to Lenin's description, the dictatorship was exercised by the working class, but the working class, in turn, was led by the party. The party, in its turn, was led by its Central Committee, which in 1920 was a group of only nineteen men. The day-to-day work of the party and the government was carried on by a still smaller group, a five-man political bureau (Politburo) elected by the Central Committee. Legally speaking, power was exercised by the government in the name of the proletariat. However, Lenin said, no important decision was ever made by the government without instructions from the party leadership. Power was exercised on behalf of the people by a party controlled by a group of five men. "This," Lenin concluded, "is a full-fledged 'oligarchy'" (1920: 371). Although he put the word *oligarchy* in quotes, it accurately described the regime he headed.

Oligarchy means rule by the few. The political philosophers of the ancient world classified governments according to the number of people who shared political power. At one extreme was autocracy, a government in which one person ruled as a dictator or a king. At the other extreme was democracy, a government in which the people ruled. A third type of government was an oligarchy. During most of its history, the Soviet political system has been an oligarchy in which political power has been concentrated in the small group of party leaders who sit on the

1

Politburo. In theory, the Politburo is accountable to the Central Committee, but the Central Committee is also a small group; thus even if the true locus of political power were the Central Committee rather than the Politburo, the Soviet system would still be an oligarchy.

During one period in Soviet history the oligarchical structure was replaced by an autocratic structure, and the system was ruled by a dictator, Josif Stalin. Stalin was one of the original oligarchs in Lenin's government. After Lenin's death in 1924, a prolonged struggle for power took place during which Stalin defeated the other leaders of the regime, beginning with Lev Trotskii. Most other opposition leaders were put on public trial, found guilty of political conspiracy, and executed during the great purges (1936–1938). Trotskii was forced to leave the country in 1929, and in 1940 he was murdered. The period of dictatorship, or autocracy, lasted approximately fifteen years, from the period of the purges until Stalin's death in 1953.

The political system then reverted to its earlier oligarchical structure. Within the Politburo in the post-Stalin period, one man has usually been recognized as leader, but there has been no dictator. Lenin had been premier, or head of the government, but since Lenin's death, the dominant political leader has always been the party's head, who usually holds the title of general secretary. Since 1953, the head of the party, like Lenin, has had to share power with the other members of the Politburo. During much of this time, the general secretary has had a state appointment as well—either as head of government (premier) or chief of state (president). But the political authority of the general secretary comes from the position of head of the party (see Table 1.1).

VISIONARY MARXISM AND PRAGMATIC LENINISM

The USSR is called a Communist country, but that designation is somewhat misleading. The only political party in the country is the Communist party, so the USSR might better be called a Communist-ruled country. *Communism* refers to a particular kind of society that will develop some time in the future. The USSR, even according to its own official ideology, is not a Communist country: It is a country that is building toward communism.

Lenin claimed to be a Marxist; yet to develop a consistent theory he had to make some crucial changes in Marxism. As a "master propagandist" (Sowell 1985: 210), Lenin was able to gloss over these changes and to present his own theory as a continuation of Marxism. As a Marxist, Lenin believed that the divisive forces in modern society were the result of economic exploitation. History, in this view, was mainly the history of class struggle—a protracted conflict between the ruling class and

TABLE 1.1
Political Leaders in the USSR

	Party Office	Government Office
V. I. Lenin	---	Premier 1917-1924
J. V. Stalin	General Secretary 1922-1953	Premier 1941-1953
N. S. Khrushchev	First Secretary 1953-1964	Premier 1958-1964
L. I. Brezhnev	First Secretary 1964-1966	
	General Secretary 1966-1982	President 1977-1982
Iu. V. Andropov	General Secretary 1982-1984	President 1983-1984
K. U. Chernenko	General Secretary 1984-1985	President 1984-1985
M. S. Gorbachev	General Secretary 1985-	

those whom the rulers exploit. Marxism taught that after the socialist revolution, exploitation would vanish, and social conflict would disappear. Lenin regarded himself as a political realist and repeatedly denied that he was a utopian thinker. Yet if Lenin was a realist, he was also a visionary: He expected that after the revolution, a new and happier society (Lenin called it a "Communist" society) would eventually emerge. His vision of the future was set down in *State and Revolution* (1918a), though glimpses of the vision also appear in some of his other writings. Lenin's vision must be understood because in his mind it justified the policies that he followed as head of the Soviet government. Lenin acknowledged that the government was a dictatorship in which the Communist party ruled alone, but he also believed that the dictatorship was only temporary: It would eventually fade away, and a happier, more abundant society would emerge.

Like Marx, Lenin believed that the state was a product of the class struggle. By definition, the state is an instrument of repression, which the ruling class uses to maintain itself in power. When exploitation has been abolished, the class struggle will be over, and the state will no longer be needed. All this, however, lay in the future. In the period immediately after the revolution, the proletariat (now the "ruling class," according to Lenin) also needs the state. Under proletarian rule, the nature of society gradually would change.

The change would come in two phases. In the lower phase, which Lenin called socialism (1918a: 297), the state and the bureaucracy that serves it would still exist. The state would still be a dictatorship, but for the first time it would be a dictatorship of the majority. Gradually, the old exploiter class would disappear. All men would go to work, and all would be paid in accordance with their contribution to society. [To ensure this, the socialist government would enforce the principle: "He who does not work, neither shall he eat" (Lenin 1918a: 297). This supposedly socialist principle is from II Thessalonians 3:10.]

In the higher phase of development, repression would no longer be needed. The achievement of socialism will release tremendous productive powers, and the new society will be a society of great affluence. Because there will be plenty for all, a cumbersome bureaucracy will no longer be needed to allocate society's resources. Administration would be simplified and would contain no professional bureaucrats because the management of public affairs could be left in the hands of any literate citizen. The difference between rulers and ruled will disappear, and the new society will be a classless society. Every person will share in the fruits of society, and every able-bodied person, as a matter of conscience, will work to fullest capacity. The capitalist, exploiter society would be replaced by a new, Communist society. Since repression will be unnecessary, the state itself would simply disappear. Or as Lenin himself put it, the state would "wither away."

All this, however, lay in the future. Lenin did not say how long the transition would take. At one point he wrote that a "whole historical period" would separate the eras of capitalism and communism (1918a: 234), but he was never more precise.

Thus the purpose of the Russian revolution was to create a Communist society, a society of abundance, without class conflict and without the instrument of repression called the state. Objective Western observers disagree on how much of Lenin's visionary program has actually been achieved, but even according to Soviet sources, the higher or Communist phase still lies in the future. Bertrand Russell, who visited Soviet Russia only two years after the revolution, concluded that the great experiment had already failed and the vision had been lost. What had emerged from the revolution was not a socialist or Communist society but a regime "painfully like the old government of the Tsar—a system which is Asiatic in its centralized bureaucracy, its secret service, its atmosphere of governmental mystery and submissive terror" (Russell 1949: 119). On the other hand, Russell suggested that perhaps the regime was now motivated by a new and different vision: not the original vision of a Communist society but a vision of a powerful, industrialized state.

In many ways, he said, Russia's Communist leaders could be compared to the rulers of a colony. Like the British rulers of India, for example, the regime stood for "civilization, for education, sanitation, and Western ideas of progress; it is composed in the main of honest and hardworking men, who despise those whom they govern but believe themselves possessed of something valuable which they must communicate to the population, however little it may be desired" (Russell 1949: 119). Russell decided that as an experiment in communism the Soviet system was already a failure. On the other hand, the system might be defended as a method of achieving the rapid industrialization of a backward and underdeveloped country (Russell 1949: 119).

As John Plamenatz has pointed out (1954: 245), Lenin had no practical experience in government when he wrote *State and Revolution*. As he acquired more experience, he became less optimistic. His later writings take on a more practical, less visionary quality. Like all rulers, Lenin came to demand first the acceptance of Soviet authority, which meant acceptance of dictatorship: "It would be extremely stupid and absurdly utopian to assume that the transition from capitalism to Socialism is possible without coercion and without dictatorship" because the country cannot immediately rid itself of the "evil heritage of capitalism" (1918b: 461, 475). He wrote that socialism can only be built with the "human material" left over from capitalism—and that this material is poorly educated and undisciplined and in need of strong leadership (Lenin 1920: 373). On the other hand, Lenin also acknowledged that in the capitalist countries where the socialist revolution had not taken place, the workers were better educated and better disciplined, and the society was more productive (1918a: 468, 470).

Lenin had mixed feelings toward both the people that his government ruled and the capitalist societies that he wanted to replace. Russell was correct when he wrote that Lenin's government despised the people it ruled and yet felt driven to serve them. Throughout Lenin's writings after 1917, this ambivalence is evident: A deep hatred for capitalism is mixed with barely disguised envy for what capitalism has achieved. The greatest task facing the government, Lenin wrote immediately after the revolution, was to raise the productivity of labor—which meant raising the educational and cultural level of the people, lifting it to a level comparable with that in the Western, capitalist societies. Building socialism meant bringing to Russia the "up-to-date achievements of capitalism" (Lenin 1918b: 468, 471).

In Lenin's 1920 treatise he advised the reader not to take the theory too seriously. In fact he explained that his own party was successful because it overcame certain leftist deviations (1920: 356). A strong and disciplined party organization is necessary to ensure that the party can be flexible and can make compromises when necessary and above all to allow the party's leaders to use their knowledge, experience, and political instinct (1920: 394). In this treatise Lenin used an expression often quoted and just as often misunderstood (1920: 397): "Our theory is not a dogma, but a *guide to action*" (emphasis in original). Lenin is telling his followers that Marxism is only a general guide, not a doctrine that should be followed blindly and without thinking.

Lenin's more pragmatic and flexible position was almost certainly the result of three years of practical experience in guiding the Soviet state through an extremely difficult period. His success merely in surviving for three years convinced him of the ultimate rightness of his cause and also that the crucial factor in this success was not Marxist theory but what he called "political instinct." All Lenin's successors have relied on their own instincts. They have quoted Marxist-Leninist theory, when they could, to justify their own actions. They have not allowed the theory to determine their actions. One precept from *State and Revolution*, however, has affected the course of the Soviet government: Lenin's definition of the state as an instrument of repression. All the men who have led the regime since Lenin have shown a strong bias toward the use of force, rather than persuasion or other nonviolent means, to accomplish their program. The regime certainly has relied heavily on persuasion, as can be seen from the massive program of indoctrination and internal propaganda. But the leaders have always seemed to believe that their survival, in the final analysis, depends on repression. This belief can be explained in part by Lenin's teachings from *State and Revolution*.

AUTHORITARIAN POLITICS

In his description of the Soviet oligarchy, Lenin showed how power is exercised in the name of the masses but is actually concentrated at the top. The people delegate power to the government, the government delegates power to the party, and finally the party delegates its authority to the Politburo, so the Politburo rules in the name of the people. This substitution principle is one of the basic operating rules of the Soviet system, and it comes up frequently in this study. A second important principle, made explicit by Lenin (1920), is the guiding role of the party. The Communist party dominates the entire political order. Basic political decisions are made by the party leadership, and no organized opposition to the party is tolerated. The third basic rule is the principle of solidarity, or monolithic unity. This principle has its roots in Lenin's constant insistence on centralism and discipline, but the formulation of the principle of solidarity belongs to Stalin, not to Lenin (Towster 1948: 123, 174). The rule of solidarity gives the Politburo its power: So long as the Politburo presents a monolithic, united front, the Central Committee will follow it without question. No one outside the Central Committee can legitimately challenge the Politburo's authority.

A regime structured in this way is classified as authoritarian by political scientists. An authoritarian regime can be defined as a political system in which no opposition to the government in power is legal or permitted. Although authoritarian regimes exist in several forms, two basic distinctions within the classification should be familiar to anyone studying the Soviet system. The first is the difference between traditional authoritarianism and modern authoritarianism. Traditional authoritarianism has been the dominant type of political order throughout history: Most of the governments that existed before the end of the nineteenth century belong to this category. Modern authoritarianism is a phenomenon of the twentieth century. The two types are distinguished in that a modern authoritarian system claims to be democratic: It claims to rule in the people's best interest and to have their support. Indeed a modern authoritarian regime may have widespread popular support, although the extent of this support cannot be tested because of the nature of the authoritarian system. Traditional authoritarianism is the rule of the few in the name of the few; "modern authoritarianism is the rule of the few in the name of the many" (Perlmutter 1981: 2). Modern authoritarianism is characterized by extensive efforts to influence public opinion, to generate mass support, and often to mobilize the population in pursuit of the regime's goals. Modern authoritarian regimes are most typically oligarchic (Perlmutter 1981: 7) and are dominated by an oligarchic political elite. Autocracy within modern authoritarian regimes is rare. The outstanding examples are the USSR under Stalin and Nazi Germany under Hitler (1933–1945).

The second distinction is between authoritarian and totalitarian systems. Political scientists do not wholly agree on what this second term means, so the precise difference between the two types cannot be set down. Generally speaking, totalitarianism is an extreme form of authoritarianism. For some Western writers, the essence of totalitarianism is the deliberate use of terror to control the population. For others, the essential feature of totalitarianism is ideology: A totalitarian regime is motivated by a doctrine (ideology) directed toward the total transformation of society. The USSR under Stalin and Nazi Germany under Hitler (1933–1945) are classic examples of totalitarian systems.

Indeed some Western scholars define totalitarianism as a form of autocracy, so that totalitarianism cannot exist without a dictator. J. J.

Linz (1975), however, accepted the position that a totalitarian regime can be oligarchic in its structure. This example points up the difficulty that Western scholars have met in attempting to formulate a simple definition of the term.

Perhaps the best approach is to treat totalitarianism as an aspiration rather than a reality. W. S. Allen has suggested that totalitarian regimes are really distinguished by their claim to exercise total control over society. On close inspection the claim always turns out to be fraudulent. The Nazi regime, for example, set out to attain total control over Germany, but the effort failed (Allen 1981: 102, 106). Some evidence, presented later in this study, indicates that the Soviet regime too does not enjoy total control over Soviet society.

In addition to these three principles—the substitution principle, the guiding role of the party, and the rule of solidarity—the Soviet system is characterized by state socialism. This term means that economic and political decisionmaking are not clearly separated. Later in the discussion of the structure of the government, some offices will be encountered that have no counterparts outside the Soviet sphere: minister of precision instrument manufacture, for example. In the Soviet definition, socialism means not only that the economy is owned by the state but that the economy is planned by the government. Economic planning, in Soviet practice, means that the government sets production goals for each enterprise in the country.

One consequence of this system, which is rarely noticed by Western observers, is that the methods developed to manage the economy spill over into other sectors of Soviet society. Soviet writers frequently contrast the rational planning system of their country with the supposedly anarchic order of Western, nonsocialist countries. In the USSR, planning is supposed to make the most efficient use of the resources of society, and it is not limited to industry. Planning covers almost everything from the output of social services to the production of the movie studios and the training of students in the universities: In theory, all is rationally planned by the government. This phenomenon can be called the cult of planning; it is an important characteristic of the Soviet authoritarian system.

THE BUREAUCRATIC MODEL

Soviet politics is bureaucratic politics. This basic fact has two important consequences for the student of Soviet society. First, political decisions are made in closed rooms by people acting on bureaucratic advice, and much of the discussion and conflict around these decisions does not become public. Not everything is done in secret: Soviet policy issues do sometimes become a subject of open discussion, although the discussion is muted by the nature of the system. Often the discussion of serious policy issues is confined to the scholarly journals and does not reach the mass media. For example, possible reform in the management of the Soviet economy has been discussed extensively. The Soviet economists have enjoyed considerable freedom to develop and discuss various proposals (although most of their ideas have been rejected by the political leadership). However, the forum for this discussion has been limited: the economic journals, newspapers published for industrial managers, and closed meetings of professional economists. The general public has not participated, and none of this discussion has been aired in television programs or mass-circulation magazines.

Second, an understanding of the bureaucracy is essential to an understanding of the political process in the USSR because the bureaucracy, not elected bodies like the USSR Supreme Soviet, is influential. When a bill is introduced in the Supreme Soviet it is the end, not the beginning, of the legislative process.

"Bureaucracy" is a value-laden word. However, for social scientists it is also a technical term: A bureaucracy is an organization that has certain characteristics, and a bureaucrat is an official who serves in a bureaucracy. Anthony Downs (1967: 24–25) has developed a model that describes bureaucracy in terms of four characteristics.

1. *A bureaucracy is a large organization.* Of course, "large" is a relative word. A bureaucracy is too large for every member to know personally every other member. Although personal relationships are important in bureaucratic behavior, because a bureaucracy is a large and impersonal organization, the relationships among its members must be somewhat formal and impersonal.

2. *The members of the bureaucracy are fulltime employees who depend on the organization for their livelihood.* As a consequence, bureaucrats owe a basic loyalty to the bureaucracy that they serve, and they are likely to see the preservation of the bureaucracy as the highest social good.

3. *In hiring personnel and promoting people within the organization, the bureaucracy's decisions are based on how well people perform their organizational roles.* As a result, ascriptive characteristics (race, religion, or social class) are not the primary determinants of membership in the organization. At least to some extent, success in the organization depends on doing the job well, and promotion is based on merit.

4. *The product of the bureaucracy is not evaluated in an external market.* This part of the definition is the most important and least understood. The typical bureaucracy provides goods and services to a group of

people who can be called its clients. The clients do not pay for the benefits they receive—at least not directly. For example, every property owner pays taxes and therefore pays for the services of the public schools, even when the property owner has no children in school. As a result, the demand for the bureaucracy's services cannot be measured, and no simple way exists to evaluate the bureaucracy's performance.

In modern societies many organizations are branded as bureaucratic. Two common types of organizations have certain bureaucratic characteristics but by this definition are not true bureaucracies. The first type is the business firm operating in a free-enterprise economy. What the firm produces is distributed in an external market, and in the long run the success or failure of the firm depends on the demand for its product. The firm's output is evaluated every time a consumer decides to buy or not to buy the product. Bureaucracies are not dependent in the same way on consumer demand for two reasons: (1) Usually what a bureaucracy produces is given away without charge, and (2) the cost of operating the bureaucracy is paid by the government, not by those who benefit directly from its services.

The second type of organization is the political party operating in a competitive electoral system. In a sense, a party resembles a business: It produces output in the form of programs and policies, which it then tries to "sell" to the electorate. The party's success or failure depends on how the voter evaluates its program. In the same way that the business firm ultimately is dependent on the consumer, the fate of the competitive political party depends on voter acceptance. The USSR is a one-party, socialist state: It lacks both competitive elections and the free-enterprise economy. This fact accounts for the extensive bureaucratization of Soviet society. Most of the social decisions that in Western countries are made either by the marketplace or by the electoral process are made by bureaucratic organizations.

Two problems confront anyone who tries to direct a bureaucracy: the flow of information and the evaluation of performance. Every bureaucrat is required to provide information to superiors, and that information may be used in turn to judge the bureaucrat's work. Consequently, the temptation is to exaggerate successes and minimize failures. This situation can be called "information distortion" (Downs 1967: 116), and it is subject to a multiplier effect. In the typical bureaucracy, information passes through several layers of organization. At each level, information may be studied and evaluated, digested and summarized—and lost. Thus the director of a bureaucratic system may be deprived of essential information.

A similar process applies to information moving from the top down-ward. The orders that the director gives may be revised, interpreted, or even lost as they pass through the bureaucracy. Downs called this process "authority leakage" (1967: 134). In any modern society, government must cope with the problem of information and authority leakage within the bureaucracy. Although one might expect that authority leakage would not be a serious problem in an authoritarian system where power is concentrated at the top, it is endemic to the Soviet system.

The problem of evaluating performance is not only to obtain reliable information but to determine the criteria on which the evaluation is based. Although not limited to the economic sphere, the problem is easiest to describe in an economic context. In the Western, free-enterprise economy, a business seeks to make a profit; profit provides not only a motive for the managers of a business but much more. Profit serves as a standard for judging the firm's success. In the bureaucratic economy, the criteria of economic success are not so well defined. Generally speaking, Soviet businesses are supposed to produce as much as they can—but this criterion leads to other problems (see Chapter 10). In fact the directors of this system—the members of the Politburo—do not have a clear standard for measuring economic results.

The lack of clear standards is not limited to the economy. Consider, as one example, the output of the Soviet movie studios. If the movie studio is not in business to make a profit, then what is it supposed to do, and how will its output be judged? Clearly, the judgment will not be left to the moviegoer. I once had a conversation with a high official of the Soviet film industry, who was trying to describe the complex, bureaucratic process by which the industry decides what films to produce, when to release them, and how long they should run in the theaters. His main point was that each of these is carefully planned. I asked him why the studios were not given freedom to produce what they wished, with the audience deciding how long a film should run. The official looked at me with a shocked expression and responded: "We cannot leave the Soviet cinema at the mercy of the marketplace!" This attitude goes far beyond the film industry and explains the cult of planning among Soviet officialdom.

Authority leakage also explains the common bureaucratic phenomenon of goal displacement. In theory a bureaucracy is an administrative organization responsible to the government, which provides the resources and determines the goals of the organization. But as B. G. Peters has pointed out, in all bureaucratic organizations the goals tend to shift from the objectives set by the government to goals more aligned with the bureaucracy's own interests. Bureaucracies become less interested in the policies of the government and more interested in other goals:

building up the organization (empire building) and making the organization secure. The major goals of the typical bureaucracy become (in
order of priority): protecting the organization itself, expanding the
organization's role and usually expanding its budget, and carrying out
the policies of the government that the bureaucracy serves (Peters 1984:
132).

This view of bureaucracy is based on the Western experience, which
has been extensively analyzed by specialists in the field of bureaucratic
behavior. Certainly important differences exist between Western bureaucracies and bureaucracies in the USSR. However, there is no reason
to assume that the Soviet bureaucrat is immune to the temptations to
which Western bureaucrats have succumbed. In the following chapters,
considerable evidence is presented that indicates that Soviet bureaucratic
behavior in some important ways resembles its counterpart in the Western
world.

REFERENCES

Allen, William S. 1981. Totalitarianism: The Concept and the Reality. In *Totalitarianism Reconsidered*, edited by Ernest A. Menzes. Port Washington, N.Y.:
Kennikat Press, pp. 97–106.

Downs, Anthony. 1967. *Inside Bureaucracy.* Boston: Little, Brown.

Lenin, V. I. 1918a. *State and Revolution.* In *Selected Works*, vol. 2, pt. 1. Moscow:
Foreign Languages Publishing House, 1952, pp. 199–325.

———. 1918b. *The Immediate Tasks of the Soviet Government.* In *Selected Works*,
vol. 2, pt. 1, pp. 448–491.

———. 1920. *"Left-Wing" Communism, an Infantile Disorder.* In *Selected Works*,
vol. 2, pt. 2, pp. 341–434.

Linz, Juan J. 1975. Totalitarian and Authoritarian Regimes. In *Handbook of Political
Science*, edited by Fred I. Greenstein and Nelson W. Polsby. Vol. 3, *Macro-
political Theory.* Reading, Mass.: Addison-Wesley, pp. 175–411.

Perlmutter, Amos. 1981. *Modern Authoritarianism: A Comparative Institutional
Analysis.* New Haven, Conn.: Yale University Press.

Peters, B. Guy. 1984. *The Politics of Bureaucracy: A Comparative Perspective.* 2d
ed. New York and London: Longman.

Plamenatz, John. 1954. *German Marxism and Russian Communism.* London:
Longmans, Green.

Russell, Bertrand. 1949. *The Practice and Theory of Bolshevism.* 2d ed. London:
Allen & Unwin.

Sowell, Thomas. 1985. *Marxism: Philosophy and Economics.* New York: William
Morrow.

Towster, Julian. 1948. *Political Power in the U.S.S.R. 1917–1947.* New York: Oxford
University Press.

2
Twentieth-Century Russia

The Russian Empire was a feeble giant. In both territory and population, Russia was the largest of the European powers, but its tremendous size concealed fundamental weaknesses in its social structure, economic system, and political order. In 1917, these weaknesses brought about the collapse of the empire and led to the emergence of a new political order dedicated to making Russia strong.

RUSSIAN EMPIRE

The Russian Empire grew out of a weak Eastern European principality, the Grand Duchy of Moscow. Because Muscovy was geographically isolated, it was not greatly influenced by the movements so important in the development of European civilization—the Renaissance and the Reformation and the scientific and industrial revolutions. But by the seventeenth century, Muscovy had expanded until it confronted greater powers, such as Sweden, Poland, and the Ottoman Empire, which together formed a barrier between Europe and Russia.

In 1682, the throne passed to a young prince, Peter Alekseevich Romanov, who transformed Muscovite Russia into a monarchy of the Western type, and earned the title of Peter the Great. Peter formed the country's first standing army and first naval force. To support this new military establishment, he built factories, organized schools, and created a permanent state bureaucracy. To symbolize these changes, the capital was moved from Moscow to a new city on the coast. In the new capital at St. Petersburg, Peter took the title of Emperor instead of the traditional title, Tsar. When Peter died in 1725, the new empire was one of the European powers.

Westernization

Serious structural flaws were present in Peter's empire. Many of his reforms were superficial, even amusing, such as the law that men living in the new capital had to shave their beards and wear Western-style clothes. The schools were intended for a tiny minority from the nobility, who were to be trained as army officers or bureaucrats. The peasants, who made up the great mass of the emperor's subjects, did not benefit from the reform (they were excused from shaving their beards), and life in the villages went on much as it had before.

Peter's reforms led to a deep schism between the people and the Establishment, between the old Russia of the villages and the official Russia of the cities. It was a deep cultural division between the educated, Europeanized upper classes and the illiterate peasant masses who still lived by traditional Russian values. Nonetheless, we can judge the achievements of Peter and his successors by a simple fact of history. By the end of the eighteenth century, Sweden and Turkey were second-rate states, and Poland, Russia's traditional enemy, had disappeared from the map.

The Russian Empire claimed not only to be a European power, but also to be a part of European civilization. Neither of these claims can be denied. St. Petersburg was deliberately designed as a European city, and the poet Aleksandr Pushkin called the capital a "window onto Europe."

Russia did not simply borrow Europe's ideas and copy Europe's tastes. In the nineteenth century, the Russians themselves made great contributions to world literature and world science. Yet the deep European connection in Russian culture did not spread to the political order. One of the ironies of history is that even though Russia was opened to European influence by a political decision of its rulers, the political system itself was very resistant to change.

Peter's success in transforming Russia into a modern state prepared the way for further confrontations with the great powers for which the country was unprepared. The century before the revolution saw the Crimean War of 1853–1856, the Russo-Japanese War of 1904–1905, and finally the catastrophic war with Germany in 1914. Each of these wars had disastrous results, and each led to new efforts to reform the state from within. The reforms were too little and too late. In political and social structure, the Russian Empire never quite managed to catch up with the West. It had a traditional society, rigidly divided into classes, with the Tsar holding on to his powers and the nobles jealously guarding their rights.

At the beginning of the twentieth century, the economy was predominantly agricultural and the majority of Russians were peasants, but a new transformation was about to convulse the country. The industrial and technological revolution had now begun. From the 1890s, Russian industry developed at a rapid rate: New factories were built, new railroad lines were laid, new mines were opened.

In Soviet history books, the prerevolutionary period is called capitalistic, but capitalism, in the sense of a free-enterprise economy, never really took root in Russia. The great spurt after 1890 was not a product of the entrepreneurial spirit but of the policies of the imperial government. As a result the Russian economy, though growing at a fast pace, had a different structure from that of Western (capitalist) economies. Much of the capital to finance economic growth came either from the government or from foreign investors. Although Russia was acquiring a modern economy, it lacked some of the most familiar components of capitalism, such as a streamlined credit system or a class of capitalist entrepreneurs. The people who ran the economy, if not actually employees of the government, often looked on themselves as servants of the state rather than businessmen.

Put to the test of war against a modern industrialized power, both the economy and the political order proved to be inadequate. At the beginning of World War I, a wave of patriotic sentiment developed, but disillusionment soon followed. Russia's defeat in World War I was partly the result of economic weakness, but it was also a failure of political will and a lack of administrative know-how.

The Tsarist Political System

The Russian Empire was the only European state that officially proclaimed itself to be an autocracy. Under Tsarist rule, the Russian government was a typical example of traditional authoritarianism. In theory, all legal power was vested in the person of the Tsar. The ministers of the government were his personal appointees, and until 1905 there was no premier who could coordinate policymaking. The laws of the empire were the Tsar's edicts. Since no legislature was elected, there was assumed to be no need for political parties. Before 1905, all political groupings that might voice opposition to the government were outlawed.

However, the form of autocracy should not be confused with the reality of dictatorial power. Tsarism fell not because it was too despotic but because it was too weak to accomplish social change. Although the Tsar's will could not be questioned, his government was concerned mainly with matters of high policy: diplomacy, the army, and finance. The Tsar himself lived remote from the people, in the Winter Palace at St. Petersburg or in other palaces maintained for his use. The distance that separated them was measured in the words of the peasant who said: "Heaven is high above, the Tsar is far away." Generally, the peasant's only contact with the government was through two officials: the army recruiter and the tax collector.

The word "intelligentsia" was coined in Russia, where to be an intellectual meant to be an enemy of the system. Even people with moderate political views came to believe that Russia had to either completely change its system of rule or undergo a revolution. One of these moderate liberals was the political philosopher Boris Chicherin (1828–1904). In an anonymous pamphlet, *Russia on the Eve of the Twentieth Century* (1900), Chicherin called on the Tsar to abandon autocracy and to summon an elected assembly that would write a constitution and establish a system of responsible government. Chicherin's warning, like that of other liberals, was ignored.

The appeal for liberalization of the political system was opposed from two sides, the Left and the Right. The rightists, who defended the traditional institution of autocracy, argued that parliamentary government was a European system that Russia could not accept. K. P. Pobedonostsev, an apologist for the autocracy, insisted that parliamentary government was "the great falsehood of our time" (1965: 32). Some defenders of the established political order argued that a parliamentary government might work in a small country like England or France but Russia was too vast, its society too primitive, and its people too ignorant to understand any system but Tsarism.

Most of the revolutionaries would have agreed that parliamentary government was a great falsehood. To them constitutional government was a system devised by decadent bourgeois democracies to preserve capitalism. If Russia had a liberal constitution and responsible government, that would only mean that Russia had become capitalistic.

The autocracy was a weak system of government. The prohibition of all political organizations (until 1905) was certainly an indication of weakness rather than strength. Until 1905, all publications were subject to governmental censorship, which only encouraged underground organizations and an illegal press. The Tsarist censorship was primarily political: Literature and science were generally free of government control, but criticism of the Tsar or the government was not permitted.

Denied any legitimate form of expression, the opposition to Tsarist rule took an illegal and sometimes violent form. Although the revolutionary movement had no organized leadership, the radicals generally went under the name of the social revolutionary party. In March 1881, a group of revolutionary terrorists succeeded in assassinating Emperor Alexander II (reigned 1856–1881). The response of his son Alexander III (reigned 1881–1894) was a regime of suppression, and the assassins were executed. In 1905, in the wake of defeat in the Far East a revolution erupted against the autocracy, and Tsar Nicholas II gave some ground.

The censorship was ended, as was the formal ban on political parties. An elected national assembly, the Duma, was created. Even with these reforms, the Russian political system remained essentially autocratic: The Duma had limited powers, and the ministers were still responsible to the Tsar, not to the Duma.

Tsarism was finally overthrown not by revolution but by war. The disruption of services and the bureaucratic mismanagement of the wartime economy caused severe hardship. After three years of war a serious shortage of food had developed, and the revolution actually began, in March 1917, with bread riots in Petrograd (as St. Petersburg was called after the war began). When the disorders started, the Tsar was at army headquarters and his ministers were unable to deal with the crisis (Katkov 1967: 282–284). Nicholas tried to return to Petrograd to take command of the situation, but the imperial train was diverted by hostile railroad workers. The monarchy and the bureaucracy that served it disintegrated. Nicholas gave up the throne while stranded at a railroad siding between his headquarters and his capital. Russia fell into political chaos, which ended eight months later when the Communists seized power.

The Bolsheviks

A Marxist party of sorts had existed in Russia since 1898, when a small group organized the Russian Social Democratic Labor party (RSDLP), and some Russian radicals had embraced Marxism even earlier. The Social Democrats were destined to remain a minority among the Russian revolutionaries. The mainstream of revolutionary thought and action was represented by the Social Revolutionary party (SR), which inherited the spirit of the nineteenth-century revolutionary movement. The Social Revolutionaries (SRs) had a considerable following in the villages, and in the free elections of 1917, they outpolled the Social Democrats. Unlike the Social Democrats, the SRs expected the coming Russian revolution to be a spontaneous national uprising unconnected with any European movement. Although they were both revolutionary parties, the SRs and the Social Democratic party disagreed fundamentally on both the tactics of the revolution and the course to be followed after. The two parties were not able to cooperate before 1917, and there was little hope that they would work together in a postrevolutionary government.

Just as the whole revolutionary movement was split among the Marxists, the SRs, and other groups like the anarchists, the Social Democrats themselves were badly divided and eventually broke into two parties. In 1903, the RSDLP held its second congress to set up a formal organization; far from uniting the party, the congress only resulted in a permanent schism. The delegates to the congress were divided over various issues, but the crucial question was party leadership. Those in the majority at the end of the congress accepted the leadership of Lenin. From the Russian word for majority (*bolshinstvo*), his followers took the name Bolshevik. The minority, who were opposed to Lenin's leadership, were derisively called the minority (Mensheviks). By accepting Lenin's leadership, the Bolsheviks took a new departure in the Russian revolutionary movement: They rejected the established leaders of the party, such as Georgii V. Plekhanov (1856–1918), the founding father of the party and the only Russian Marxist at that time with an international reputation.

The key to the Bolsheviks' eventual success was their belief in highly disciplined organization. Lenin envisaged the party as a small and tightly knit group of professional revolutionaries who would sacrifice everything to the aim of revolution (Lukacs 1971: 25). Although the party was supposed to be the vanguard of the working class, most Bolshevik leaders were intellectuals who had never worked in a factory. As a party, they were held together by their fanatical loyalty to Lenin and his vision of the revolutionary future. Anyone who joined the Bolsheviks was expected to accept the authority of their leadership, which in turn accepted the authority of Lenin. In 1917 the Bolsheviks had a great advantage in organization. When compared with the other revolutionary parties, the Bolsheviks appeared not only to be well organized but also to be united around a coherent program and a dynamic leader. In a country with a tradition of autocratic rule, this was a good image to have.

THE REVOLUTION

The revolution of 1905 seemed to be a dress rehearsal for the great upheaval of 1917. In the latter year, the government was again demoralized by military defeat and showed no great determination in the face of a popular uprising. However, two important differences should be pointed out. First, in 1905 the army remained loyal and put down the uprisings in the cities; in 1917, however, the trained garrison of the capital had been sent to the front, and the poorly trained troops that remained behind went over to the side of the revolutionaries. The Tsar had to abdicate because he could not control his capital.

Second, in 1905 the revolution seemed to be groping for organized leadership, which it found only at year's end when the rebellion had run its course. At that time, the revolutionaries in St. Petersburg tried to organize a general strike and created a coordinating committee called the St. Petersburg Council of Workers' Deputies. In Russian, the word for council is *soviet*: The Russian revolution had found its characteristic institution. Although the soviet came into existence too late to play a decisive role, the vice-president of the St. Petersburg soviet, a flamboyant youth named Lev Trotskii, acquired considerable notoriety until he was arrested. In 1917, a new Petrograd soviet was summoned almost at the first moment of revolution. Similar soviets sprang up in other cities and villages. In July, the leaders of the soviet were able to call an all-Russian Congress of Soviets in the capital.

The Soviets

The soviets were not Bolshevik organizations. The St. Petersburg soviet of 1905 was dominated by the Mensheviks (Trotskii did not join the Bolsheviks until 1917). The soviets of 1917 had representatives from several revolutionary parties, and the Bolsheviks were in a minority. In the all-Russian Congress of Soviets, the largest party was that of the Social Revolutionaries (Schapiro 1960: 164). In the revolutionary situation of 1917, political power was not measured by votes, and the soviets were not parliamentary bodies. They were revolutionary assemblies that claimed to represent the people in revolt, but the deputies to the soviet were often confused and unsure of their aims. In these circumstances, the Bolsheviks were easily able to take the lead.

The Provisional Government

After Nicholas II abdicated, the legal authority in Russia was a provisional government, headed first by the liberal Prince Georgii Lvov and later by the moderate socialist Aleksandr Kerenskii. The provisional government could hardly be called democratic, although its leaders proclaimed that eventually a liberal and constitutional government would be formed in Russia (Katkov 1967: 410). This aim was precisely the bourgeois democracy that the Bolsheviks despised. The country was still at war with Germany, and the provisional government put off the question of a constitution to a later, calmer time. The government did summon a constituent assembly, which was duly elected with an SR majority. But the Bolsheviks (who were by then in power) broke up the assembly with force.

In retrospect, it is easy to see that the provisional government made a crucial blunder when it decided to continue with the war. The war created the conditions that led to the collapse of the old autocratic regime, and the abdication of the Tsar had not really solved the underlying problems.

The leaders of the soviet opposed the war, but they also opposed Lenin, who seemed to be advocating unilateral surrender. The soviet did not fully accept the authority of the provisional government, but, on the other hand, it did not seek to overthrow it. In fact, the soviet resolved to obey the government only insofar as the policy of the government was consistent with the aims of the soviet. Thus came the dual power of 1917—a weak, unstable government confronted with a revolutionary assembly that claimed to speak for the masses but that was not yet ready to take power in its own name.

This was the uncertain situation that Lenin found on his dramatic return to Russia in April 1917. In a brief statement (the April Theses), Lenin laid down his own program, including two major demands: (1) The war must end, and (2) the soviet should seize power. For three months, Lenin and the other Bolshevik leaders pursued these aims openly—an end to the war, a soviet republic, and eventually a socialist state. In July 1917, violent demonstrations erupted in Petrograd under the slogan "All Power to the Soviets!" The demonstrations failed in their purpose, and Lenin was forced to go underground until November, when he emerged as the premier of the Soviet Republic.

The October Coup

In his theoretical model of the revolutionary process, Crane Brinton (1952: 153) argued that the typical revolution involves a struggle between moderates and extremists, and the extremists will win and drive the moderates from power. That was the pattern in 1917, as the Russian revolution drifted from the moderates who created the provisional government to the Bolsheviks who seized power in October.

In autumn 1917, the Bolsheviks were, for the first time, winning majority support in some of the soviets, including the crucial soviet of Petrograd. The second all-Russian Congress of Soviets was to meet in November, and although the Bolsheviks did not have a majority there, they were the largest single party. Lenin and Trotskii (who had by now become the Bolsheviks' chief tactician) resolved on a coup d'etat to coincide with the meeting of the Congress of Soviets. Under Bolshevik command, armed workers seized strategic points in the capital (the central telegraph office, for example) early on the morning of November 7. The members of the provisional government were arrested, although Kerenskii managed to slip away. The all-Russian Congress accepted the seizure of power and voted to approve the new "Soviet government," with Lenin at its head.

SOVIET RUSSIA UNDER LENIN

Many Russians and Western observers believed that the Bolsheviks were anarchists who would destroy all organized authority and drive the country further into chaos. Since the popular mood in 1917 was one of simple opposition to all established authority, the Bolsheviks did not discourage this impression. For tactical reasons, Lenin embraced some of the anarchists' demands, but he did not embrace their philosophy. The goal of the Bolshevik movement was not to destroy authority but to take power and use it to accomplish a socialist revolution (Lenin 1918: 317).

The dictatorship of the proletariat soon became a dictatorship of the Bolshevik party. The regime adopted some revolutionary imagery to conceal this fact. Spurning the title of ministers, which was associated with both Tsarism and the provisional government, the members of Lenin's government were called people's commissars. The government itself was called the Council of People's Commissars (Sovnarkom). When a new army was organized in 1918, it became the Workers' and Peasants' Red Army. The party itself changed its name to the Communist party to distinguish it from the Social Democrats of Western Europe, who were generally opposed to Lenin's regime.

Despite the revolutionary style, many of the practical measures of the new Soviet government looked like the familiar process of modernization and secularization, and not socialism. The leaders of the great French revolution had thrown out the old calendar and introduced a radical new one beginning with the year I. The Soviet leaders, on the other hand, were content to abandon the archaic Russian calendar and to adopt the calendar used in Western countries. The Bolsheviks quite literally brought Russia up to date. In other ways, too, Russia was now brought into step with Western societies. In a sense, Lenin's revolution was a culmination of the reforms of Peter the Great. The church was separated from the state; divorce and civil marriage were made legal; and the education of children was made the responsibility of the civil authority. All formal distinctions of class and status, which had been preserved under Tsarist law, were abolished.

The program of the new government was well calculated to appeal to the masses. Lenin did not concern himself with the constitutional structure of the state. He simply assumed that the Congress of Soviets represented the will of the masses, and that was all the legitimacy he needed. Nor did Lenin come forward at this point with a comprehensive program for the socialization of Russia. His program was more specific and had two key planks: (1) an end to the war and (2) a redistribution of the land.

When the Soviet demand for a general cease-fire was ignored, Lenin entered into direct negotiations with the Germans. The war finally ended on the eastern front with the treaty of Brest-Litovsk in March 1918. Russia paid a high price for peace because it had to give up a large amount of territory, including some major industrial areas. The Bolsheviks could have been (and were) accused of betraying Russia. But within a year, Lenin's policy proved to be brilliantly successful. The Germans themselves were defeated by the Western Allies, and the Soviet government was able to repudiate the treaty. In the meantime, Lenin gained valuable time—a breathing space—in which to consolidate his position.

The Civil War

The consolidation of power took more than three years. Some of the former Tsarist generals organized anti-Bolshevik troops and began a civil war around the periphery of central Russia, which remained under Bolshevik control. Some moderate political leaders who had supported the provisional government joined the anti-Bolshevik forces. A threat also arose from the Left: Some of the Mensheviks and SRs looked on the Bolshevik government as counterrevolutionary and hoped to replace it with a genuinely revolutionary government.

The anti-Bolshevik or White forces were given support by the Western Allies, who sent their own troops into Russian territory. The official justification for this Allied intervention in the Russian civil war was to help in the war against Germany: If the Soviet regime could be overthrown, perhaps the government that succeeded it would renew the fighting on the eastern front and take some of the pressure off the Allied forces in France. However, the intervention continued after the armistice was signed because the overthrow of the Bolsheviks had become an end in itself.

Why did the Bolsheviks, who had come to power in a country torn apart by revolution and war, win the civil war? Part of the answer lies in the weakness and confusion of the Whites, who were never able to organize a united coalition. The Whites included monarchists who hoped for a restoration, outright reactionaries who would have been content with a military dictatorship, liberals, and some socialists. Geography was also on the Bolsheviks' side. The White forces occupied the rimland of the former empire. The new Red Army had the advantage of occupying the interior lines.

In addition, the Allied intervention, although not strong enough to be a decisive factor in the military struggle, tipped the balance against the Whites on the political front. The Whites were made to look like foreign agents, whereas the Bolsheviks could claim to be defending the Russian homeland. General Aleksei Brusilov, who had commanded the Tsar's armies against the Germans, issued a plea to other officers of the old army to support the government, not in defense of Bolshevism, but in defense of Russia.

It would be a serious error, however, to attribute the Bolsheviks' victory to their enemies' mistakes. The Bolsheviks had the will to win, and their leaders threw themselves into the struggle with tremendous energy. Trotskii, as commissar for war, found a natural outlet for his great gifts of revolutionary leadership. Within a few months, he managed to organize a new Red Army of half a million men, many of them veterans of the war against Germany who now committed themselves to a new cause. Although when compared with the Tsarist army this force was not large, the Red Army was adequate for waging a civil war largely fought in small skirmishes. Thus, a country accustomed to vacillation in policy and inefficiency in administration found itself under the rule of people who seemed to know what they wanted and how to get it.

At the beginning of the revolution, the Soviet government passed a decree on land, which had little effect except to legalize what the peasants were doing on their own—seizing the land from the landowners. This forcible redistribution of the land did not, of course, solve the economic problem of feeding the cities. Since the normal system of supply had completely broken down, the government relied on requisition by force. Armed detachments, usually led by party members, roamed the countryside and forced the peasants to turn over their produce for distribution in the cities. The result, as could have easily been foreseen, was that the peasants lost the incentive to produce. Enough food was found to keep the workers from starving, but overall food production fell sharply.

In the industrial sector of the economy, too, the Bolsheviks were to some extent swept along by events. Many industrial enterprises were taken over by the workers in the name of workers' control, which sounded more like anarchism than Lenin's socialism. The Bolsheviks' program called for national economic planning and for centralized control over industry, but early efforts in this direction ended in failure. Industrial production by 1921 has been estimated at about 15 percent of the prewar level.

Throughout the civil war, some opposition existed within the Communist party to the policies of the leadership. The so-called left Communists opposed the treaty of Brest-Litovsk and tried to prevent its ratification. A somewhat more dangerous group from Lenin's viewpoint was the Workers' Opposition, which included many trade union leaders. The Workers' Opposition demanded, among other things, that the unions should enjoy a direct voice in the management of industry. Although this was not the same thing as workers' control, the demands of the Workers' Opposition still ran counter to Lenin's own plans for the management of industry. Moreover, the very name Workers' Opposition cast some doubt on the claim that the government already belonged to the workers and peasants of Russia. Until 1921, however, none of these groups presented any threat to Lenin's leadership within the party. The threat to Soviet rule from outside the party helped to unite all dissident groups within it.

The New Economic Policy

By 1921 the outside threat had disappeared. The civil war had ended in military victory for the Red Army, but it had also led to economic disaster. Fields lay untended, and industry was in shambles. As the White armies were defeated one by one and the Allied forces were withdrawn from Russian territory, it became obvious that a change of course was needed. Lenin's government now introduced a new economic policy (NEP) to restore order and to reconstruct the economy. The essence of NEP was a partial restoration of capitalism, though under strict government control. As Lenin frankly admitted, it was a retreat. The government began by making broad concessions to the peasants. Food was not to be forcibly requisitioned; instead, the peasants were to turn over part of their produce as a tax to the government and could sell the rest on a free market. The peasants thus were encouraged to produce as much as they could.

This move was followed by a partial return to private enterprise in light industry and trade, and the currency was stabilized to make this possible. Heavy industry, which Lenin called the "commanding heights" of the economy, remained in the hands of the government. The last vestiges of workers' control disappeared, and each state-owned enterprise was put under the control of a manager appointed by the government. The enterprise was to operate on commercial principles and to show a profit. This system was hardly free enterprise, but it was still not socialism. Lenin himself called the new economic order "state capitalism."

During the chaotic conditions of the postrevolutionary period and the civil war, Lenin had had little time to concern himself with the long-range problem of the development of Russia. The immediate problem was survival. Lenin gave first priority to the task essential to the development of Russia: reestablishing governmental authority in a country that had drifted into anarchy. For this purpose, he was prepared to make compromises, like the Brest-Litovsk treaty or the NEP.

With the end of the civil war, the Soviet government was firmly established in power. The authority of the Communist party within the government was virtually unquestioned. This development was not, however, inevitable. At the beginning of the revolution, a clear demarcation was evident between the soviets and the party, and several parties and groupings existed within the soviets. For a short time, some left-wing members of the SR party were actually members of the Soviet government.

In theory, the Sovnarkom was responsible to the all-Russian Congress of Soviets and not to the party. But one by one, the other parties had been driven underground and were eventually destroyed (Schapiro 1955). The Congress of Soviets met for only a short time each year, and in fact the congress came under the control of the Communist party. Thus under Lenin's leadership the unique pattern of the Soviet political system evolved (Rigby 1979: 176–177). Soviet Russia became a one-party state, with the party leadership enjoying clear predominance over the government. Although no opposition to the government was organized, various groups within the party, such as the Workers' Opposition, converged in 1921 to present a threat to Lenin's leadership. To many members of the party the NEP was not merely a retreat in policy but an abandonment of socialist doctrine. This doctrinaire attitude led to a political crisis within the party early in 1921.

At the 10th Party Congress in March, Lenin succeeded not only in winning acceptance for NEP but in passing a resolution that forbade all organizations like the Workers' Opposition within the party. A resolution on party unity, as approved by the congress, prohibited party members from organizing any groups with an independent political program. A secret clause in the resolution, later made public, authorized the party's Central Committee to expel members who violated the new rule. This resolution did not end opposition within the party. Throughout the 1920s, bitter conflict existed within the leadership over policies and personalities. The resolution made such opposition illegal, thus putting a powerful weapon in the hands of anyone who could claim to be the party's official spokesperson.

The resolution was a significant turning point in the history of Soviet politics. Although the party was always authoritarian in its organization, it had tolerated some opposition within its membership. Now a paradoxical situation had developed: In economic policy, the party was taking a step backward in the direction of capitalism; yet politically, it was giving up inner party democracy. The introduction of NEP had thrown open for discussion the whole question of the future of the Soviet system. If the country was not moving toward socialism, then where, in fact, was it going? The decree on party unity cut off discussion of this question and ensured that the future of Russia would be decided by the party leadership.

Lenin's last writings suggest that he was greatly concerned about the future of the Soviet state (Lewin 1970), but he was not to take part in the decision. In May 1922, he suffered a stroke from which he never fully recovered, and in January 1924, he died. During the last two years of his life, NEP appeared to be a success. Under the stimulus of the free market, agriculture recovered quickly. Although industry was much slower to recover (not for several years did Russian industry return to the prewar level of output), some improvement could be seen. After seven years of war, revolution, and famine, Russia was at peace; the peasants seemed to have a secure hold on their land, and it could be hoped that prosperity might finally reach this troubled country. Moreover, the political atmosphere in the mid-1920s was relatively relaxed. No party line was established on literature, science, or philosophy, and for a brief time, the intellectual life of the country flourished.

SOVIET UNION UNDER STALIN

Although the NEP was successful for the short term, critical economic problems remained. The country still had not fully recovered from the war. Recovery, moreover, would be only a first step toward the long-run goal of creating a modern industrial society on the wreckage of the empire. These economic problems could not be resolved until the Bolsheviks solved their political problems. The regime now faced a succession decision: Either the authority Lenin had exercised had to pass on to some new leader or some form of group leadership had to be agreed upon.

Beyond the immediate question of Lenin's successor lay the problem of the political institutions to guide Russia from backwardness to modernity. What was to be the ultimate relationship between the party and the state? How could the vast human resources of the country be mobilized most effectively? How was the Russian population to be educated to the life of an urban and industrial society? And finally, what form was the new society to take? The only available examples of industrial societies were capitalist. If they agreed on nothing else, the Soviet leaders were determined that the new society they were creating would not be capitalistic. In fact, in the 1920s the leadership was arguing not only over the succession to Lenin but also over national goals.

The First Succession Struggle

The obvious candidate to succeed Lenin was Trotskii. As head of the Red Army, he had a powerful base from which to seize power. Yet his very prominence tended to unite the other party leaders against him. Moreover, he was a latecomer to the party—he had joined the Bolsheviks only in 1917—and this was a black mark in the eyes of those who had worked with Lenin in the dark years of exile before the revolution. Partly for these reasons, Trotskii found little support among the professional party administrators who were increasingly in control of the party's affairs.

Even before Lenin died, a powerful coalition of party leaders organized to stop Trotskii: the *troika* of Georgii Zinoviev, Lev Kamenev, and Josif Stalin. Stalin was head of the party's central office, and Zinoviev and Kamenev controlled the party organizations of Petrograd (soon to become Leningrad) and Moscow, respectively. The troika was able to dominate the party machinery so effectively that if Trotskii had chosen to stage a coup, it would have appeared as a move against the party—that is, as an attempt at counterrevolution.

The personalities of the contenders undoubtedly contributed to the bitterness of the political conflicts of the 1920s. Stalin (born Josif Dzhugashvili in 1879) was an ethnic Georgian who had been trained for the priesthood but had become involved in the revolutionary movement in his native region and had eventually joined the Bolsheviks. Throughout the prerevolutionary period, Stalin had remained in the Bolshevik underground inside Russia, until he was caught by the Tsarist police. Although he was a senior leader of the party in 1917, Stalin did not play a prominent role in the revolution. In Lenin's government, as commissar of nationalities, he was responsible for the affairs of the non-Russian peoples of the empire.

In 1922, Stalin was made general secretary of the party, a job supposed to be concerned with administration. Lenin soon realized that Stalin was developing this position into one of great power and recommended that the party find a way to remove Stalin. His advice was never carried out.

Trotskii's personality differed sharply from Stalin's. Stalin seemed to be a colorless and even diffident man, whereas Trotskii was a gifted orator and a charismatic leader, a Jewish intellectual who had spent much of his adult life in the West. Zinoviev, who eventually joined Trotskii in a leftist opposition to Stalin, was also a Jewish revolutionary who had chosen exile in the West to the more dangerous life of the underground in Russia. Before 1917, he was probably the Bolshevik leader closest to Lenin. The other leading figure in the political drama of the 1920s was Nikolai Bukharin, the theoretical spokesman for the regime.

Although Stalin was eventually proclaimed to be a great theoretician, his real abilities lay in the realms of organization and administration. Under his leadership as general secretary, the permanent administrative staff of the party, the apparatus, gradually acquired control over the entire party organization. Stalin's ultimate political success was a result of a determined effort to make the apparatus the ruling force in the country. He used his position as general secretary to make strategic appointments in the organization, and he was able to use this organizational power within the party to oust his opponents.

In the early 1920s, when this process began, the trend of events was not at all obvious. Most of the Bolshevik leaders were not aware of the enormous potential of the office of general secretary. They were more afraid that Trotskii might be a "man on horseback," and they joined with Stalin against Trotskii. Stalin was not seen as a serious contender for power.

Policy Conflicts

Most Communists believed that in the long run the revolution could succeed in Russia only as a part of an international socialist revolution. Without explicitly abandoning this idea, Stalin called upon the party to concentrate on Russia's own internal development, leaving the rest of the world to find its own way to socialism. Trotskii's program, on the other hand, acquired the label of permanent revolution: At home, it meant a crash program of industrialization, and in the rest of the world, it advocated active Soviet assistance to other revolutionary movements.

Politically, Trotskii's program was not popular except with the most militant members of the party. It certainly entailed great risks, both at home and abroad. Stalin called his own program Socialism in One Country. Essentially, Stalin promised a continuation of NEP for an indefinite period.

In the context of Soviet politics, Stalin's program was rightist and Trotskii's belonged on the Left. The rightists in the party, including Bukharin, were those who supported Stalin against Trotskii, and later against Zinoviev and Kamenev. The leaders of the Left were removed from positions of power, and some were expelled from the party. Trotskii was eventually deported from the USSR. Then, in 1928, Stalin made a sudden shift. Without admitting it, he became a leftist and initiated a series of programs that were to transform Russia.

Until the Russian revolution, the capitalist experience provided the only historical examples of industrialization. Capitalism brought a market economy and development toward a liberal democracy. In the classic capitalist model of economic development, the stimulus of growth comes from private enterprise. Capital is invested in enterprises in the hope of a profitable return. In an underdeveloped society, capital for economic growth may come from foreign investors, as French capital had once flowed into Russia. But the Soviet regime was prohibited by its doctrine from using private investment as a source of capital, even if it had been available. The government did hope to find foreign funds in the form of credits, and for this reason it sought to normalize diplomatic relations. In the early 1920s, it was already apparent that unless the Soviet regime were replaced by one friendly to capitalism, Russia would have to rely on its own resources for economic development.

All the party's leaders agreed on the need for economic growth. They wanted not only to restore the economy, but also to catch up with and overtake the great industrial powers. The leaders were agreed on a further point: This process of economic growth was to be socialist and not capitalist. Yet no one was sure exactly what socialist meant in this context. Marxist theory had always assumed that the socialists would come to power in a mature capitalist system and that the socialist government would not have to grapple with the problems of economic growth.

Only very slowly and after several false starts did the outline of a truly socialist economic system take shape in Russia. Politically, however, the meaning of Soviet socialism was quite clear: The party was to maintain its monopoly of decisionmaking power, and the development of the economy was not to follow a course that would imperil Communist rule.

In the 1920s, the regime faced two possible strategies or alternative courses of action for economic growth (Spulber 1964). One was to continue along the present course of state capitalism and NEP, allowing for a slow accumulation of capital to support the development of new industry. A second strategy was to abandon NEP and embark on a crash program of industrialization. This second strategy, that of the Left, aimed at a complete transformation in the shortest possible time. All available resources were to be channeled into the development of heavy industry. The production of consumer goods, already at a low level, would fall still further. The peasants, in particular, would suffer. Indeed, the essence of the leftists' strategy was to make the peasants pay the cost of industrialization. This policy involved not only economic costs, but serious political risks. If the standard of living were depressed too low, another great revolution might occur.

The strategy of the Right, although addressed to an economic problem, was political. The rightists pointed out that NEP had brought stability, which had to be preserved if the economy was to prosper. Above all, NEP had mollified the peasants; any change of course would provoke a reaction and might be self-defeating.

The peasants held the key to economic growth for two reasons: (1) Farm products were the country's main source of foreign exchange, which would be needed to pay for foreign machinery, and (2) what the peasants produced would be needed to feed the urban workers, who would grow in number. Following the leftist strategy would have risked starving the cities. Thus this strategy could succeed only if the regime found some means of controlling the peasant.

Collectivization and the Five-Year Plan

The original impetus for Stalin's dramatic change of course in 1928 was a critical shortage of grain. The NEP solution no longer worked: The peasants were producing, but they were not bringing their produce to market. Using one of his typical methods, Stalin solved this problem with an organizational change. The entire agricultural system of the country was reorganized, and the peasants were brought into collective farms.

The collective farm (*kolkhoz*) was a voluntary organization in which the peasants pooled their resources and worked together for greater efficiency. In fact, the peasants were driven into the collective farms by force: Peasants who refused to be collectivized were arrested and often shot. On the other hand, party organizers who went into the villages to manage the collectivization process were sometimes taken captive by the peasants and tortured or killed.

The collectivization of agriculture could not have been accomplished without these party organizers. A decade earlier during the civil war, the government had attempted the forcible requisition of grain. Although this technique had been partially successful, the government was not able to bring the peasants under control. Now the party had the capacity to mobilize and redirect the lives of millions of peasants.

The result of the collectivization process, as Leonard Schapiro (1960, pt. 3) described it, was a "third revolution," a social revolution that transformed rural Russia. It took several years to accomplish, but in the end, the regime realized its goal. The kolkhoz did not contribute to the growth in agricultural productivity (Western economists almost all agree that the kolkhoz is relatively inefficient), but it was an effective mechanism for extracting grain from the peasants to feed the cities.

Earlier, the peasant problem had been the main obstacle to the industrialization of the USSR. Having found a temporary solution, Stalin was able to turn to the basic problem of development. Along with the drive for the collectivization of agriculture, the USSR embarked on its first five-year plan (1928–1932) for the development of industry. The plan was essentially a set of target figures showing the level of output to be reached over five years. Industrial production was to grow 100 percent overall. The cost of this tremendous increase was to be borne by the Russians themselves. All possible effort was thrown into the drive to raise industrial production, which meant a deliberate decline in the already low standard of living.

As the collectivization effort revealed, Stalin was prepared to use drastic force to carry out his program. But he understood that his chances of success were much greater if the regime could generate genuine enthusiasm in the population, instead of relying entirely on force. So he instituted an elaborate propaganda program, designed to instill in the worker and peasant the virtues of hard work, devotion to the national cause, and a faith in a brighter future. This program added a new function to the responsibilities of the Communist party: agitation and propaganda, or *agitprop*. The plan became the single theme of literature, movies, and art. A typical Soviet novel of the period focused on the construction of a new enterprise, and all characters were totally devoted to filling and overfilling their work quotas. The aim of this propaganda campaign was to persuade the nation that the plan was not only a program for economic growth, but also the basis for new, Communist society.

The Transformation of the Party

By the early 1930s, Stalin had established himself in a position of unprecedented power. The leading bodies of both the party and the government were, for the most part, filled with men whose first loyalty was to him. Both the Left and the Right oppositions appeared to have been crushed. But Stalin's position was not unassailable. The country was being driven at a terrible pace, and the accumulated resentment of the people could possibly lead to revolt. Since Stalin had seen two great revolutions in his lifetime, his own sense of insecurity is easy to understand.

In fact, at the time of the 17th Party Congress in 1934, an effort was under way to replace Stalin as general secretary. Resentment still stirred against him within the party organization, and furtive anti-Stalin leaflets were passed from hand to hand. Stalin must have believed that if this latent opposition could have found a leader to rally the people and the party, a revolt might have arisen against his rule.

Some of the former opposition leaders were still at liberty, though they were discredited and had no political power. Among Stalin's own followers, people could be found who might have led a movement against him. Sergei Kirov, who had succeeded Zinoviev as the party leader in Leningrad, was a possible candidate. In December 1934, he was murdered under mysterious circumstances that have never been fully explained. In the course of investigating Kirov's murder, Stalin's government mounted a reign of terror that peaked four years later.

In 1936 the leaders of the old Left opposition were tried and executed. These show trials were the most dramatic and puzzling aspect of the great terror. One by one, former leaders of the Communist party, many of whom had been in Tsarist prisons, stood up in open court to confess to a great political conspiracy against the Soviet state. In new trials in 1937 and 1938, the leaders of the Right were also sentenced to death. But the purge of the 1930s went much further than the top-ranking leaders on public trial; the total number of arrests ran into the millions. Possibly more than a million were executed, some without even the pretense of a trial. Many remained in prison or concentration camps until Stalin died, and the entire population was terrorized.

Although we would like to know what forces in Stalin's own personality could have driven him to use terror to reinforce his own authority and why the opposition leaders cooperated with the prosecution, the importance of the terror lay not in its psychological aspects but in its results. First, although the wave of organized violence and mass arrests ended in 1938, a numbing sense of fright hung over the party and the nation until Stalin's death: Stalin had now acquired the ultimate power of life and death over the entire Soviet leadership. Second, those who were purged had to be replaced. A new generation of party leaders moved into the party apparatus as well as into the government. They were younger men who had come into the party after the revolution, and they owed their allegiance to Stalin. The result of the purges was a new leadership, the men who ran the Soviet Union in the 1940s and who for the most part remained in power after Stalin died. Most of these men were not old Bolsheviks or Leninists, and they were not revolutionaries. The purges thus produced a new political elite, men who had not known Lenin and owed their careers to Stalin's favor.

The New Autocracy

What happened during the purges to the revolutionary tradition of the party? The answer is that this tradition was Stalin's main target in the great terror of the 1930s, and the target was effectively destroyed. To be sure, the party still called itself Communist, and the government was still theoretically a dictatorship of the proletariat. But Stalin proved to be a cautious and even conservative ruler. The revolutionary imagery of the past was allowed to disappear. The army, for example, had once been noted for its revolutionary elan. Now, in the 1930s, the old Tsarist-style uniforms and ranks reappeared, and a greater distinction developed between officers and enlisted forces. This process was accelerated during World War II when the regime tried to appeal to traditional patriotism as well as to loyalty to communism. The Red Army finally became the Soviet Army. The commissars were called ministers after 1946.

As a consequence of the purges, the Soviet political system differed markedly on the eve of World War II from what it had been under Lenin. The country was in fact, though not in theory, an autocracy. The purges had prepared the way for a new generation of political leaders who had been educated under Soviet rule and owed their positions to Stalin. The people who had actually led the revolution were dead, in prison, or in exile, and only a few believed that the regime was revolutionary.

The Stalinist period of Soviet history is sometimes referred to as a period of totalitarianism, and a comparison is often made between it and the period in German history under Hitler. The comparison should not obscure the real differences between Hitler's regime and Stalin's. For one thing, Stalin was committed to a practical goal: the transformation of Russia into a powerful industrialized state. Where Hitler was a gambler, Stalin was cautious, especially in foreign policy. Another difference is that the Nazi system was based explicitly on the leadership principle (*Führerprinzip*), and its adherents openly admitted that it was a one-man dictatorship. Now in practice, Stalin's system degenerated into one-man rule, but in theory, it remained the rule of the Communist party. Thus after Stalin died in 1953, the collective leadership of the party was able to reassert itself.

Stalinism in Perspective

N. S. Timasheff (1946) described the 1930s as a "great retreat": a retreat from the revolutionary tradition back to the established order of autocratic rule, authoritarian government, and Russian nationalism. In the nineteenth century, an apologist for the Tsarist system had recommended the slogan, "autocracy, orthodoxy, nationalism." This could very well have become Stalin's slogan, except that the orthodoxy (*pravoslavie*) of the established church was replaced by the new orthodoxy (*ortodoksalnost*) of the official Marxist-Leninist ideology. Timasheff described from historical perspective what Bertrand Russell had foreseen in 1919—the power of the authoritarian, Tsarist tradition in Russia.

Nonetheless, Stalinism and Tsarism differ in several important ways. It would be a serious mistake to interpret Stalin simply as a counter-revolutionary or as a despotic ruler who was a new Tsar in all but name. Stalin's regime can be seen as a period of transition between the traditional autocracy of Tsarism and the modern authoritarianism of contemporary USSR. Stalin himself described his system as "revolution from above." He dedicated his regime, with great singleness of purpose, to the transformation of Russia. This meant the development of a powerful industrial base. The country's new heavy industry was to provide the military hardware that would prevent any repetition of the catastrophe of Russia's past wars.

As the period of the first five-year plan was ending, many Russians expected a breathing space and an end to the crash program of industrialization. Stalin, however, planned to go on with a second five-year plan to continue the rapid pace of industrial growth. In a frank speech to a group of industrial managers in 1931, Stalin defended the new five-year plan out of considerations for national security:

> It is sometimes asked whether it is not possible to slow down the tempo somewhat, to put a check on the movement. No, comrades, it is not possible! The tempo must not be reduced. On the contrary, we must increase it as much as is within our powers and possibilities. This is dictated to us by our obligations to the workers and peasants of the U.S.S.R. This is dictated to us by our obligations to the working class of the whole world.
>
> To slacken the tempo would mean falling behind. And those who fall behind get beaten. But we do not want to be beaten. No, we refuse to be beaten! One feature of the history of old Russia was the continual beatings she suffered because of her backwardness. She was beaten by the Mongol Khans. She was beaten by the Turkish beys. She was beaten by the Swedish feudal lords. She was beaten by the Polish and Lithuanian gentry. She was beaten by the Japanese barons. All beat her—because of her backwardness, military backwardness, cultural backwardness, political backwardness, industrial backwardness, agricultural backwardness. . . .
>
> We are fifty or a hundred years behind the advanced countries. We must make good this distance in ten years. Either we do this, or we shall be crushed. (Stalin 1931: 455–456)

This speech seems all the more remarkable when we recall that the German invasion came ten years and four months later.

The 1931 speech was an appeal to traditional nationalism, but Stalin did not rely on patriotic fervor alone. He called for a "struggle with backwardness," for the transformation of Russian society along new lines. This notion of development and change, of harnessing modern technology to traditional national values, was also a significant departure from Tsarism.

Stalin's regime was the classic model of the mobilization system (Apter 1965). Under Stalin, literature, the arts, philosophy, the social sciences, and to some extent the natural sciences were all exploited to mobilize the human resources of the country in the interests of economic development. Unlike the Tsars, Stalin was always interested in building public support. He ruled in an age of mass politics, and he required more than just subservience. The success of the plan to industrialize Russia, in particular, demanded the active and enthusiastic support of the masses who were now moving from the village to the city.

AFTER STALIN

Stalin died March 5, 1953, and with his death the era of personal dictatorship ended. Although Nikita Khrushchev became the dominant political leader he was never an autocratic dictator. He was a ruler with limited powers, and eventually he was removed in a palace coup in October 1964. Leonid Brezhnev (who died in office in November 1982) was, like Khrushchev, a ruler with limited powers. Unlike Khrushchev, Brezhnev understood and accepted the limitations on his authority.

As S. F. Cohen (1984) pointed out, the dominant theme of Soviet politics in the post-Stalin period has been the issue of reform versus conservatism. Put another way, the issue was how much of the Stalinist machinery was to be dismantled and how much saved. Khrushchev was a reformer whose slogan might have been "Back to Lenin!" Like Lenin himself, Khrushchev was something of a visionary, although he lacked Lenin's political genius. In 1956, in an astounding speech to the 20th Communist Party Congress, Khrushchev denounced Stalin and painted a grim picture of Stalin's crimes. Thus Khrushchev's program of reforms was sometimes called de-Stalinization. No doubt, for a time Khrushchev was a popular hero. His program of reform contained two elements that guaranteed his popularity: (1) He restricted the power of the political police, so that organized terror was no longer used as an instrument of government, and (2) he tried to change the priorities of economic policy to put more emphasis on consumer goods and improve the Soviet standard of living.

Like Stalin, Khrushchev began with the support of the party apparatus. Later, like Stalin, he found the party a hindrance to his own freedom of action. Unlike Stalin, Khrushchev could not use the political police to terrorize the apparatus and remove his opponents. Instead he attempted a series of bureaucratic reforms designed to rejuvenate the party from within. The reforms failed, and Khrushchev alienated the very people on whom he most depended: the professional apparatus of the party. These people conspired to remove him in 1964 and put Brezhnev in his place.

Brezhnev epitomized the conservative approach in style as well as substance. Where Khrushchev was ebullient, Brezhnev was reserved and remote. Khrushchev was continually announcing new ideas that were denounced after his removal as harebrained schemes. Brezhnev promised order, stability, and an end to political experiments. On the other hand, some of the reforms of the Khrushchev regime survived under Brezhnev. The standard of living continued to improve, although at a slower pace under Brezhnev. For a time it appeared that Brezhnev might succeed in a crucial area of policymaking where Khrushchev had tried and failed:

improving relations with the United States. In some ways, indeed, Brezhnev appeared to be more liberal than Khrushchev. Until about 1980, the regime was much more tolerant of political dissent than it had been under Khrushchev.

Although Khrushchev and Brezhnev had quite different styles and pursued different policies, they operated in much the same institutional framework. Thus a modern authoritarian regime evolved out of the Stalinist system but differed from it. The remaining chapters of this book will examine the institutions of that post-Stalin political order.

REFERENCES

Apter, David E. 1965. *The Politics of Modernization.* Chicago: University of Chicago Press.

Brinton, Crane. 1952. *The Anatomy of Revolution.* New York: Prentice-Hall.

[Chicherin, Boris.] 1900. *Rossiia nakanune dvadtsatogo stoletiia.* Berlin: Hugo Dietz Verlag.

Cohen, Stephen F. 1984. The Friends and Foes of Change: Reformism and Conservatism in the Soviet Union. In *The Soviet Polity in the Modern Era,* edited by Erik P. Hoffmann and Robbin F. Laird. New York: Aldine, pp. 85–104.

Katkov, George. 1967. *Russia 1917: The February Revolution.* New York: Harper & Row.

Lenin, V. I. 1918. *State and Revolution.* In *Selected Works,* vol. 2, pt. 1. Moscow: Foreign Languages Publishing House, pp. 199–325.

Lewin, Moshe. 1970. *Lenin's Last Struggle.* New York: Vintage Books.

Lukacs, Georg. 1971. *Lenin: A Study on the Unity of His Thought.* Cambridge, Mass.: MIT Press.

On Party Unity. 1921. *Resolutions and Decrees of the Communist Party of the Soviet Union,* edited by R. H. McNeal. Vol. 2. Toronto: University of Toronto Press, 1974–1982, pp. 119–121.

Pobedonostsev, Konstantin P. 1965. *Reflections of a Russian Statesman.* Ann Arbor: University of Michigan Press.

Rigby, T. H. 1979. *Lenin's Government: Sovnarkom 1917–1922.* Cambridge: Cambridge University Press.

Schapiro, Leonard. 1955. *The Origin of the Communist Autocracy: Political Opposition in the Soviet State, First Phase 1917–1922.* Cambridge: Harvard University Press.

———. 1960. *The Communist Party of the Soviet Union.* New York: Random House.

Spulber, Nicholas. 1964. *Soviet Strategy for Economic Growth.* Bloomington: Indiana University Press.

Stalin, J. 1931. The Tasks of Business Executives. In *Problems of Leninism,* 11th ed. Moscow: Foreign Languages Publishing House, 1953, pp. 447–458.

Timasheff, N. S. 1946. *The Great Retreat.* New York: Dutton.

3
The Collective Society

One of the consequences of modernization and industrialization in all parts of the world is the breakdown of the old class structure. The new social groups that arise are differentiated not on the traditional basis of class and status, but on the basis of the social or economic role that they play in the new society. Before 1917, the people of Russia were primarily engaged in agriculture and were mostly illiterate. The successful industrialization of Russia would require that millions of people be moved from the village to the factory and that they be taught to read and write in the process. Their lives would now be governed not by the seasonal changes of the village but by the daily routine of the factory. In the USSR as in other developing countries, social transformation has complicated the task of ruling the country. In place of a mass population of peasants who knew little of life outside the village, the Soviet regime rules a people who are far better educated than the subjects of the Tsar and who are eager to know more about the world outside the USSR.

As described in Chapter 2, Stalin's regime opted for a crash program of industrialization, giving highest priority to heavy industry and to the needs of national defense. The industrialization program then created new problems that called for new decisions. The standard of living was deliberately depressed as one way of paying the costs of industrialization. The industrial workers, whose numbers were rapidly growing as more and more peasants moved into the cities, were crowded into urban slums where only the most essential services were provided. The newly arrived worker was likely to get nothing more than a cot in a dormitory and a vague promise that eventually he would be assigned more living space so that his family could join him. When they did, an apartment might be divided up to accommodate two families instead of one and then be divided again until an entire family might get only a single room. In addition, women by the millions were taken out of these crowded apartments and put to work in factory and office. These changes had a drastic effect on family life as well as on the overall social structure.

Workers must be trained to operate the complicated tools of modern industry. A peasant can be handed a shovel on the first day in the city and put to work at a construction site, but a hundred or more peasants are needed to do the work of a single bulldozer. On the other hand, one person may require months to learn to operate a bulldozer properly. Furthermore, the bulldozer economy requires an elaborate infrastructure to keep it going: mechanics to repair the equipment, factories to supply spare parts, planners and engineers to supervise the work. In the first five-year plan, trained personnel at all levels were in short supply: There were just not enough skilled workers, engineers, or technicians, and the economy had to rely very heavily on the peasant with a shovel. The long-range solution, of course, was mass education, which would provide trained men and women not only for the factories, but also for the bureaucracy that managed the system.

In addition to the problem of education, there was the problem of incentive. The regime could promise the workers and the peasants very little material reward for their contribution to the industrialization program. Stalin relied on the collectivization of agriculture to provide a means whereby the peasants could be forced to supply food to the cities. Ruthless as he was, Stalin understood the limits of force. He knew that the system would be far more efficient if people could be persuaded to work rather than driven to it by fear. Thus, the five-year plans were accompanied by the most intensive efforts at propaganda and political indoctrination. The regime tried to persuade the population that everyone had a contribution to make to the overall goal of the transformation of Russia. Work was to be its own reward. T. H. von Laue (1971: 155) suggested that one aim of Communist ideology was to instill the drive and motivation that in the Western world were called the Protestant work ethic.

In the long run, the motivation was the promise of material reward. The people were urged to work hard because eventually there would be a payoff, and the new factories being used to produce machine tools and armaments would be converted to the production of consumer goods. Of course, Stalin recognized that in the short run, too, there had to be some material incentive for hard work. Skilled workers were paid more than the untrained, and managers and engineers were paid more than workers at the bench.

SOCIAL STRATIFICATION

In the early years of the Soviet regime, self-conscious effort was made to achieve genuine egalitarianism. Under Lenin's rule, no member of the government could earn more than the wage earned by a skilled factory worker. For a time, indeed, the worker was a member of a privileged class. Men of lower-class origin, and especially factory workers, were given preference in admission to the Communist party and to the universities and in the assignment of apartments in the crowded cities.

The "great retreat" of Stalinism meant the abandonment of this early, idealistic effort to create a classless society. Stalin put a higher priority on industrial development than on making a reality of Lenin's vision. The Stalin constitution of 1936 (art. 12) contained the formula: "From each according to his ability, to each according to his work." People were to be rewarded in proportion to the contribution they made to the fulfillment of the plan. In 1931 Stalin called for an end to the "naive idea" that all should be paid equally. He denounced this as equality mongering (*uravnilovka*, literally, "leveling") and called for payment of differential wages to create incentives:

> We cannot tolerate a situation where a rolling mill operator in a steel plant earns no more than a janitor. We cannot tolerate a situation where a machinist in the railroad industry earns only as much as a typist. Marx and Lenin said that the difference between skilled and unskilled labor would exist even under socialism, even after classes had been abolished, that only under communism would this difference disappear and that, consequently, even under socialism "wages" must be paid according to work performed and not according to needs. (Stalin 1953: 464)

Along with payment of higher wages to skilled labor, Stalin insisted on recognition of the importance of managers, administrators, and other white-collar workers. He referred to this group as the "industrial and technical intelligentsia." As a consequence of Stalin's policy, the working-class mythology became less important. Society in the Soviet Union became stratified, with men and women organized into various distinct social groups (Inkeles 1971: 137; Kerblay 1983, ch. 8).

DIMENSIONS OF SOCIAL CLEAVAGE

In all modern societies people are divided into groups on the basis of social and economic status, race and nationality, religion, and occupation. The USSR is no exception. These divisions into religious, ethnic, or economic groups are called social cleavages.

When does social cleavage become political cleavage? When does a dimension of social cleavage, such as religion, take on political significance? The comparative analysis of societies suggests that when different dimensions of social cleavage divide people into the same groups, then social cleavage becomes mutually reinforcing and politically divisive. If, for example, low-income status is associated with a particular ethnic or racial group, then these two dimensions of cleavage are felt more strongly and people develop a sense of belonging to a group rather than to the society as a whole. The Soviet regime has made a deliberate effort to prevent this from happening.

Within the USSR four important dimensions of social cleavage can be distinguished: (1) social class, (2) nationality, (3) religion, and (4) membership in the Communist party. In addition a division is formed between the urban population and the peasants, which requires special treatment.

Social Class

Soviet practice recognizes three basic social groups: (1) workers, (2) peasants, and (3) intelligentsia. These could more accurately, of course, be called occupational groups. In Soviet social statistics, the adult citizen is assigned to a social group on the basis of the work that he does, and children are assigned to the social class of the person who supports them. The terms of worker and peasant have obvious meanings, but the Soviet concept of intelligentsia requires some explanation.

Before 1917, the term intelligentsia generally referred to the left-wing intellectuals who were part of the revolutionary movement. Since the revolution, however, the term has been applied very broadly to persons who do not work with their hands or, in Soviet terminology, to persons of intellectual labor (*umstvennyi trud*). Thus, the intelligentsia embraces several groups: personnel in the bureaucracies, professional people, such as doctors, teachers, and engineers, rank-and-file white-collar workers, and intellectuals in the narrow sense of the word, such as writers, artists, and scientists. Stalin (1953: 685) once said that the USSR consisted of two classes, the workers and the peasants. Under this formulation, the intelligentsia was called a stratum (*prosloika*) rather than a class. This theory remains the official one, although it is no longer attributed to Stalin. In fact, the intelligentsia is a complex and highly stratified social group, which includes the highest-ranking members of the various elites as well as ordinary office workers.

On the basis of a study of former Soviet citizens, Alex Inkeles (1971: 151–152) found that the three social groups were in turn divided into at least ten subgroups. Certainly the subdivisions within the intelligentsia are the most important politically. The Soviet intelligentsia appears to be divided into at least three different levels: the elite, the general intelligentsia, and the white-collar workers.

The Elite. This level consists of the most prominent and most highly paid people in each professional group. The elite can in turn be classified into (1) the political elite, which consists of the highest-ranking leaders of the party and government—a group of a few hundred men who have direct influence on political decisions; (2) the managerial elite, the men who actually operate the government, the economy, the armed forces, the police apparatus, and other parts of the Soviet system; and (3) the cultural and scientific elite, the artists, scientists, writers, performers, and scholars.

The General Intelligentsia. This level can be classed into two groups: (1) the bureaucrats, who staff the government, the economy, and the armed forces and who provide middle-level leadership throughout the political system; and (2) the professional people, who are persons with advanced technical training such as doctors, engineers, or lawyers.

The White-Collar Workers. These workers are the lower-level clerks, technicians, secretaries, and teachers.

These groups can be differentiated on the basis of political influence, social status and prominence, and rewards. The political elite consists of those who have a place in the Communist party hierarchy. Milovan Djilas (1957) called the political elite a "new class": the political bureaucracy that rules the USSR through the Communist party.

The political elite is exclusively male. Female apoliticism—the tendency for women not to be involved in political life—is found in all traditional societies and is particularly pronounced in the USSR. This apoliticism is reinforced by the dual structure of the Soviet political system. Women frequently hold office in local government, but they rarely occupy decisionmaking positions in the local organizations of the party. This phenomenon is even more obvious in Moscow. As Gail Lapidus has pointed out, women can be found in certain ceremonial roles, but within the top-level party leadership, "politics remains a male affair" (1978: 200).

In Djilas's view, the managerial and the cultural-scientific elites were merely officials who served under the control of the new class. The managerial elite, though not without political power, is composed of people who have nonpolitical careers. Although the cultural and scientific elite has far less political influence, it enjoys much greater prominence, and the members of this group are often more visible and better paid than the managers or the political leaders. Some of the members of this elite group do not belong to the Communist party.

Soviet society has an elite of privilege, not an elite of wealth. The difference between the elites and the average Soviet citizen is not measured in rubles. Members of the elite enjoy a variety of nonmonetary privileges, such as better housing, access to special stores, and educational and cultural opportunities (Matthews 1978: 43–52; Djilas 1957: 45; Sakharov 1975: 25). But these privileges come with the job: A person who drops out of the elite may lose all such privileges. This system of distributing privilege on the basis of elite status prevents the accumulation of wealth and makes every elite member dependent on the regime not only for income, but for life-style.

Nationality

The population is divided into a large number of distinct ethnic groups of whom the Russians count for slightly more than half. Many of the recognized nationalities are small groups of people living in isolated parts of the country. But there are still twenty-three major nationalities in the USSR. In Soviet practice, nationality is determined primarily by language, and nationalities are classified according to linguistic features. From the viewpoint of the relationship between nationality and the political system, somewhat different criteria can be employed. The major nationalities can be classified into the following groups.

Eastern Slavic Peoples. The Russians, Ukrainians, and Belorussians together account for about three-fourths of the total population.

Western Peoples. The Western group includes the Estonians, Latvians, Lithuanians, and Moldavians, who were brought under Soviet rule as a consequence of World War II. The three Baltic peoples had lived under Tsarist rule for almost two centuries and yet were highly westernized. Unlike the other nationalities in the USSR, they use the Western (Latin) alphabet. In religion, they are Lutheran or Roman Catholic. The regime has always looked upon the Baltic region as an area of potential political dissidence. The Moldavians speak a language close to Rumanian, but they write in a Russian (Cyrillic) alphabet. In religion, the Moldavians are Orthodox.

Caucasian Christian Peoples. The Caucasus is a checkerboard of many small ethnic groups, of whom three fit the description of major nationality: Georgians, Azeri, and Armenians. The Georgians, who were converted to Christianity in the fifth century A.D. (that is, about 500 years before the conversion of the Russians), have spent a large part of their history under foreign rule and yet have maintained a high sense of national identity. The Armenians, too, have a long history. But unlike the Georgians, the Armenians have dispersed beyond their homeland.

Islamic Peoples. The territory once called Turkestan was incorporated into the empire during the nineteenth century. The natives were Islamic, and most spoke a Turkic dialect. These Turkic-speaking Muslims are also found in the Caucasus (the Azeri) and in the Russian republic (the Tatars, for example). In Central Asia, the Tsarist government did not interfere with the Islamic social structure and made no serious effort to modernize the population. Before the revolution, most people remained illiterate and continued to live under the rule of native emirs.

Soviet rule brought revolutionary change to the entire country, but especially to the Islamic regions. The government has tried to root out some aspects of the Islamic tradition (particularly the subordination of women). Central Asia has been an area of rapid economic growth, especially after World War II but the society has not been completely westernized. Foreign visitors to Tashkent (the largest city in Soviet Central Asia) feel that they are in the Middle East. On the streets some women still wear veils.

Nonterritorial Nationalities. Most major nationalities are organized into separate republics within the USSR (see Chapter 7 for an examination of the internal structure of the republics). Having the status of a republic brings some distinct advantages, including the right to educate children in the national language rather than in Russian. Three of the major nationalities do not enjoy this status: the Germans, the Poles, and the Jews. These might be called the nonterritorial nationalities (Aspaturian 1968: 143).

Religion

The Soviet state is officially atheist. Some religious organizations are tolerated, but the state does not take a position of neutrality on this question. After a period of initial conflict during the 1920s, the state and the churches arrived at a tacit understanding not to interfere in each others' affairs. This understanding came about because the government was preoccupied with other things, and most Communists believed that religion would simply die a natural death under the new social order. At the same time, the most important religious organization, the Russian Orthodox Church, had a long tradition of subservience to the state—a tradition that the revolution did not destroy.

This arrangement came to an end in 1929, when the party took on a more hostile attitude toward religion. A national organization called the League of the Militant Godless was created to disseminate antireligious propaganda. Hardly by accident the campaign against religion was launched at the same time as the collectivization drive. Religious faith was thought to be especially strong among the peasants, and the party's apparent aim was to destroy the church as a social institution in the countryside.

The antireligious campaign died away in the course of the great retreat. The government restored the seven-day week, with Sunday set aside as a day of rest. Later, during the war, church-state relations improved dramatically. Stalin met with the head of the Russian Orthodox Church, and a modus vivendi was developed. Stalin welcomed the support of the church in the fight against the German invaders, and the church in turn received greater freedom. In particular it was allowed to reopen some of its seminaries. The League of the Militant Godless was eventually disbanded.

Religion was an important exception to the general pattern of post-Stalin liberalization. In 1954, a secret party decree resumed the antireligious campaign (CC Decree of July 7, 1954). Over the next several years, there was a gradual tightening of religious activity, and Stalin was criticized for being overly tolerant toward religion. In 1959 an intense antireligious campaign was begun, which continued until the ouster of Khrushchev in 1964. This campaign was probably motivated by Khrushchev's desire to advance the country more rapidly toward Lenin's idea of a socialist society.

Despite the hostility of the government, religion has survived in the USSR. Since official statistics on church membership are not available, it is impossible to give exact figures or even to offer reliable estimates, but undoubtedly millions of believers are practicing various faiths in the USSR.

Religion is closely associated with nationality. The Orthodox faith is the predominant one of the Russians, Ukrainians, and Belorussians, and it is also the traditional religion of the Georgians and Moldavians. Walter Kollarz (1961: 32) estimated the number of Orthodox believers at between 20 and 30 million, and that figure could be too small. A Soviet dissident (Shafarevich 1972: 43) put the number of Orthodox believers at 70 million.

Among the Russians, the second most numerous church group is the Old Believers, who adhere to an ancient Orthodox tradition but who were separated from the official church in the seventeenth century. The Old Believer faith, even more than other religions, seems like a relic of a distant past. The Tsarist authorities, who supported the patriarchal church, refused to recognize the Old Believers and tried without success to suppress them. The Soviet authorities have been more tolerant with respect to this particular group.

The largest Protestant group in the USSR is the Baptists. Although the Baptists are officially tolerated, they have not achieved the kind of informal understanding that appears to operate between the Orthodox church and the state. One group of Baptists (the *initsiativniki*) has broken away from the recognized church and functions illegally. Of the remaining Christian churches, the best established are the Lutherans (who are strongest in Latvia and Estonia), the Roman Catholics (in Lithuania), and the Armenian church.

Geoffrey Wheeler (1969: 189) estimated the number of Muslims in the USSR at between 25 and 30 million. It might be assumed that the Muslims felt the shock of Soviet rule even more than the Christians. The leaders of the revolution were committed to uprooting some of the deepest traditions of the Islamic faith—and, in particular, they were committed to improving the status of women. Indeed, the early Soviet efforts to emancipate women were deeply resented by the Muslim men. Women who shed the veil were sometimes attacked and even killed. But there can be no question that the younger generation in the Muslim areas welcomed the new opportunities brought about by the revolution for education and for cultural and economic progress. Further, Soviet rule brought a heightened sense of national identity to the peoples of Central Asia. The regime has been tolerant of Islam as an institutionalized religion, and the mosques and medressahs continue to function.

In a sense, the citizen who is a religious believer has opted out of contemporary Soviet society. Certainly he is disqualified from membership in the Communist party. Therefore some professional careers, such as those in the army and the higher bureaucracy, are closed to him. Any open manifestation of religious belief would disqualify a person from the teaching profession or any other job carrying responsibility for the young. A Soviet teacher of French (Shchipkova 1979) described how she lost her job and then had her Ph.D. taken away when the fact that she was a practicing Orthodox believer became known.

Thus religion serves as a type of cleavage that cuts deeply into Soviet society and separates the majority of the population from the very substantial minority who are believers (*veruiushchie*). Probably a great many believers are able to reconcile in their own minds their religious faith and their loyalty to the Soviet state. The party leadership, however, has not been reconciled to the survival of religious faith. They do not look upon religion as a harmless relic of the past, but rather as an impediment to social progress.

Party and Nonparty

The fundamental political cleavage is that between party members and nonparty people, between *partiinye* and *bezpartiinye*. The Communist party is supposed to be the leader of Soviet society, but it should not be supposed that party members are always the bosses and that nonparty people merely make up the rank and file. Although a strong tendency does exist for party membership to be more concentrated in the higher ranks, this rule is by no means universal. In a classroom, some students may be party members whereas the professor is not. In a factory, a worker may belong to the party whereas the factory manager may not. Consequently, the division between party and nonparty is not that between the rulers and the ruled or between the affluent and the lower classes: It is a distinction between those who have made a commitment and entered the party's ranks and those who have (for whatever reason) stood aside.

The party member does not wear a badge or a uniform, and in appearance, he cannot be distinguished from other Soviet citizens. Furthermore, the party member is found at almost every level in the society—in the collective farms, the factories, and the universities, as well as in the bureaucracy. The citizen is frequently reminded of this division into two groups. Almost every Soviet document asks the citizen to declare party status: All those who apply for a marriage license, for admission to a university, or for a job must announce whether they belong to the party. It is hard to convince the *bezpartiinye* that this entry on the application form does not make some difference. This factor has some importance in Soviet society. Alex Inkeles and Raymond Bauer found: "In the mind of the population, the distinction between party and nonparty is apparently one of the most meaningful and significant bases of social differentiation (although not of political cleavage) and one which looms as large as any other" (1959: 300).

SOVIETIZATION OF THE VILLAGE

The differences between rural and urban life are probably greater in the USSR than in any other industrial society. The explanation must be found in two facts: (1) The extreme backwardness of village life before the revolution has not been overcome by half a century of rapid development, and (2) the Soviet leadership has given a low priority to the problem of improving rural conditions.

Village Life Under the Tsars

Until the middle of the nineteenth century, the twin processes of modernization and westernization had little impact in the Russian village. Most Russian peasants lived under a form of serfdom that did not differ much from slavery. The peasant was legally bound to the land, and since the land was thought to be the property of the noble class, the peasant could be bought and sold much like a slave. Nikolai Gogol's famous novel *Dead Souls* was a grim satirical indictment of the institution of serfdom.

Peasant life was organized around the village commune. D. M. Wallace (1961: 166, 175) called the commune "the most peculiar of Russian institutions." It was an authoritarian institution where power rested in the hands of the household heads and the village elders, who made all the important decisions. The peasant could not leave the village even temporarily without the permission of the elders.

In 1861, the institution of serfdom was abolished by imperial edict. But although the peasants acquired some legal rights that they had not enjoyed before, economically they were still tied to the land and to the village commune. Some enlightened Russian thinkers called on the government to abolish the commune and to encourage the development of individual farming on a commercial basis. For a long time this argument fell on deaf ears. Most Russians, of both Left and Right, had a sentimental attachment to the commune. Conservatives looked on the commune as a barrier to the spread of radical ideas among the peasantry. The commune kept the peasants in the fields and in the church and away from the cities. In contrast, some revolutionaries looked upon the commune, with its supposedly collectivist institutions, as the harbinger of a new society, and they feared that the abolition of the commune would encourage the growth of capitalism and individualism.

The Stolypin reforms (named for the prime minister who was assassinated in 1911) allowed the peasant family to opt out of the commune under certain conditions. Stolypin hoped that eventually Russia could become a nation of small farmers—men and women working their own land and producing meat, milk, and grain for the market.

These reforms were carried through with great caution, and by the time of the revolution, only a small part of the land had been transferred into private hands. The Soviet government thus fell heir to an agricultural system that was collectivist in its social institutions and backward in its technology.

Collectivization

The archaic social organization of Russian agriculture almost certainly facilitated the collectivization program of the early 1930s. Traditionally, the Russian village was a cluster of small houses where families lived close together. Even in some areas where the Stolypin reforms had been carried out and the land had been marked into private holdings, the families remained in the village rather than moving onto their own land. The careful study by Moshe Lewin (1968) provides a detailed picture of village life after the revolution. Farming methods had changed little since the time of Peter the Great, and modern techniques such as crop rotation were virtually unknown. Millions of peasants still used the wooden plow and harvested their grain by hand.

Since the forced collectivization of 1929-1930, most peasants have lived on collective farms, or *kolkhozy*. An alternative form of agriculture enterprise is the *sovkhoz*, or state farm, which is owned and operated by the government. The kolkhoz is managed by a chairman, who is formally elected by the members but whose selection is actually subject to the approval of the local party organization, and the chairman can be removed if necessary. The farm is required to sell a large part of its produce to the state at fixed prices. In the past, the prices for these compulsory deliveries were kept artificially low, so that the peasants in effect were subsidizing the rest of society. Since Stalin's death, the prices paid by the state have gone up, and price increases by Brezhnev led to a marked rise in farm income. But the peasant still makes considerably less income than the industrial worker.

After the collective farm has met its obligations under the compulsory delivery system, it can sell additional grain and other farm products to the state, usually at a higher price. The kolkhoz can also sell food products directly to the consumer in a free market, where prices find their own level in accordance with the law of supply and demand. Such an open kolkhoz market can be found in most Soviet cities and is an important part of the Soviet second (free) economy.

Kolkhoz members are required to work parttime in the collective farm's fields, for which they are paid somewhat irregularly. They also have the right to work small plots of land of their own and to sell this produce at the kolkhoz market. For this purpose, the collective farm allots to each peasant household a small private plot that is typically no more than an acre and a half but is worked intensively. For many peasant families, the private plot is the main source of income. Frequent complaints are heard that the peasant gives too much attention to his plot to the detriment of the kolkhoz's collective effort. No doubt the regime would like to abolish the institution of the private plot, but so far it has not taken the risk. Certainly, the private plot is an anachronism— a tiny island of free enterprise within the socialist economy. The peasants will never be fully integrated into the Soviet system so long as this peculiar institution survives.

POLITICAL SOCIALIZATION

Socialization is the process by which a growing child becomes a member of society. It embraces the entire social and educational process wherein the individual learns the rules of behavior and internalizes the values of society. Political socialization is the process by which the individual assimilates the political beliefs, such as attitudes toward authority, which are predominant in society. Political socialization occurs in every society and takes place in many settings—the family, school, and formal and informal youth organizations. It involves both overt political socialization, that is, deliberate political education, and more subtle and indirect methods of indoctrination.

In studying Soviet patterns of child upbringing and education, we can see a variety of ways in which individual children learn political values characteristic of the behavior of Soviet adults. One important value is respect for authority. "First of all, a child must be *obedient* toward his parents and other adults, and treat them with respect. . . .

The child must fulfill requests that adults make of him—this is the first thing the child must be taught" (emphasis in original). This advice comes from an authoritative Soviet textbook on raising children (quoted in Bronfenbrenner 1970: 10). Permissiveness or overindulgence in the whims of children is frowned on. The goal, however, is not just to instill blind obedience to established authority but also to internalize this respect for and acceptance of authority.

The second important value is the role of the collective in setting standards and regulating social behavior. From earliest childhood, the Soviet citizen is taught to identify with a group, and far less emphasis than in U.S. society is placed on the needs and aspirations of the individual. The peer group is the collective of children, and the individual child is encouraged to take pride in the achievements of the collective. In childcare centers, the emphasis is on collective play; very young children are deliberately given toys that are too large or too complex for a single child to play with alone (Bronfenbrenner 1970: 21). Further, from an early age, children are trained to criticize the behavior of others from a collective viewpoint.

The Family

The history of Soviet policy toward the family is a good example of the great retreat. Some Communists looked on the family as an instrument of capitalist exploitation and expected the family to disappear altogether after the revolution. Lenin was not an extremist in this respect, but his government did carry out a revolution in the field of family relations. The only legal requirement for divorce was that the party desiring to break up a marriage register the fact of divorce with the authorities. At first, no provision was made for the children of a broken marriage.

Beginning in the 1930s, this radical approach to the family was abandoned. Soviet social scientists had discovered an unacceptable increase in the number of homeless children and in the incidence of juvenile delinquency. The government took some steps to provide homes for children without parents, and the police began a campaign against juvenile crime. But it was soon recognized that the best long-range solution to this problem was to strengthen the institution of the family. A 1936 law made it much more difficult to get a divorce, especially where children were involved.

Perhaps nothing affords better evidence of the essential social conservatism of Stalin's regime than this decision to reverse the trend toward the breakdown of the family. From this point on, Soviet propaganda was directed at refurbishing the institution of the family and at strengthening the authority of parents. Although some important changes in family policy have evolved since 1936 (Juviler 1967: 29),

Soviet policy has been fairly consistent in trying to reinforce the family relationship and to make the upbringing of children a parental responsibility.

Educational Opportunity: The Schools

In a society that has an elite of privilege rather than an elite of wealth, educational opportunity is of crucial importance. It has been called the filter that determines access into the elite (Lane 1976: 185). David Lane, relying on Soviet data, has argued that the offspring of white-collar workers and officials have an advantage in educational opportunity over the children of workers and peasants. Statistics show that only about one-fourth of those who enter school at age seven actually complete the ten-year program of secondary education. The children of workers and peasants are much more likely to leave school before finishing. The ninth and tenth classes, which prepare students for higher education, contain a disproportionate number of children from upper-class families.

Soviet school teachers devote a considerable amount of care to socialization in the broader sense of preparing children to become well-adjusted members of society. Children as individuals are not encouraged to compete with others but rather to do their share within the group. For instance, a Soviet text for teachers states that it is wrong to say: "Children, sit up straight." Instead, the teacher should look over the rows of children sitting in the classroom and say: "Let's see which row can sit the straightest" (Bronfenbrenner 1970: 53). With this challenge from the adult authority in the room, each row will try to be best. And each child in the row will look upon others with a critical eye and ask the question: Who is letting the row down?

Higher Education

The Soviet system of higher education is maintained to train specialists. The universities are only a small part of the whole system of higher education. Most advanced education is acquired in specialized institutes that function to train professional workers—doctors, engineers, teachers, managers. The universities are devoted primarily to training scholars and research scientists. The universities, institutes, and other centers of higher education are collectively known as *vuzy* (*vysshie uchebnye zavedeniia*, or higher educational institutions).

Higher education is intensely specialized. The future Soviet doctor (who is likely to be a woman as in the following example) normally enters medical training right after leaving school at about age eighteen. She will not have the luxury of spending four years in college, getting a general education, and pondering her future. During the first year in the medical institute, she must decide whether to train to be a surgeon or to enter some other medical specialty. Once her career decision is made, it is not easy to change. The future doctor attends a separate medical institute that has no connection with a university. In the classroom, in the dormitory, in the library, and very likely in much of her social life, she sees only other medical students.

An important consequence of this educational system is that most professional groups in the USSR are very closely knit in a way found only in military life in the United States. In each bureaucracy that oversees a branch of industry, the managers generally have attended the same schools, lived in the same dormitories, and held the same jobs during their careers.

Few drop out of Soviet vuzes. Competition is extremely stiff, and admission is granted on the basis of competitive examinations. In the most prestigious institutions (such as the universities at Moscow or Leningrad, the Bauman Technical School, or the Leningrad Polytechnical) the admission rate may be as low as one applicant out of fifty, and no doubt the children of white-collar families have a better chance of gaining entry. Nonetheless, since the revolution the USSR has made impressive progress in opening up new channels of educational opportunity—and hence career opportunities—to all classes of society.

Once admitted, the student can look forward to a secure future. He has few personal decisions to make in the course of his education, since much of the curriculum consists of required courses. After five years of study, he will be assigned to a job where he must normally stay for three years. There is no tuition fee, and most students receive a government stipend. In effect, the student is required to repay the state by accepting this first work assignment, wherever it may be. Once this obligation has been paid off, the young specialist is free to accept employment elsewhere if he can find it.

Although the primary function of the vuz is to train professional specialists, it is also an instrument of political socialization and recruitment. More overt political indoctrination takes place there than in the schools. The primary channel of political socialization, however, is not through the formal curriculum but through the Communist youth organization.

The Komsomol

The political education of school-aged children and youth is the responsibility of two organizations that function under the watchful eye of the party leadership: the Young Communist League and its junior affiliate, the Young Pioneers. The Young Communist League, or Komsomol, is a mass organization open to all from ages fifteen to twenty-eight, inclusive. (The term *Komsomol* is an abbreviation for *Vsesoiuznyi kommunisticheskii soiuz molodezi*, which means All-Union Communist League of Youth.) The Young Pioneers is open to younger children beginning at age ten.

The Komsomol serves three basic functions in the Soviet system. First, it is an instrument of political indoctrination and social control among the country's youth. As the only national youth organization in the USSR, it provides a channel of communication by which the regime's message, in both subtle and unsubtle ways, can be transmitted to young people. Second, the Komsomol sometimes serves as a mobilizing organization. Through it, the normal interests and enthusiasms of young people can be directed toward the regime's program.

The third major function of the Komsomol is to recruit future political leaders. The structure of the Komsomol is almost identical with the organization of the Communist party. In every factory, military base, or university—wherever there is a party organization—there is bound to be a Komsomol organization too. Like the party, the Komsomol has its own bureaucracy—the Komsomol apparatus—which is subordinate to the party apparatus. The young leaders of the Komsomol are regarded as potential party leaders. Many Komsomol leaders, however, are not so young. To ensure effective party control, those who work in the Komsomol apparatus are exempt from the general rule that members must leave the organization at age twenty-eight (Kassof 1965: 52). Many of the leaders are over thirty.

As discussed later, the Communist party of the Soviet Union is a highly selective organization. Those who apply for party membership must satisfy several requirements, and a young person who wishes to join the party must present a good Komsomol record. Increasingly, the Komsomol serves as a screening organization for the party. But unlike the party, the Komsomol is a mass organization. The standards for admission are not as rigorous, and the party expects the Komsomol to reach out to all Soviet youth.

The Komsomol is not yet an all-encompassing organization: Only about half of the eligible Soviet young people actually take the trouble to join the Komsomol. The organization appears to be strongest in those areas of Soviet life where political controls are most important to the regime—especially in the universities and in the armed forces. Komsomol organization is not so widespread among working-class youth or among the peasantry. Still, as Allen Kassof pointed out, the influence of the Komsomol is almost universal because no other youth organization exists. Extracurricular activities in the schools and leisure-time activities among young workers are organized to a great extent by the Komsomol.

CITIZEN, PARTY, AND STATE

The political education of the Soviet citizen does not come to an end when he leaves school. Indeed, the party goes to great lengths to maintain an extensive system of internal propaganda in a continuous effort to get its message across to the population. The aim of this propaganda is not merely to ensure the loyalty of the population or to shut out hostile ideas: The Soviet regime seeks much more than passive acceptance of its authority. Its purpose is to stir up positive and enthusiastic support for the party's program and the policies of the government. Every method of reaching the consciousness of the citizen has been utilized for this purpose: the printed word, the arts, and movies and television. The party also puts great stress on word-of-mouth propaganda, or what it calls agitation.

Public Opinion and the Media

The Soviet press is not actually government controlled, since the most important newspapers are published by the party. The press is supervised by the party's department of propaganda. The most authoritative newspaper in the country, the daily *Pravda*, is the official organ of the Central Committee of the party. The other main Moscow daily, *Izvestiia*, is published by the government. In the provincial cities, the main daily newspapers are all organs of the regional party office.

The major professional groups have their own daily newspapers, published in Moscow and circulated throughout the country. These special papers include *Krasnaia zvezda* (*Red Star*), the military newspaper, which is published by the Ministry of Defense; *Gudok* (*Whistle*), published by the Ministry of Transportation and directed toward railroad workers; and *Komsomolskaia pravda*, published by the Komsomol.

The specialized newspapers carry the same general news found in *Pravda* and *Izvestiia*. In addition, they carry news of interest to their class of readers. For example, *Pravda* carries stories about the work of local party organizations that are not printed in the other newspapers. The Soviet citizen may thus depend primarily on one paper both for general news and for information of professional interest. A person in the military might read *Krasnaia zvezda* whereas the physician reads *Meditsinskaia gazeta*.

Agitation is an important part of the propaganda effort and reaches the consciousness of the citizen in two distinct ways. First, the agitator—a particularly important institution in the industrial plant where he is usually a worker—is given time off to speak to small groups about the current party line. The other channel of oral propaganda is the well-established institution of the public lecture. The Znanie (knowledge)

Society, which operates under the direct supervision of the party, sponsors an extensive system of lecture programs. Every Soviet city of any size has a municipal lecture hall operated by the Znanie Society, where one can hear lectures on subjects ranging from modern mathematics to classical music. Political lectures are also available on such topics as international relations, racism in America, and the efforts to overfulfill the current five-year plan.

One important reason for the survival of these face-to-face propaganda mechanisms in the era of mass television is that they provide two-way channels of communication. Through the factory agitator and the Znanie Society, the party not only passes on information to the Soviet citizen but also acquires information about the state of public opinion. The regime is deeply interested in knowing what the public thinks, and the central party office compiles regular reports for the leadership on the mood of the population. These data are apparently based on such sources as letters from newspaper readers, questions asked of Znanie lecturers and agitators, and police reports.

The obvious question—How much of the official propaganda line is believed?—is impossible to answer. Soviet citizens are exposed all their lives to the principles of the official ideology and have practically no opportunity to hear opposing viewpoints. Much of the indoctrination inevitably takes hold even on nonmembers of the party.

Inkeles and Bauer (1959: 179) found that the official propaganda line did have a profound influence on the "basic thought processes" of the individual. Their analysis of popular attitudes toward society, the party, and the Soviet state showed many instances where defectors from the Soviet system continued to use the language of the party line and to accept many of the values of the official ideology.

Participation and the Saliency of Politics

Several studies of public opinion in modern political systems have shown that the mass public tends to have a rather low level of interest in politics, and most people seem to be poorly informed about the political life of their own country. The USSR does not differ greatly from other modern countries in this respect. Indeed, there is some reason to suspect that the level of interest in the USSR may be even lower than in Western countries. In a nation with a competitive political system, national politics has some of the quality of a contest between two or more opponents seeking the same office. People take an interest in the election campaign because of the excitement of the contest. They want to know who will win, although their interest may subside considerably once the outcome is known. But in the USSR, there is no contest or no public contest anyway.

Getting Ahead in the System

The industrialization of society creates great problems, but it also creates new opportunities. The process of modernization breaks down the traditional barriers of class and status and makes possible a high rate of upward mobility. Inkeles and Bauer found that the mobility rate in the USSR was much like the mobility rate in other modern and industrialized countries.

Inkeles and Rossi (1971) studied the popular ratings given to occupational prestige in six societies, including the Soviet Union. They found that the ratings followed much the same pattern in all six countries. Doctors were given a very high rating in each case. Among the other high-ranking jobs were professor, scientist, and engineer, whereas ordinary jobs in industry and agriculture were rated much lower. Of course, these results are not surprising. What is important is the similarity of the ranking across national and cultural borders. Inkeles and Rossi concluded that the structure of modern society tends to create a common sense of values more or less independent of cultural and political variables.

The rankings of various occupations by former Soviet citizens are shown in Table 3.1. In this survey, the subjects were asked to rank various occupations in terms of their desirability as a career. An interesting result is that the party official was given a rather low rating on this scale. In fact, the job of party secretary was given a lower ranking than worker. David Lane (1976: 182) reported the results of some Soviet studies of occupational rankings in the 1960s. The results are similar to those in Table 3.1, except that the occupation of party secretary was not included in the Soviet data.

In every industrial society, education is the key to a successful career. The situation in the USSR is no exception. Since educational opportunities are not evenly distributed, a certain inequality in career opportunities results. However, a political career—that is, a career in the party apparatus—would appear in many ways to be an exception to this basic fact. A study of the family background and educational patterns of the present party leaders would show that many came from lower-class families and nonprestigious schools. Many, indeed, were educated relatively late in life. Former General Secretary Konstantin Chernenko, for example, completed his higher education when he was in his forties and already held a high party position.

One important conclusion that can be drawn from this information is that a party career is a channel of upward mobility in Soviet society. In prerevolutionary Russia, only an estimated 2 or 3 percent of the population had any real chance at a career that could lead to a position

TABLE 3.1
Evaluation of Occupations by Soviet Citizens*

Occupation	Rating
Doctor	75
Scientist	73
Engineer	73
Factory manager	65
Accountant	62
Armed forces officer	58
Teacher	58
Worker	48
Party secretary	41
Collective farm chairman	38
Collective farmer	18

Source: Based on a survey in Alex Inkeles, Social Change in Soviet Russia (New York: Simon and Schuster, 1971), p. 77.

*In this survey, each person was asked, "Taking everything into account, was the job of _____ in the Soviet Union: very desirable, desirable, so-so, undesirable, or very undesirable?" The answers were scored on a scale of 0 (very undesirable) to 100 (very desirable). This table gives the average rating for each job.

of power in society (Adeen 1960: 279). In the contemporary Soviet Union, not every youngster has a full opportunity for the kind of education that would let him become an engineer, a scientist, or a factory manager. But anyone, provided that he meets the political standards, can join the party—and through the party can advance into the ranks of the highest elite.

REFERENCES

Adeen, A. 1960. The Civil Service: Its Composition and Status. In *The Transformation of Russian Society*, edited by C. E. Black. Cambridge: Harvard University Press, pp. 274–292.

Aspaturian, Vernon. 1968. The Non-Russian Nationalities. In *Prospects for Soviet Society*, edited by Allen Kassof. New York: Praeger, pp. 143–198.

Bronfenbrenner, Urie. 1970. *The Two Worlds of Childhood: U.S. and U.S.S.R.* New York: Russell Sage Foundation.

CC Decree of July 7, 1954. On Serious Shortcomings in Scientific-Atheistic Propaganda and Measures To Improve It. In *KPSS v rezoliutsiiakh i resheniiakh sezdov, konferentsii, i plenumov TsK*, vol. 6. 8th ed. Moscow: Politizdat, pp. 501–506.

Djilas, Milovan. 1957. *The New Class: An Analysis of the Communist System.* New York: Praeger.

Inkeles, Alex. 1971. *Social Change in Soviet Russia.* New York: Simon and Schuster.

Inkeles, Alex, and Raymond Bauer. 1959. *The Soviet Citizen.* Cambridge: Harvard University Press.

Inkeles, Alex, and Peter H. Rossi. 1971. National Comparison of Occupational Prestige. In Inkeles, *Social Change in Soviet Russia*, pp. 175–212.

Juviler, Peter H. 1967. Family Reforms on the Road to Communism. In *Soviet Policy-Making*, edited by Peter Juviler and Henry Morton. New York: Praeger, pp. 29–61.

Kassof, Allen. 1965. *The Soviet Youth Program.* Cambridge: Harvard University Press.

Kerblay, Basile. 1983. *Modern Soviet Society*, translated by Rupert Sawyer. New York: Pantheon Books.

Kollarz, Walter. 1961. *Religion in the Soviet Union.* New York: Macmillan.

Lane, David. 1976. *The Socialist Industrial State: Towards a Political Sociology of State Socialism.* London: Allen & Unwin.

Lapidus, Gail Warshofsky. 1978. *Women in Soviet Society: Equality, Development, and Social Change.* Berkeley: University of California Press.

Lewin, Moshe. 1968. *Russian Peasants and Soviet Power: A Study of Collectivization.* London: Allen & Unwin.

Makarenko, A. S. 1967. *The Collective Family: A Handbook for Russian Parents.* New York: Doubleday.

Matthews, Mervin. 1978. *Privilege in the Soviet Union: A Study of Elite Life-Styles Under Communism.* London: Allen & Unwin.

Sakharov, Andrei. 1975. Soviet Society. In *My Country and the World.* New York: Vintage Books, pp. 11–50.

Shchipkova, Tatiana. 1979. Imeet li pravo sovetskii prepodavatel na svobodu sovesti? *Vestnik russkogo khristianskogo dvizheniia* 130: 345–354.

Shafarevich, I. P. 1972. *Zakonodatelstvo o religii v SSSR.* Paris: YMCA Press.

Stalin, J. 1953. *Problems of Leninism.* 11th ed. Moscow: Foreign Languages Publishing House.

von Laue, Theodore H. 1971. *Why Lenin? Why Stalin? A Reappraisal of the Russian Revolution, 1900–1930.* 2d ed. Philadelphia: Lippincott.

Wallace, Donald Mackenzie. 1961. *Russia on the Eve of War and Revolution.* New York: Random House.

Wheeler, Geoffrey. 1969. National and Religious Consciousness in Soviet Islam. In *Religion and the Soviet State*, edited by Max Hayward and William C. Fletcher. New York: Praeger, pp. 187–198.

4
Soviet Political Ideology and Doctrine

Political culture means the set of attitudes, beliefs, and political values generally shared by the members of a society. Political culture includes political style and the rules of the game played by the political elite, but it also includes the almost subconscious attitudes that people have about themselves, about authority, and about the society in which they live. What society does one identify with, for example? Does an Uzbek peasant think of himself as a Muslim, an Uzbek, or a citizen of the USSR? He is, of course, all three, but which group receives his deepest loyalties—the nation, the faith, or the state? On the other hand, Soviet political culture also includes the official doctrine of Marxism-Leninism, as formulated by the party, taught in the schools, and tirelessly repeated in the press, on television, and in the lecture hall.

IDEOLOGY VERSUS DOCTRINE

In the analysis of Soviet political culture, we need to distinguish between ideology and doctrine. Doctrine denotes the authoritative and usually well-publicized ideas that make up the official philosophy of Marxism-Leninism. Ideology is those political values that are parts of the belief system of the individual. In contrast to doctrine, ideology tends to be ambiguous, inconsistent, and even irrational.

This definition of ideology corresponds to the usage of most political scientists. Unfortunately, some writers on Soviet politics use the term in a different sense. C. J. Friedrich and Z. K. Brzezinski (1965: 22) defined ideology as an official body of doctrine. But whatever the terminology, most Western specialists would agree on the basic distinction between doctrine (or what is sometimes called official ideology) and ideology as defined here.

In every political system, ideology influences the way in which people relate to authority and the way in which political decisionmakers approach their problems. What is distinctive about the USSR is the regime's insistence on maintaining an official doctrine. The doctrine is maintained because it performs some essential functions in the political system. Every party member is expected to be familiar with the principles of Marxism-Leninism and to continue to study the doctrine using textbooks that the party provides. Marxism-Leninism provides the language of political discourse in the USSR.

The doctrine also serves to legitimize the regime. In fact, Marxism-Leninism performs a function in some ways analogous to the role of the Constitution in the United States or the Crown in Great Britain. The Soviet leaders may disagree on what the doctrine actually means (just as U.S. politicians may disagree in their interpretation of what the founding fathers meant), but they are united in their professed loyalty to the doctrine and in their determination not to allow any other doctrine to be accepted.

Finally, the doctrine helps to mobilize the people and to generate support for the regime. Some people believe that they are sharing in a program of historical proportions, or what is referred to in the USSR as the building of communism. It is doubtful if the regime could have demanded, or would have received, the enormous sacrifices that the people have made if they did not have a deep-seated belief in the righteousness of the Soviet cause.

Do people in the USSR actually believe what the doctrine teaches? In Chapter 3, Alex Inkeles's and Raymond Bauer's (1959) conclusion— that the official doctrine does have an influence on the basic thought processes of the Soviet citizen—was presented. Some of the official doctrine apparently has been accepted and has entered into the ideology of the average Soviet citizen, and some has not.

Do the leaders believe in the doctrine? Some Western scholars have assumed that the doctrine is an operational code that the leaders follow. Robert C. Tucker (1971) called this "ideological determinism." Lenin himself warned that a political leader must be flexible, open-minded, and able to adapt to changing circumstances. Lenin also said that the theory was only a "guide to action" and not a detailed plan to follow. However, certain aspects of Marxism-Leninism clearly have been internalized by the leaders and have become a part of their ideology and thus influence their decisionmaking behavior. Although the idea of ideological determinism can be rejected, ideology still does in some complex way influence behavior.

In fact, the question about ideology, doctrine, and policymaking cannot be answered without first examining the content of both the ideology and the doctrine. Contemporary Soviet political culture is a complicated web of beliefs derived from many sources, including the early revolutionary movement and classical Marxism. The political culture has also been influenced by the Russian political tradition.

RUSSIAN TRADITION

The religious philosopher Nicolas Berdyaev (1955) has emphasized the Russian roots of Soviet communism. The character and the content of Soviet political culture have been formed by Russian history, and according to Berdyaev, a knowledge of Marxism will not help to understand this culture. Two elements in the Russian past are of primary importance in understanding the contemporary political culture: (1) the tradition of autocracy and (2) the long and painful experience of westernization and modernization.

The Westerners

In the last century, the question of the national tradition and the relative value of Russian culture versus Western influence became the subject of bitter philosophical controversy. Two schools contended over this issue—the Westerners and the Slavophiles. The Westerners accepted the fact of Western influence and insisted that historically Russia should be a part of Europe. Westerners were just as patriotic as their antagonists. Although they had no specific political and social program, the Westerners did insist that if Russia were to play its proper role in Europe's affairs, it would have to continue the economic and political development begun more than a century earlier with Peter the Great. The Westerners left no movements or party, but westernism survived into the twentieth century and represented an attitude or state of mind that might be defined as a willingness to accept the modernization of Russia along European lines.

But what is Europe? Western Europe is a diverse civilization. Russian intellectuals, both Slavophiles and Westerners, looked to Europe and saw what they wanted to see. A small number of Westerners were converted to the Roman Catholic faith because they saw in the church the epitome of European civilization. Other Westerners were converted to Marxism.

The Slavophiles

The Slavophiles recognized that Europe was economically stronger and politically more powerful than Russia; yet they insisted that in a moral sense Russia was more pure and less corrupt than the West. Such opinions are not, of course, unusual in developing societies that have come under European influence. Slavophilism was, in fact, a psychological reaction against the westernization of Russian society.

Slavophile thought was based on a fundamental dichotomy between two worlds—Russia and the West, or "we" and "they" (Riasanovsky 1952: 60). The Slavophile historians looked upon Russian civilization as unique, a society in which the great virtues of the past had been preserved uncorrupted by modern life. The West was corrupt: It was a society of sin, lust, decadence, and rationalism. In the Slavophile view, the outstanding feature of Western society was its individualism. The Russian ideal was the collective, in which the rights and selfish interests of the individual were subordinated to the good of the whole. This collectivism was embodied in two Russian institutions: the peasant commune and the Orthodox Church.

The Slavophiles were religious romantics, and the political aspects of their philosophy are confused and contradictory. But the Slavophiles did agree that the Russian people were essentially apolitical. Neither the commune nor the church, which reflected the peculiar genius of the Russians, was a political institution. In the ideal vision of the Slavophiles, Russian society was harmonious and free of class strife. For these reasons, political activism or organized political parties were not needed.

This concept of the apolitical character of the people could be translated into an apology for autocracy to justify the idea that all power should be left in the hands of the Tsar. Stephen White (1979) took note of the importance of the autocratic tradition. This tradition is important because of the deeply held view that the people are apolitical and not really interested in ruling themselves.

RUSSIAN SOCIALISM

Aleksandr Herzen (1812–1870) was the first Russian socialist. Although Russians before Herzen had written about the injustices of Russian society and had conspired against the Tsarist regime, Herzen was the first Russian radical to openly embrace socialism as a political philosophy. Herzen believed deeply in individual freedom, and he was eager to liberate the country from the Tsarist autocracy. He had no specific economic program, and certainly he did not plan the nationalization of industry or the creation of central economic planning. In fact Herzen seems to have been generally opposed to industrialization.

By socialism Herzen meant the complete transformation of society— not merely the destruction of Tsarism but the creation of a new and more equitable social order (Malia 1961: 6). In his early career, Herzen was a Westerner. Later, he was won over to some of the ideas of the Slavophiles, although he did not abandon his political radicalism. His contribution to the development of Russian political ideas lay in the combination of socialism with the Slavophile philosophy. Herzen wrote not only that Russia might become socialist, but that having done so, it might then lead the way for Western Europe. Russia did indeed have a mission, not a religious mission but a political one—to open the way to socialism.

Under Herzen's influence, a new political movement was born: the *narodnichestvo* (from *narod*, or people), a socialist movement that was Russian in origin and owed little to Western ideas. In the Social Revolutionary circles, which inherited the *narodnik* idea, the coming revolution was planned, organized, and dreamed about—but never carried out. Still, the revolutionary movement of the twentieth century owes much to the thinking of these early Russian socialists.

Tkachev: Conspiracy of the Minority

In 1876 the socialist Petr Tkachev (1844–1886) published a short pamphlet on *Revolution and the State*, anticipating the book Lenin was to write on the same subject. Tkachev argued that a political revolution must come before the transformation of society: The revolutionaries must seize power before they can carry out their program. The revolution would be a conspiracy undertaken by a small group on behalf of the masses. Once in power, the new government would carry out a "revolution from above" using the organized power of the state. Thus the immediate aim of the revolution was to seize power and create a revolutionary state (Tkachev 1876: 141).

Although he was sometimes called "the first Bolshevik," Tkachev was not a Marxist. Unlike the Marxists who were his contemporaries, Tkachev believed that the world socialist revolution would begin in Russia and then spread to the West. In an open letter to Marx's friend Friedrich Engels, Tkachev expressed great confidence that Russia was close to revolution—much closer, in fact, than the developed countries of Western Europe (Tkachev 1874: 88–98). However, Tkachev warned that if the revolutionaries did not seize power when the opportunity arose, it might not come again. Tkachev emphasized what would later be called the subjective factors in the revolution.

Lavrov: The Revolutionary State

A more detailed vision of the future revolution is provided by Petr Lavrov (1823–1900), who anticipated the strategy and tactics of the Bolshevik regime after 1917. Lavrov developed two fundamental ideas: (1) the role of the party, both before and after the revolution, and (2) the transitional dictatorship that would bridge the gap between Tsarism and the new, socialist order. In Lavrov's vision of the future, the party was to be a group of "critically thinking individuals," intellectuals drawn together for the common purpose of revolution. In the *Historical Letters* (1967), first published in 1868-1869, Lavrov laid down a program of political action that became the strategy of the Social Revolutionary movement. His critically thinking individuals were described as "more capable and vigorous than other men." A small group of these individuals compose the "sole instruments of human progress" (Lavrov 1967: 141, 171, 174). The revolution will not happen suddenly, but the idea of revolution will grow slowly, and the critically thinking individuals will eventually form a political party.

Lavrov assumed that Tsarism would fall as a consequence of a mass uprising. But even though the masses could overthrow the Tsar, they could not create a new regime. That was the task of the party. In *The Element of the State in the Future Society*, written in 1875, Lavrov said that the party must be prepared to go into action when the moment of revolution arrived. Once in power, the party would proceed with the revolutionary transformation of Russia.

The primary task of the new government would be to reeducate the masses. In a revealing passage, Lavrov argued that the masses would be indifferent to the revolution and perhaps even hostile to the revolutionary government. The population would be the same on the day after the revolution as on the day before: ignorant or poorly educated, and accustomed to the ideas and values of the old order. The old ideas would not be easy to shake off. Therefore, a long period of transition would be required, during which the people would be taught to accept and support the revolutionary order. In the meantime, Russia would be ruled by a temporary dictatorship of the Social Revolutionary party.

The confused and disoriented state of the masses dictated the structure of the revolutionary state. It would be too dangerous to introduce genuine democracy at once. During the transitional period, the party would rule through institutions controlled by party members. The government would be an executive council controlled by the party. The council would appoint (not elect) a national assembly in which reliable nonparty persons would be included. Eventually, when the masses came to accept the new political order, the national assembly could be chosen by election. Bolshevism was to combine this distrust of the masses with the doctrines of classical Marxism.

MARXISM IN RUSSIA

Unlike Lavrov, Marx offered no blueprint for a revolutionary government to follow. Marx did predict that private enterprise would be abolished, social classes based on economic inequality would disappear, and eventually the state, too, would be gone. Marxism is primarily an economic theory, but it is also a theory of revolution, and this latter aspect explains its appeal in Russia. The theory teaches that capitalism must collapse from its own internal contradictions, and the working classes oppressed under capitalism will rise up to destroy it. Although Marx did not say this, his writings were interpreted in Russia as teaching two ideas: (1) The theory is equally applicable to all countries, and (2) the revolution is inevitable. Marxism appeared in Russia at a time when the revolutionary movement was in a crisis of confidence, and the movement itself was split over the question of tactics. Marxism offered the revolutionaries a message of hope and optimism, for it seemed to predict the inevitable fall of the hated Tsarist regime.

The first Marxist political organization was created by Georgii V. Plekhanov (1856–1918). In 1883, together with Vera Zasulich and a small group of Russian revolutionaries living in Western Europe, Plekhanov organized the Liberation of Labor group. The organization was dedicated to propagandizing the ideas of Marx among the Russian revolutionaries. Marxism did not enjoy instant success, and the *narodnik* idea remained predominant. Nonetheless, for the reasons suggested, Marxism gradually acquired more and more followers.

The immediate message that Plekhanov and his group sent back to Russia can be summed up in a few words: Patience and forebearance! Plekhanov's theory of revolution taught that the country was under a "double yoke" of the Tsarist autocracy and the capitalist economy, and this double yoke would be thrown off in two stages. First, the people would have to overthrow Tsarism and only then could they rise up against capitalism. Thus the country had to pass through two revolutions: (1) a democratic revolution against Tsarism, and (2) a socialist revolution, which would lead to a new economic order.

The logical conclusion from this theory was that the Marxists should not immediately agitate for a socialist revolution. Instead, they should cooperate with liberals and moderates in the effort to achieve a democratic order. Only then, under the protection of democracy, could they agitate for socialism. The more militant Marxists felt uncomfortable with Plekhanov's theory, and when the moment for the seizure of power arrived, the theory was ignored. It was left to Trotskii to formulate a new theory that justified, in Marxist language, a strategy of seeking an immediate advance toward socialism. This was his theory of permanent revolution.

LENINISM

Marxism provided a justification for the revolution, but it did not provide a plan. Lenin claimed only that he was applying Marx's theories to specific Russian conditions, but in fact he changed Marxism considerably. As John Plamenatz (1954: 221) pointed out, Lenin thought of himself as a "defender of a pure faith," but he made changes in the theory that "turned Marxism inside out."

At the beginning of the twentieth century, Marxist parties were able to operate with considerable freedom in the Western countries. Their members were called socialists or social democrats, and they avowedly pursued the aim of destroying capitalism. However, the Western parties were already becoming "deradicalized" (Tucker 1969). Because they were able to function in a competitive political system, the Western parties relied on traditional political methods, with the aim of getting votes and winning elections. By contrast all political parties were illegal in Russia until 1905. Russia's brief experiment with electoral politics did not persuade the Bolsheviks that there was any hope in that direction. The Bolsheviks called themselves social democrats, but they were deeply divided from the social democrats of the West.

This political situation had a direct influence on the development of Leninism. Under the conditions that existed in Russia, the only tactics that held any hope of success were those of illegal struggle, and the only prospect of winning power was the forceful overthrow of the existing order. The Tsarist government was not democratic, and Lenin did not intend to replace it with a democratic order. He openly acknowledged that his aim was to establish a revolutionary dictatorship. As already described, Lenin justified the dictatorship with the argument that it was only temporary.

Although Lenin supported his ideas with constant references to Marx, he was also influenced by Russia's own revolutionary tradition. Many parallels can be found between Lenin's ideas and the ideas of Lavrov, in particular. The justification of the transitional dictatorship is one example (Hammer 1971).

Lenin was an organizer and leader, rather than a political philosopher. He was not as original as Plekhanov or Trotskii, the two major theoreticians of prerevolutionary Russian Marxism. Still, in his capacity as a leader and organizer, Lenin demonstrated a masterful insight into political motivations and questions of strategy and tactics in a revolution. The description by Alfred Meyer is accurate: "Lenin was a revolutionary of a rare type: a revolutionary with a bureaucratic mind, for whom a high degree of organization in human affairs represented progress, order, and rationality" (1957: 98).

The Revolutionary Party

In *What Is to Be Done?* (1902), Lenin argued in favor of an authoritarian and highly centralized party. The party was not to be a mass organization but a small group of professional revolutionaries. Of greatest interest in this book, however, are not the details of party organization but the assumptions about human society and human nature with which Lenin justified his ideas.

In Western societies, a Marxist party might seek to be a genuinely democratic organization. In Russia, where the masses were barely literate and were tied in thought and spirit to the village, Lenin insisted that a democratic mass organization could accomplish nothing. On this point he agreed with Tkachev and Lavrov. The message of *What Is to Be Done?* was that the revolutionary idea would not develop within the working class but would have to be introduced from the outside. This task belonged to the party, the "vanguard of the working class." Lenin angrily denounced the belief that leadership could spring from the masses themselves. Having somewhat contemptuously dismissed the possibility of a spontaneous working class movement, Lenin went on to argue that the workers' party should not base itself on the working class alone or appeal only to working class interests. The party should appeal to all people who felt themselves oppressed by the Tsarist system. Lenin's idea of the party thus is based on the conviction that only a minority of educated people are able to guide the masses, and they should be entrusted with the power to lead. Trotskii criticized Lenin's ideas about party organization: "These methods lead to this, that the party organization takes the place of the party itself, the CC [central committee] takes the place of the party organization, and finally a 'dictator' takes the place of the CC; and also to this, that the committees provide the 'direction' while the 'people keep silent'" (1904: 54). Lenin responded with a defense of centralized organization: "In its struggle for power, the proletariat has no other weapon except organization" (1904: 644).

The Revolutionary State

The essence of Bolshevism (Plamenatz 1954: 285) was the idea that the revolutionary party should first seize power and then use the authority of the state to accomplish the transformation of society. This was a radical revision of Marxism, but it did not originate with the Bolsheviks; this same idea can be found in Tkachev and Lavrov. Like Lavrov, Lenin believed that the only government that could succeed in the chaotic conditions of the revolution was a dictatorship of a well-organized and disciplined minority. Lenin was an orthodox Marxist in his view that every state was a dictatorship. For him the only question was: Which minority will rule?

Yet at the end of his life, Lenin expressed deep concern about the growing complexity of the governmental apparatus, which seemed to be leading the country toward greater bureaucracy rather than toward socialism. As Moshe Lewin (1970: 124) pointed out, bureaucracy is a serious problem in any developing country. In the early stages of development, not enough well-trained persons are available to staff the administrative machine. The Soviet government thus was forced to rely on officials left over from Tsarist days, just as in the Third World newly independent countries must retain some of the civil servants of the former colonial power. In his last writings, Lenin complained about the problem but could not find a solution.

In 1918 and 1919, these problems still lay in the future. The long-range objective of building communism became less important than the immediate problem of survival. Like Lavrov, Lenin believed that survival would require not only defeat of the regime's enemies but the rehabilitation and reeducation of the masses. He called for ceaseless effort at education in the spirit of the new order.

> The dictatorship of the proletariat is an unending struggle—bloody and bloodless, violent and peaceful, military and economic, educational and administrative—against the forces and traditions of the old society. The force of habit of millions and tens of millions is a terrible force. Without an iron party tempered in the struggle, without a party which enjoys the full confidence of the honest segment of the working class, without a party which is able to watch over and influence the mood of the masses, the struggle cannot be won. (Lenin 1920: 367)

Thus Lenin transferred his concept of the party to the organization of the Soviet state. The quoted passage contains the essence of Leninism.

TROTSKYISM

Trotskii's criticism of Lenin put him at odds with the Bolsheviks until 1917 when he finally came over to Lenin's side. From then until Lenin's death, Trotskii was the second-ranking leader in the regime, although he did not abandon his earlier ideas. Even when he held office in the Soviet government, Trotskii began to criticize the tendency toward bureaucratism and the domination of the party by its bureaucratic apparatus (1965: 15, 37). After he was expelled from the country, Trotskii continued to criticize Stalin's regime in such works as *The Revolution Betrayed* (1937).

Like so many Russian political thinkers, Trotskii looked on the state as a powerful institution. Unlike Marx, for whom the state was merely an instrument of class rule, Trotskii wrote that the state was a creative force in its own right. In Russia, "capitalism seemed to be an off-spring of the state" (1962: 173)—a remarkably un-Marxist statement. Both Lenin and Trotskii reinterpreted Marxism to conform to their own ideas, but Trotskii did this openly whereas Lenin insisted that he was faithful to the original Marxist teachings. Trotskii did not look on Marxism as a closed doctrine. He wrote: "Marxism is above all a method of analysis—not an analysis of texts, but analysis of social relations" (1962: 196). From this perspective, Trotskii tried to revise Marxism in the light of the special circumstances of Russian history.

Marx, or so Plekhanov had taught, treated the revolution as the product of an inevitable historical process. Trotskii put more stress on what he called the subjective factors in history: the readiness of the revolutionaries to seize power. This approach led him to a startling conclusion: "It is possible for the workers to come to power in an economically backward country sooner than in an advanced country" (1962: 195). If this were to happen in Russia, then the working class would have to proceed directly to the establishment of a socialist system without pausing for the first, or democratic, revolution.

STALINISM

Stalin's most important contribution to the Soviet doctrine was the idea of "socialism in one country." This is not really a theory: It was a policy and a slogan, formulated to meet the needs of a postrevolutionary state exhausted from war and civil strife. As a policy, socialism in one country was a brilliant conception. Stalin was urging the country to turn away from its preoccupation with revolution and to concentrate instead on reconstruction at home. The policy of socialism on one country was the first step in the great retreat. The program allowed Stalin to appeal over the heads of Trotskii and the more radical members of the leadership to the patriotic spirit of the people. Trotskii once said that without European help, the revolution in Russia would collapse. Stalin was saying something like this: "Trotskii underestimates the power of the people. Let us forget about Europe and Europe's problems, and devote our energies to building a powerful socialist state in our own country."

As Robert Daniels (1960: 252) pointed out, socialism in one country was a major turning point in the history of the Soviet ideology. Stalin was not only turning inward toward the country's internal problems; he was also turning backward away from Marxism and toward the traditions of the Russian socialists. This change brought a new conception of Russia itself and its place in the world—at least a conception that was new to the Marxists. Stalin conceived of the country as alone and isolated, surrounded by a hostile "capitalist encirclement." He looked on the world as divided into two camps: the camp of socialism and that of imperialism (1919: 240–244). Or as he put it, in language that recalled the Slavophiles, *our* camp and *their* camp.

In the early years of Stalin's rule, the doctrine seemed to emphasize the subjective factors in politics. At one point, Stalin (1953: 200) wrote that the major weakness of his opponents was lack of faith. Faith was, indeed, very important to Stalin. To succeed, it was not enough for the party to have the correct policy. Equally important was that the people have faith in the policy (1953: 140). If faith were strong enough, there was no limit to what could be done. As Stalin put it, "There are no fortresses that Bolsheviks cannot take" (1953: 458).

However, as Stalin grew older, he became both more conservative and more cautious, and these changes were reflected in Soviet doctrine. In the last years of Stalin's regime, there was less talk about the great power of faith. His writings show a concern with stability and order and a concern about preserving the institutions that he had created. In his last work (1952) Stalin wrote about the objective processes in society and said that a government could not repeal the laws of nature.

DISSIDENCE AND DISSENT

Marxism-Leninism, as interpreted by the Soviet leadership, is an authoritarian doctrine that does not tolerate open dissent. Any disagreement with the general line of Marxism-Leninism is unacceptable. The Soviet attitude is revealed in the very term used for dissident—*inakomysliashchii*—which literally means "one who thinks differently." Yet in spite of the authoritarian tradition of Russian society, dissidence and political protest have a long history, and they have not disappeared in the Soviet Union. Dissidence virtually disappeared under Stalin because of the massive terror, but it reappeared after Stalin died. The most prominent of the early dissenters was Alexander Esenin-Volpin, son of the poet Sergei Esenin. Esenin-Volpin was a philosopher who specialized in mathematical logic and was an accepted member of the scientific community until he began to write political works. In 1961 a U.S. publisher released a translation of his *Philosophical Treatise*. This document, which had already circulated in samizdat form in the USSR, contained an attack on the philosophical foundations of Marxism as well as political criticism of the Soviet leadership. The regime denounced Esenin-Volpin in the most abusive language, and he was confined to a mental institution for a time (*Pravda*, Dec. 22, Dec. 27, 1962). Esenin-Volpin was forcibly hospitalized again in 1968, but he was later released and allowed to emigrate (Shatz 1980: 179). Esenin-Volpin's book was the first of an outbreak of dissident writing, which was widely circulated in manuscript form and developed into the samizdat network. The closing words of Esenin-Volpin's book provided the inspiration for the new movement: "There is no freedom of press in Russia, but who can say that there is no freedom of thought?" (1961: 171)

It should not be forgotten, however, that this movement includes only a tiny minority—a few hundred courageous men and women who have been willing to voice opposition to the regime. According to Andrei Amalrik (1970: 13), one of the best known of the dissenters, the democratic movement included only a few dozen activists and several hundred sympathizers. Furthermore, it was a movement without a political leader and without any concrete program. Most of the dissidents seemed to have agreed on the need for freedom of expression and for limitations on the operations of the political police. But the movement included a wide range of divergent views, the most important of which are probably the following: a neo-Slavophile school oriented toward Russian nationalism and the Orthodox faith, and liberals whose long-range goal was political reform along Western, constitutional lines. In addition, the dissident movement included professed Marxists whose aim was to restore "genuine" communism (or Leninism) and nationalists from the non-Russian republics of the USSR.

None of these tendencies has any mass base. Amalrik expressed considerable pessimism about the success of Soviet dissent because of the "paradox of the middle class": The natural supporters of the movement should be the middle class, but in the USSR the middle class consists almost entirely of employees of the regime—functionaries of the economic bureaucracy or the government or party apparatus. In Amalrik's words: "They regard the regime as a lesser evil than the painful process of changing it" (1970: 21).

Nonetheless, the dissident movement is an important element in the USSR. In the absence of a free press, samizdat has provided the only outlet for open political discussion. And the most interesting and provocative discussion about the country's problems has come from the dissidents; an ongoing debate about the USSR and its future can be found among the pages of samizdat.

The neo-Slavophile tendency is represented by the novelist Aleksandr Solzhenitsyn, who was forcibly expelled from the USSR in February 1974, and the liberal tendency by the physicist Andrei Sakharov. For years the regime tolerated Sakharov, apparently afraid to expel him because (unlike Solzhenitsyn) he knew too many secrets, especially about defense capability (Sakharov 1978: 18). Finally, in January 1980, Sakharov was exiled to Gorkii, a city in an area closed to foreigners. He has remained in Gorkii, isolated from other dissenters, ever since.

Solzhenitsyn's political program was set out in his *Letter to the Soviet Leaders* (1974), which he wrote shortly before his expulsion. This program can be summed up as a rejection of Western society and as an urging to return to the Russian past (Kelley 1982). Solzhenitsyn specifically rejected Marxism-Leninism because he saw it as another import from the West that had poisoned Russian society. He also rejected Western democracy, which he described as a source of confusion and crisis (Solzhenitsyn 1975: 24). His ideal seems to be a more traditional form of authoritarianism in which there would be an open competition of ideas, without the political struggles that are a disease of Western democracies. In defense of this idea, Solzhenitsyn offered two arguments. First, he pointed out that most human societies, during most of history, have existed under some form of authoritarian rule. Therefore, provided that authority is kept within certain limits, an authoritarian regime should be as tolerable as a democratic system (1975: 23). Second, he argued that Russian society is, in any case, not ready for a democratic order: It would be easier and more natural to make the transition from one authoritarian system to another rather than make a complete break with the past and try to create a democratic order. In any case, Solzhenitsyn argued, the country had a brief experiment with democracy in 1917 and the results of that experiment were not encouraging.

Sakharov first appeared on the dissident scene in 1968, with his essay "Progress, Coexistence, and Intellectual Freedom" (1974: 55–114). This essay presented a highly idealistic (perhaps one should say utopian) view of the future: The USSR and the USA would "converge," so that the United States would become more socialist whereas the Soviet Union would become more democratic and provide greater protection for individual rights. After 1968, Sakharov became less utopian and perhaps more pessimistic (Shatz 1980: 130), and he called himself a liberal rather than a socialist. Most of his writings have been in the Western liberal tradition: He called for tolerance for dissent and voiced concern about human rights and the rule of law. Yet as Shatz (1980: 167) reminded us, Sakharov's liberal philosophy is outside the Russian political tradition. Solzhenitsyn is much closer to that tradition, and for that reason he probably has a larger following within the USSR.

Sakharov refused to accept Solzhenitsyn's conclusion that the country was in some sense not ready for democracy. Furthermore, in response to Solzhenitsyn's *Letter*, Sakharov said that he could not accept the division of the world of ideas into Western and Russian. In contrast to Solzhenitsyn, Sakharov defended science and technological progress and insisted that this progress must be a "world-wide process."

> Our country cannot live in economic and scientific-technical isolation, without trade, including the exchange of the nation's natural resources. It cannot live alienated from world scientific and technical progress, which

not only represents a danger, but simultaneously the only real chance for saving mankind. This rapprochement with the West must . . . be accompanied by democratic reforms, part voluntary and part compelled from within by economic and political pressures in the USSR. (1977: 299)

Solzhenitsyn, like James Madison (*The Federalist*, no. 10), is opposed to political parties. Sakharov, on the other hand, is in favor of a multiparty system (1975: 102).

Despite their differences, Sakharov and Solzhenitsyn agree on one fundamental point: They oppose revolution, and both hope that somehow their programs can be realized through peaceful change. Sakharov and two other dissidents issued a manifesto that called for the democratization of the country (Sakharov 1974: 115). Like Solzhenitsyn's *Letter*, it was addressed to the leaders of the Soviet government.

SOVIET IDEOLOGY TODAY

The regime has a powerful compulsion to impose control, order, and discipline where it perceives anarchy and confusion, and ideological conformity is an important characteristic of the system. In practice, ideological conformity means accepting the current interpretation of the doctrine or what is called the general line of the party. The doctrine changes in accordance with Lenin's admonition that the party must be flexible and able to adapt to changing circumstances. The requirement for conformity, however, does not change. The Soviet term for this is *partiinost*, an untranslatable term that means conformity to the party line.

Creative Marxism

The source and inspiration for the doctrine are still Lenin, but the recent trend has been to insist that the basic principles are not taken from books but from the practical experience of the USSR in building a Communist society. M. A. Suslov, who until his death in 1982 was the regime's leading specialist on ideology, put it this way:

The founders of Marxism-Leninism, with true genius, laid down the basic direction, the main principles of the historical transition from capitalism to socialism, and of the development of socialist society into Communist. But, in distinction to the utopian socialists, they never claimed that they could foresee the specific, concrete details of this transition. . . . V. I. Lenin noted that "we do not and cannot know by what phases or what practical measures mankind will reach this high aim." . . .

In the practice of socialist construction there have arisen and there continue to arise countless problems which had never been encountered before. In order to find their solution, what is needed is not only a knowledge of the general theoretical principles of the development of socialism, but also a deep understanding of . . . a real socialist society. (1972: 495–496)

This doctrine of creative Marxism is useful to the Soviet leadership for two reasons. First, the doctrine seems to justify almost any program or policy line dictated by practical experience. At the same time, the regime can insist that the principles of Marxism-Leninism, as developed and interpreted in the USSR ("a real socialist society"), are the basis for scientific communism that ought to be accepted in other countries.

The Basic Principles of Ideology

It is not easy to determine what the ideology teaches. The brief statement that follows is an attempt to summarize some of the basic principles of the ideology of the Soviet leadership. These principles can be extracted from official texts, primarily from those by Lenin. They are important, however, not because of their author but because they are a part of the operational code of the regime.

The Masses. The revolution of 1917 was carried out in the name of the workers and peasants, and the regime today claims to represent the whole people. However, the leadership has the ambivalent attitude toward the people seen in Lenin. Left to themselves, the people are incapable of arriving at the truth or making independent judgments about the policy of the regime. The people are capable of heroic deeds but only if they are mobilized and led.

Although the USSR still does not have a classless society, much of the class prejudice of the old order has disappeared. Leninism is an authoritarian doctrine, but it is not necessarily elitist. The ideology does not teach that any race or social group is inherently superior or that any particular class of people has been chosen to lead the masses. The Soviet leadership, like the Communist party, is open to people of quite diverse educational, social, and ethnic backgrounds. The leadership's attitude toward the masses is not directed at lower-class people as individuals.

As a whole, however, the masses have not reached a sufficiently high level of social consciousness to be allowed meaningful participation in the affairs of government. This does not mean that the masses can be ignored. Like any modern authoritarian government it tries hard to generate public support.

Social Anarchy. This conception of the masses contributes to a second idea: the natural anarchy of society. Marx described capitalism as economic anarchy, and for him, socialism meant an end to anarchy in production and the organization of society on a more orderly basis. This attitude is the antithesis of the liberal idea of the "invisible hand," or what is sometimes called the "natural identity of interests." Nothing could be more alien to Soviet thinking than laissez-faire. The Soviet view is that if society is left alone, it will just run down—or worse, it will come apart.

Compulsion Toward Order. The party leaders believe that they have a mission to impose order and discipline on a chaotic and disorderly world. Of course this compulsion toward order has a practical side, too. The regime not only governs the country but is the employer of practically every worker. Like bosses everywhere, the regime is interested in economy and efficiency. But this compulsion extends beyond the workplace to every facet of the society. It is the basis for what was earlier called the cult of planning.

Authoritarian Role of Party. The party is seen as the engine that drives Soviet society. The party leadership, like Lenin, fears spontaneity and leaves nothing to chance. Thus the society must be controlled and the economy planned under the leadership and the inspiration of the party.

The State. "That government governs best which governs least"—this bit of American folk wisdom is wholly alien to Soviet thinking. The Soviet view is that the state (and its government) must play a central role in the life of society. The official doctrine still teaches that eventually the state will wither away, but according to the current thinking, some of the institutions of the state (especially the administrative system) will survive. The doctrine also teaches that the USSR is a state of "a newer and higher type" than any previous state. Individuals are presumed to be dependent on the wisdom and power of the state for their own welfare, rather than dependent on their own initiative.

Ideology and Reality

These ideas appear to a great extent to be shared by the population at large. Certainly there is no reason to believe that the majority of the population hold beliefs hostile to Soviet rule. On the contrary, a number of Western studies have concluded that the people believe in the positive value of a strong and paternalistic state and in the importance of social order (Inkeles and Bauer 1959: 250). These studies confirm Amalrik's "paradox of the middle class."

The tenets of the belief system must not be confused with the facts about the real world. An ideology is a statement about an ideal world, a set of ideas which describe what *should* be, and not what *is.* It was already suggested that the Soviet ideology was totalitarian in its aspirations, in its belief that all social life should be centrally planned. The Soviet leaders have by no means achieved this grand design, and Soviet society is not totalitarian. Indeed the reality of Soviet society would confirm the worst fears of the leadership: It is contradictory and confused, torn by tense conflicts that only a strong government can control.

REFERENCES

Amalrik, Andrei. 1970. *Will the Soviet Union Survive Until 1984?* New York: Harper & Row.

Berdyaev, Nicolas. 1955. *The Origin of Russian Communism.* London: Geoffrey Bles.

Daniels, Robert. 1960. *The Conscience of the Revolution.* Cambridge: Harvard University Press.

Esenin-Volpin, Alexander. 1961. *A Leaf of Spring.* New York: Praeger.

Friedrich, C. J., and Z. K. Brzezinski. 1965. *Totalitarian Dictatorship and Autocracy.* 2d ed. New York: Praeger.

Hammer, Darrell P. 1971. The Dictatorship of the Proletariat. In *Lenin and Leninism,* edited by B. W. Eissenstat. Lexington: Heath, pp. 25–42.

Herzen, Alexander. 1963. *From the Other Shore and the Russian People and Socialism.* Cleveland: Meridian Books.

Inkeles, Alex, and Raymond Bauer. 1959. *The Soviet Citizen.* Cambridge: Harvard University Press.

Kelley, Donald R. 1982. *The Solzhenitsyn-Sakharov Debate: Politics, Society and the Future.* Westport, Conn.: Greenwood Press.

Lavrov, P. L. 1875. *Gosudarstvennyi element v budushchem obshchestve.* In *Sobranie sochinenii,* vol. 7. Petrograd: Kolos, 1920.

——— . 1967. *Historical Letters,* translated by James P. Scanlon. Berkeley: University of California Press.

Lenin, V. I. 1902. *What Is To Be Done?* In *Selected Works,* vol. 1, pt. 1. Moscow: Foreign Languages Publishing House, pp. 203–409.

——— . 1904. *One Step Forward, Two Steps Back.* In *Selected Works,* vol. 1, pt. 1, pp. 410–656.

——— . 1920. *"Left-Wing" Communism, an Infantile Disorder.* In *Selected Works,* vol. 2, pt. 2, pp. 341–434.

Lewin, Moshe. 1970. *Lenin's Last Struggle.* New York: Vintage Books.

Malia, Martin. 1961. *Alexander Herzen and the Birth of Russian Socialism, 1812–1855.* Cambridge: Harvard University Press.

Meyer, Alfred. 1957. *Leninism.* Cambridge: Harvard University Press.

Plamenatz, John. 1954. *German Marxism and Russian Socialism.* London: Longmans, Green.

Plekhanov, G. V. 1961. *Selected Philosophical Works,* vol. 1. Moscow: Foreign Languages Publishing House.

Riasanovsky, Nicholas. 1952. *Russia and the West in the Teaching of the Slavophiles.* Cambridge: Harvard University Press.

Sakharov, Andrei. 1974. *Sakharov Speaks.* New York: Random House.

——— . 1975. *My Country and the World.* New York: Random House.

———. 1977. On Aleksandr Solzhenitsyn's *Letter to the Soviet Leaders*. In *The Political, Social and Religious Thought of Russian 'Samizdat'—An Anthology*, edited by Michael Meerson-Aksenov and Boris Shragin. Belmont, Mass.: Nordland, pp. 291–301.

———. 1978. *Alarm and Hope*. New York: Random House.

Shatz, Marshall. 1980. *Soviet Dissent in Historical Perspective*. Cambridge: Cambridge University Press.

Solzhenitsyn, Aleksandr. 1974. *Letter to the Soviet Leaders*, translated by Hilary Sternberg. New York: Harper & Row.

Solzhenitsyn, Alexander, Mikhail Agursky et al. 1975. *From Under the Rubble*. New York: Little, Brown.

Stalin, J. V. 1919. Two Camps. In *Works*, vol. 4. Moscow: Foreign Languages Publishing House, 1953, pp. 240–244.

———. 1952. *Economic Problems of Socialism in the USSR*. New York: International Publishers.

———. 1953. *Problems of Leninism*. 11th ed. Moscow: Foreign Languages Publishing House.

Suslov, M. A. 1972. *Izbrannoe: rechi i stati*. Moscow: Politizdat.

Tkachev, P. N. 1874. Otkrytoe pismo g. F. Engelsu. In *Izbrannye stati na sotsialno-politicheskie temy*, vol. 3. Moscow: Izdatelstvo Politkatorzhan, 1933, pp. 88–98.

———. 1876. *Revoliutsiia i gosudarstvo*. In *Sochineniia*, vol. 2. Moscow: Mysl, 1976, pp. 141–153.

Trotskii, L. 1904. *Nashi politicheskie zadachi*. Geneva: Izdanie Rossiiskoi Sotsialdemokraticheskoi Rabochei Partii.

———. 1937. *The Revolution Betrayed*. Garden City, N.Y.: Doubleday, Doran.

———. 1962. *Permanent Revolution and Results and Prospects*. London: New Park Publications.

———. 1965. *The New Course*. Ann Arbor: University of Michigan Press.

Tucker, Robert C. 1969. *The Marxian Revolutionary Idea*. New York: Norton.

———. 1971. *The Soviet Political Mind*. Rev. ed. New York: Norton.

White, Stephen. 1979. *Political Culture and Soviet Politics*. New York: St. Martin's Press.

5
The Communist Party

Modern authoritarian regimes make a continual effort to generate public support. In the Soviet Union, the need for a strong popular base led to a new kind of political system: the single-party regime. One of the functions of the Communist party is to mobilize public opinion behind the regime and its program and to hold together the oligarchical leadership, the masses, and the various bureaucratic structures in between.

PARTY COMPOSITION

More than 18 million Soviet citizens belong to the Communist Party of the Soviet Union (CPSU), either as regular members or as probationary (candidate) members. Yet the CPSU includes only about 6.5 percent of the total Soviet population, or about 10 percent of the adults. Party membership does not bring tangible rewards, although it does open some career opportunities that may be closed to non-Communists.

The Party Under Khrushchev and Brezhnev

The party has come a long way from Lenin's original conception, but it still claims to be composed of only the vanguard of Soviet society—the most advanced and politically conscious Soviet citizens. In the post-Stalin period, the social and ethnic composition of the party changed: The recruitment of workers was emphasized (Table 5.1) and the number of party members from the smaller nationality groups increased (Table 5.2). Initially, Khrushchev encouraged rapid growth in party membership, but toward the end of his administration he had second thoughts: In 1963, he confessed that some party members did not really deserve to belong to the party of Lenin (Hammer 1984: 199). After Khrushchev's resignation, one of the first acts of the new regime was to clamp down on the recruitment of new members (Hammer 1971).

Party saturation (Rigby 1968) is defined as the level of party membership within a specific group in the population. Approximately one

TABLE 5.1
CPSU Under Khrushchev and Brezhnev: Social Composition

	Percent of Total Membership			Average Annual Rate of Increase (%)	
	1957	1964	1971	1957-1964	1964-1971
Workers	32.0	37.3	40.1	10.2	5.9
Peasants	17.3	16.5	15.1	5.8	2.9
White-collar and others	50.7	46.2	44.8	4.9	3.9
CPSU Total				6.7	4.5
Total members (millions)	7.495	11.022	14.455		

Source: Partiinaia zhizn 19 (1965): 11; Kommunist 15 (1967): 95;
Pravda, March 31, 1971.

TABLE 5.2
CPSU Under Khrushchev and Brezhnev: Nationalities

	Membership (thousands)			Average Annual Rate of Increase (%)	
	1961	1964	1969	1961-1964	1964-1969
Russians	6,117	7,335	8,390	5.7	3.6
Ukrainians	1,412	1,813	2,154	8.1	4.7
Belorussians	287	386	464	9.9	5.1
Uzbeks	143	194	245	10.2	6.7
Kazakhs	149	181	220	6.1	6.7
Georgians	170	194	225	4.0	3.9
Azeri	106	142	181	9.6	6.9
Lithuanians	43	62	81	12.5	7.8
Moldavians	27	41	52	14.6	7.0
Latvians	34	44	55	8.8	5.9
Kirgiz	27	35	42	8.1	4.7
Tadzhiks	33	42	51	8.0	5.5
Armenians	161	188	212	4.7	3.2
Turkmen	27	32	39	5.3	5.1
Estonians	24	34	41	11.1	5.4

Sources: Partiinaia zhizn 1 (1962): 49; 10 (1965): 12; and
Partiinoe stroitelstvo (1970: 65).

of every four white-collar workers belongs to the CPSU, so party
saturation is 25 percent. The comparable figure for the peasantry is one
out of twenty. Compared to the level in other occupational groups, party
saturation is high among officials of the government, industrial managers,
and military officers. Although party saturation among workers and

TABLE 5.3
Education of CPSU Members
(as percentage of total membership)

Category	1927	1939	1946	1952	1961	1971	1983
Higher	0.8	5.5	7.3	8.9	13.2	19.6	29.5
Incomplete higher	---	2.0	2.2	2.8	3.0	2.4	2.2
Secondary	9.1	12.5	23.3	22.2	26.2	34.3	43.0
Incomplete secondary	---	13.6	24.6	27.6	28.6	24.9	15.7
Elementary	63.0	46.1	34.4	31.4	25.8	18.8	9.6
None	27.1	20.3	8.2	7.1	3.2	---	---

Source: Kommunist 15 (1983): 22.

TABLE 5.4
CPSU Members by Age Group
(as percentage of total membership)

	%
25 and younger	6.4
26-30	11.2
31-40	20.8
41-50	25.4
51-60	21.1
61 and older	15.1

Source: Kommunist 15 (1983): 25.

peasants is lower, these groups are by no means excluded from the party's ranks. On the contrary, party members are to be found in every walk of life and every profession except the clergy. Not surprisingly, the party finds its greatest strength among the bureaucrats and managers, but the recruitment policy aims at bringing in the best people from all elements of Soviet society, so that party influence can be felt in the field and on the assembly line.

The educational level of party members has increased markedly. The data in Table 5.3 show, however, that the party is not just an organization of the well educated. J. F. Hough (1976) developed an estimate of party saturation among men over thirty, classified by level of education. Almost 85 percent of party members belong to the over-thirty category (Table 5.4). About 75 percent are men. Hough calculated that among men over thirty with a higher education, party saturation is somewhat above 50 percent. This result is not surprising, since the Soviet Union draws its managers and officials from this group. Yet even in this important category, almost 50 percent have chosen not to join the party.

Although the Brezhnev regime slowed down the expansion of party membership, it continued Khrushchev's policy of recruiting workers. T. H. Rigby concluded that "the main motive for the drive to increase manual worker recruitment is to strengthen the regime's links with the working class and to offset the growing influence within the party of the technical intelligentsia" (1976: 330–331). This interpretation seems to be confirmed by Soviet statements on recruitment policy. Party Secretary Ivan V. Kapitonov said that worker recruitment was emphasized to ensure "a strengthening of the party's ranks, and a growth of its authority among the populace" (1982: 12).

CPSU ORGANIZATION

The CPSU is not democratic, even in its formal structure: It is an authoritarian and highly centralized organization. Two operating principles maintain the authoritarian character of the party: (1) indirect election and (2) the substitution rule. At each level of organization, the same three-part structure is found: An assembly (or conference or congress) represents all the members of the organization; the assembly delegates its authority to a committee, which in turn delegates its authority to an executive board (*buro*). Within the buro, which is the decisionmaking body, the dominant member is the party secretary. Except at the very lowest level (the primary party organization), elections are indirect: The primary organization sends delegates to the local conference and the local conference in turn sends delegates to the next higher level of the organization.

The party undoubtedly attracts individuals with authoritarian attitudes. The authoritarian personality, as defined by behavioral scientists, tends to be deferential toward authority and conformist both in behavior and in social attitudes. As we shall see later in this chapter, the process by which new members are recruited for the party seems designed to screen out nonconformists and to bring into the party individuals who are personally authoritarian in their attitudes.

According to the Party Statute (art. 19) the basic rule of party organization is democratic centralism, which is defined as follows.

1. All leading party organs are elected from below.
2. Periodic accountability of party organs to their organization and also to higher organs is required.

3. Strict party discipline and subordination of the minority to the majority is mandatory.
4. The decisions of higher organs are absolutely binding on lower ones.

An organization based on democratic centralism will appeal to the individual with authoritarian attitudes. A second rule of party organization is the territorial-production system. The party organizations generally correspond to territorial units such as cities and republics. However, the primary party organization follows the production principle (described in the next section).

Primary Party Organization

The production principle means that the party members belong to primary organizations associated with their workplaces. This close relationship between the party and the workplace makes the party an integral part of the working lives of its members. The primary party organization is the link that connects the Communist party to the rest of Soviet society. Primary organizations are supposed to be small enough so that the members know each other well, and the average primary organization has forty-three members. A very large primary organization, in a large industrial plant for example, will be divided up into shop organizations.

The structure of the primary organization varies with its size. A general meeting of all the organization's members is convened once a month. The general meeting is the only level at which rank-and-file members of the party participate directly in decisions, but even the general meeting delegates its authority. Every primary organization elects a secretary to manage its activities. Larger primary organizations (more than fifteen members) also elect a buro. Very large organizations elect a party committee (*partkom*) as well as a buro.

Kapitonov (1982: 13) described the primary organization in one Soviet factory, the Moscow Electric Lamp Plant. The partkom had forty-four members, half workers, the others management personnel, engineers, and the secretaries of the shop organizations. The committee met once every six weeks. The buro had thirteen members and met two or three times a month.

Most primary organizations perform three basic functions: recruiting new members, ideological work and political indoctrination, and monitoring the work of the parent organization. Although these functions are important, the primary organization is not intended to replace the management of the parent institution. In a recent Soviet novel, the hero Glebov is the secretary of a partkom in a large factory. Glebov describes his own functions this way: The partkom is not supposed to take the place of the plant director or the chief engineer. "What is the main thing in the work of the partkom? People, and a concern about their education" (Shevtsov 1970: 29).

Most Soviet membership organizations contain a "party group," which is similar to a primary party organization. The Party Statute (art. 67) provides that such a group must exist in any organization that has three or more CPSU members. The function of the group is to assure that the party's influence extends to the Komsomol, the trade unions, the soviets, and other "public organizations."

Recruitment of New Members

A party member is expected to be an activist but also a conformist. The first requirement of the Soviet citizens who seek to join the party is that they accept the program and the statutes. The procedure for admitting new members ensures that not many nonconformists find their way into the party. A person who wants to join the party must serve for a year as a candidate member. During this probationary period he is watched closely to determine if he deserves the title member of the party.

The Party as Cheerleader

Every primary organization is engaged in ideological work. The targets of this propaganda effort vary with the organization. On a kolkhoz, the primary organization may devote much effort to atheistic propaganda, since religion seems more firmly entrenched in the countryside. On the factory or on the farm, much of the propaganda effort aims at increasing production and promoting good work habits. In this effort, the party member is expected to influence others not only through formal propaganda but also by example.

Every available means is used to get the party's message to the nonparty masses, including posters and wall newspapers. The party tradition has always placed a high priority on oral propaganda by which the skilled agitator can tailor the message to the needs of the audience. There has recently been an emphasis on political information, where the role of the agitator is not only to persuade but to serve as a source of news. Many party organizations have a group of political information specialists (*politinformatory*) who carry out this function. The job of the politinformator is to counter foreign propaganda and rumors that spread through the population.

Monitoring Function

The primary organization keeps a watchful eye on the institution with which it is associated, reporting shortcomings and correcting faults where possible. This function is *kontrol*, which can be translated as monitoring, rather than control. The purpose of monitoring is to prevent authority leakage. In carrying out this function, the party organization is not supposed to interfere in management or issue any instructions. But if management fails to respond to a signal from the party, then the organization can appeal to higher-level authority—to local government or the local party organization. The primary organization serves as a monitor of the institution within which it functions. This is only the lowest level in a monitoring system that runs through much of Soviet society.

Territorial Organization

At this level the party organization consists of three bodies: the party conference, the committee, and the buro. The conference is a large body of several hundred delegates. The delegates to a city conference are normally elected by the primary organizations. The city conference, in turn, elects delegates to the conference at the next higher level, which is usually the region (*oblast*). The conference meets at least once every two and one-half years, and this meeting is usually a ceremonial event lasting only one day. The regional conference elects a regional committee, or *obkom* (*oblastnoi komitet*). This election is a formality because the regional leaders select the obkom members, and the conference merely confirms that choice.

The obkom is supposed to meet three times a year, and it represents various groups that make up the regional elite. The largest group of members comes from the party apparatus: regional secretaries and secretaries of lower-ranking party organizations. The second group comes from the governmental bureaucracy: the chairman of the regional government, the department heads, and the mayors of major cities in the region. Other institutions that are represented include the security police, industrial management, the labor union organization, and an occasional kolkhoz chairman (Stewart 1968: 46; Hough 1969: 327). The distribution of membership reflects the distribution of political influence within the region and the dominance of the party officials or apparatus.

Obkom Buro

The buro is a small group of about ten members, and all the obkom secretaries are ex officio members. Since there are usually four or five secretaries, the professional party officials are thus assured of a dominant voice in the buro. The chairman of the regional government is a member of the buro, as is the first secretary of the party organization in the major city of the region.

The buro has broad authority to supervise all activities of the region, and it has a much larger area of responsibility than has the regional government. The buro's major concern is the economic performance of the region, which is largely outside the jurisdiction of the regional government. The buro's task is to mobilize the resources of the region to fulfill the target figures set by the planners in Moscow.

Important appointments in the government or economic bureaucracy must be cleared with the regional buro, and the buro sometimes takes the initiative. In a Soviet novel, *The Regional Party Secretary* (Kochetov 1962), First Secretary Denisov finds that a chemical plant is not meeting its production quotas. Denisov contacts the minister of the chemical industry in Moscow and has the plant manager dismissed from his job.

This same structure is found at other levels in the territorial organization, although the terminology differs slightly. At the city level, the organization is referred to as the *gorkom* (from *gorodskoi komitet*, or city committee). In the party organization of the union republics, the conference is replaced by a congress of the republic party, and the committee becomes the republic central committee.

NATIONAL PARTY ORGANIZATION

The all-union congress, in theory, is the supreme authority in the party. In the first years after the revolution, the congress was in fact a powerful body where important decisions were made. Since then, several developments have weakened the congress's authority. The fact that the congress meets only once in five years ensures that the important decisions are made elsewhere, and the congress's function is simply to ratify these policy decisions. The congress has grown so large (5,000 delegates) that it is virtually impossible for the delegates to do much more than sit and listen. Indeed the main function of the congress is to provide an enthusiastic audience for speeches by the party leadership.

Delegates do not have to be members of the party organization they represent, and officials from Moscow are often elected by provincial organizations. In 1981 Mikhail Gorbachev, who was already a party secretary based in Moscow, was a delegate to the 26th Party Congress from Stavropol. As a result of this practice, officials from Moscow are overrepresented in the party congress and the regional party organizations underrepresented.

Even though it does not exercise real power, the party congress is an occasion of great ceremony where important announcements may be made. Kremlin watchers can sometimes detect signs of division within the leadership, despite the careful staging of the congress's sessions. The congress follows a standard format: an address by the general secretary, a second major speech by the premier devoted to the national economic plan, and party elections. The congress elects two bodies: the Central Committee and a Central Auditing Commission. In practice, the congress simply elects a slate determined by the leadership. The Central Committee, in turn, is charged with electing other central bodies: the Politburo, the general secretary, the Secretariat, and the Party Control Committee.

The substitution principle is at work here: The party congress elects a Central Committee and then adjourns for five years; the Central Committee, in turn, delegates its authority to the Politburo and the Secretariat. The Party Control Committee, the disciplinary court of the CPSU, has authority to hear appeals against disciplinary measures or expulsion of members from the party. The exact composition of the committee is not made public, and only the name of the chairman is known.

Under Stalin, autocratic rule reached its logical conclusion: The institutions of the national organization ceased to function. After the 18th Party Congress (1939), more than thirteen years elapsed before the 19th Party Congress met, just a few months before Stalin's death. The Central Committee, too, no longer functioned.

With the restoration of the oligarchy, this process was reversed. The Central Committee began to meet regularly in accordance with the statutes, and meetings of the party congress were held as required. This resuscitation of the national organization did not restore the congress to its former power, but it did restore the Politburo, and to some extent it enhanced the prestige of the Central Committee.

Central Committee

The Central Committee is a body of about 500 members and candidates for membership. At the time of the revolution, it had twenty-five members (four of them candidates), and it functioned as a genuine committee.

The Central Committee's members are the Soviet political elite. They are chosen primarily on the basis of the positions they hold. Some offices seem to entitle the holder, more or less automatically, to membership in the Central Committee. In addition to the national leaders, the following groups are found in the committee.

Regional and Republic Secretaries. The largest single bloc (about one-third of the total membership) consists of secretaries from the territorial organization.

Government Officials. The next largest bloc consists of officials of the central government. Most members of the Council of Ministers are elected to one of the central party bodies automatically.

Regional and Republic Government. All the republic premiers are Central Committee members, along with a few other officials of regional and republic administration.

Military. The chief of staff and the uniformed leaders of the major military commands are Central Committee members.

Ambassadors. The ambassadors to the Eastern European countries and the Communist-ruled states of Asia are normally included. These appointments, however, seem to be party positions, judging from the career patterns of the ambassadors. The ambassadors to a few non-Communist countries (often career diplomats) are also included.

Police. Under Stalin, the political police were well represented in the Central Committee. Under Khrushchev, this representation was reduced. Indeed at one point the head of the KGB (the security police) was not even a Central Committee member. This pattern was reversed after Khrushchev's resignation, and the police were once again represented.

Scientific and Cultural Establishment. The members of the scientific and cultural establishment seem to be chosen because of their positions in the bureaucracy and not because of their standing in the intellectual community. For example, the president of the USSR Academy of Sciences and the head of the Union of Soviet Writers are routinely elected to the Central Committee.

Special Positions. Certain posts appear to entitle the holder to membership in the Central Committee. These positions include the head of the trade-union organization and the head of the Young Communist League. In recent times the Central Committee has also included a collective-farm peasant and one or two factory workers.

On paper, the Central Committee is the governing body of the party. In fact its power is exercised by the Politburo, acting in the Central Committee's name. The Central Committee will not oppose the Politburo once the Politburo makes its will known. But potentially, the Central Committee can be called upon to arbitrate differences within the Politburo itself. Such an event is extremely infrequent and therefore critical. On at least one occasion in recent Soviet history, the Politburo was unable to reconcile its differences and a divided Politburo went to the Central Committee to resolve the issue. This was the anti-party affair of 1957, when a majority of the leadership wanted to oust Khrushchev from office. Khrushchev succeeded in appealing to the Central Committee, which supported him rather than those who opposed him.

Perhaps the most important fact about the Central Committee is that it is a recruiting ground for the central leadership. Politburo members are always chosen from the Central Committee. In practice, the most important limit on the Central Committee's power is that it does not elect new members, except from among candidate members who are being promoted. As discussed later, this fact is a significant limitation on the power of the national leader. The election of new members of the Central Committee is the prerogative of the national party congress.

Most Central Committee (CC) decrees are drawn up in the Secretariat and approved by the Politburo, without actually being considered by the full committee. The Soviet press may report that a meeting was held "in the CC," or that "the CC has heard a report" or issued a decision. These meetings or conferences held in the CC are not meetings of the committee: They are meetings held under the auspices of the Politburo and Secretariat, probably in the Central Committee building in Moscow. Meetings of the Central Committee, which usually take place twice a year, are ceremonial occasions.

The Politburo

Theoretically the Central Committee elects the Politburo. In fact the Politburo elects itself. The Politburo is a self-perpetuating body that tends to change rather slowly. At each party congress, normally one or two Politburo members retire, and one or two new members are elected. At the 26th Party Congress in 1981, no changes at all were made in the Politburo's composition.

Like the Central Committee, the Politburo has both regular members and candidates for membership. Although the number of members is not fixed, the Politburo typically has about twelve members and five candidates. Some members of the leadership seem fated for permanent candidate status. Petr Demichev, presently the minister of culture, has been a candidate for almost twenty years. Boris Ponomarev, a senior party secretary and director of the party's International Department, also seems to be a permanent candidate member. On the other hand, in 1985 two men were elected members without serving as candidates.

The Politburo membership, without exception, is drawn from the party apparatus and the government. The exact balance within the Politburo between officials of the government and officials of the party varies over time. Under Khrushchev, the Politburo had a preponderance of party secretaries, and that pattern was maintained in the early years of the Brezhnev regime. Occasionally government officials were brought into the Politburo, but this was unusual. In the later years of the Brezhnev period more members were added to the government: In 1973 the minister of foreign affairs, the minister of defense, and the KGB chief were rather suddenly added to the Politburo membership, and the precedent of having these officials in the Politburo has continued.

As is the case with the Central Committee, the easiest path to Politburo membership has been through the territorial apparatus. Most people who reached this level during the Khrushchev era had earlier served as regional or republic first secretaries. No one who had served an entire career in the central party office in Moscow reached this status. The next largest group in the Politburo consists of a few experienced economic managers who have reached the top of the political hierarchy.

No office automatically entitles the holder to Politburo membership. The general secretary, the premier, and the president are included but because these offices are filled from among Politburo members, rather than vice versa. The only exception is the office of first secretary of the Ukrainian party. Beginning with Khrushchev, every recent Ukrainian leader has reached at least candidate status. Another party post that usually leads to Politburo membership is the first secretaryship of the Moscow city organization. Judging from the early appointments of the Gorbachev administration, there seems to be agreement among the leaders that the KGB chairman and the minister of defense are entitled to sit on the Politburo. Some of the secretaries from the smaller republics are candidate members of the Politburo.

The Politburo meets once a week, usually on Thursdays, and in recent years it has published a brief summary of its decisions in the Friday morning newspapers. Some evidence indicates that Politburo members not resident in Moscow (republic party secretaries) do not attend each weekly meeting (*Pravda*, Dec. 7, 1984). Most members do reside in Moscow, so the Politburo can be called together on short notice. The staff work for the Politburo is done by the central apparatus under the direction of the Secretariat.

The Politburo appears to operate by consensus and discussion. Some evidence indicates that when the members are divided, the discussion goes on until they reach a general agreement, so that a vote is taken only as a last resort. The crucial question about Politburo decisionmaking is the degree of bargaining and negotiation. Will Politburo members ever trade their votes for support on another policy issue in which they are interested? Although this probably happens, no evidence of such vote-trading is allowed to leak out to the public. The rule of solidarity is the source of the Politburo's strength within the system. As long as it remains united, it is unlikely to encounter opposition within the Central Committee, and other than the Central Committee no institution in the system could seriously oppose the Politburo and its policies.

THE APPARATUS

The apparatus is the paid professional staff of the party. Although this political bureaucracy is a powerful organization, its power should not be overestimated. The apparatus operates at every level of the Soviet political system, and through the mechanism of the primary party organization, the apparatus reaches into almost every sector of Soviet life. The central apparatus in Moscow supervises all the operations of the Soviet government, and the local and regional apparatus supervises the corresponding agencies of local and regional government.

The apparatus is not an independent political force. In the language of public administration, the central apparatus is not an operating agency but a staff agency that serves the Politburo. Its function is to supervise and control the government and the other bureaucracies that run the Soviet Union but not to take their place.

A primary function of the apparatus is to process information. Every day, hundreds of reports flow into the apparatus from all levels of the Soviet system. The apparatus studies and summarizes this information and is prepared to brief the party's decisionmakers on almost any subject. The apparatus also has the task of ensuring an effective flow of information from the top downward, so that party members outside the apparatus are kept informed about the regime's current policies (*Partiinoe stroitelstvo* 1970: 271).

Another aspect of the apparatus enhances its potential power: It is the bureaucracy that has produced most of the country's leaders. Since Stalin, all persons who held the country's highest office spent most of their careers in the party apparatus. Similarly, most men (and the one woman) who have been members of the Politburo are also products of the apparatus. In the future, too, the apparatus will probably provide most of the contenders for political leadership. The exact number of apparatchiks is not known. Estimates by Western scholars range between 230,000 and 500,000 (Schapiro 1960: 525; Rigby 1976; Jozsa, 180). Although the bureaucracy is large, it is still much smaller than the party as a whole.

Some Western observers assume that a fundamental conflict exists in Soviet society between the apparatchiks and the technically trained managers. However, very little evidence is available to support this generalization. For the most part, the officials of the central apparatus seem to be well-educated and experienced in the areas of Soviet society that they supervise. There is no reason to assume that the apparatchiks are less pragmatic in their approach to problems than are the managers and the technocrats.

The Secretariat

The Secretariat is supposed to be in charge of current work within the Central Committee, especially in the fields of personnel assignment and the verification of decisions. The official description of the Secretariat's work (art. 38 of the Party Statute) states that it is not supposed to formulate policy, which is the function of the Politburo.

Although the number of party secretaries is not fixed, normally the Secretariat has about ten members. The party statutes do not assign separate responsibilities to the secretaries, except that the head of the Secretariat is designated as general secretary. Individual members shift their responsibilities according to the work load. Some secretaries (especially those who are not full members of the Politburo) specialize in specific areas of policymaking. Ponomarev specializes in international relations, and V. I. Dolgikh has special responsibility for overseeing heavy industry.

In addition to this general and shifting division of functions, a clear hierarchy of status can be seen within the Secretariat. Some secretaries are full members of the Politburo, some are candidate members, and some are outside the Politburo altogether. Sometimes, on the basis of protocol evidence, a "second secretary" can be identified, although no one has ever held a formal title of second secretary at the national level. During the brief term of Konstantin Chernenko, Gorbachev quickly emerged as the second-ranking secretary, and his succession to the office of General Secretary was no surprise.

Even more than the Politburo, the central Secretariat is dominated by apparatchiks. Most of the members of the Secretariat served as secretaries of an obkom or republic organization before they were promoted to the central Secretariat. Some of the secretaries had no experience in the central party organs until they reached the Secretariat.

General Secretary

Since the death of Stalin, we can trace the progressive institutionalization of the office of general secretary. An office is a political or administrative function understood to be separate from the individual who holds it (Weber 1964). In the early stages of the development of a political system, this distinction between the office and the individual is not made, and the idea of the office is not clearly understood. The charismatic leader derives authority from personal qualities and not from an office.

When Stalin was appointed in 1922, general secretary was a title rather than an office with clearly defined functions. He was supposed to run the party's central office, and while Lenin was alive and well, the general secretary was subordinate to the head of government. But Lenin soon became incapacitated, and Stalin exploited the great potential of this position to create a power structure in which the party apparatus dominated the government and the general secretary was superior to the premier.

After Stalin's death, the office of general secretary was not immediately filled. Khrushchev was given the title of first secretary, but he never accumulated the power that Stalin had held. When Khrushchev resigned, the position was not allowed to remain vacant, and Leonid Brezhnev was immediately elected first secretary. The people who had overthrown Khrushchev agreed that the party needed a chief executive and the Secretariat a responsible leader. Later, when the office became vacant because of the death of the incumbent general secretary, a successor was elected almost immediately.

A further step in the institutionalization of the office came in 1966, when the title of general secretary was not only restored but given a legal basis for the first time. At the 23rd Party Congress, the statutes were amended to provide for the election of the general secretary by the Central Committee. Brezhnev was elected and then reelected in 1971, 1976, and 1981, thereby setting the precedent that the general secretary's term expired with a new congress.

Although the general secretary is the most powerful leader in the Soviet oligarchy, his power is not unlimited. Significant institutional constraints are placed on his power to appoint and dismiss other leaders (Brown 1980: 149). One of these constraints is the structure of the leading organs of the party. The general secretary's leading colleagues come from the Politburo and Secretariat, and these bodies, in turn, are chosen from the members of the Central Committee. As turnover within the Central Committee and Politburo is relatively slow, the general secretary does not have a free hand to promote his own political friends. He has to find supporters among those already in the political leadership. A general secretary who has a short term during which no change occurs in the Central Committee (as was the case with Iurii Andropov and Chernenko) finds his power relatively limited.

The general secretary does have a powerful instrument under his control because he is the chief executive of the central apparatus. This control over the apparatus, together with his protocol position as the party's main spokesperson, gives the general secretary his power. He also appears to have considerable control over the flow of information into the Politburo, although he is certainly not as powerful as Stalin was in this respect. In addition, he has some control over appointments throughout the apparatus. Exactly how much power he has compared with other members of the Secretariat is impossible to determine. Perhaps the general secretary is still a potential dictator. All the evidence suggests, however, that despite the general secretary's great power, he must work together with other members of the Politburo and Secretariat.

At times the general secretary has held other posts as well. Both Stalin and Khrushchev held the office of premier. After Khrushchev left office, it was decided that in the future the two offices—head of the party and head of the government—should be kept separate (Rodionov 1967: 219). Brezhnev assumed the office of president in 1977, and that precedent was followed until 1985.

Central Party Apparatus

The central apparatus consists of about twenty administrative agencies, or departments of the Central Committee. Some of the more important departments are headed by secretaries. In the 1920s, the most important function of the apparatus was cadres work, or supervising appointments in the government and in the economy. *Nomenklatura*—or the power to control appointments—was used by the new general secretary to build up a political machine. In the 1930s during the first five-year plans, the work of the apparatus involved assigning competent managerial personnel to jobs in the expanding industrial economy. In addition to this responsibility, the party apparatus became much more active in the ideological field.

Each department of the central apparatus supervises the work of one or more ministries, as well as other government agencies and public organizations. This supervisory responsibility includes watching over appointments (through nomenklatura) and monitoring other activities. Through the network of primary party organizations, each department receives information about the agencies that it supervises. The department, in turn, is able to provide information to the Politburo not only about the activities of the government, but about every organization in Soviet society.

After half a century in power, the party can be less concerned about the loyalty or reliability of industrial managers or government officials, so the nomenklatura function should be less crucial. But many jobs in the system are still politically sensitive, and in those cases, the party continues to exercise direct nomenklatura. The party leadership holds nomenklatura over the appointment of party officials at all levels (*Partiinoe stroitelstvo* 1970: 271). The Party Statute (art. 49) provides that a party secretary at the local level must be approved (*utverzhdaetsia*) by the obkom or republic central committee.

The organizational structure of the apparatus underwent several changes under Stalin (for a history of the apparatus, see Fainsod 1953: 152–179). By 1948 the apparatus had evolved the general structure that it has today. Its structure follows the branch principle: The apparatus is divided into several departments that correspond to the organization of the government and branches of the economy. Each department is responsible for overall supervision of one sector of the Soviet system.

However, the apparatus of 1948 and that of today differ in one vital way. In 1948 the apparatus still served as an instrument of Stalin's personal dictatorship. The key organ within the central apparatus was Stalin's chancellery (or personal secretariat), which had once been called the secret department (*sekretny otdel*) and later became the special sector (*osoby sektor*) (Rosenfeldt 1978). The secret chancellery, under Aleksandr Poskrebyshev, monitored the rest of the apparatus, and it supervised the operations of the political police, carrying out some of Stalin's most sensitive political operations. In this department, apparently, the purges were planned. After Stalin's death the secret chancellery was broken up, and Poskrebyshev disappeared. Neither Khrushchev nor his successors had personal control over a secret department with this power.

Khrushchev experimented with a number of administrative reforms of the central apparatus (Hammer 1984: 195–197). The central apparatus was gradually divided into two sets of departments, with one overseeing the Russian republic and the other group overseeing the rest of the USSR, and a separate buro for the affairs of the Russian republic was created in 1956. In 1962 Khrushchev established a number of special boards and commissions to oversee the work of the apparatus departments. The boards were mainly headed by people known to be Khrushchev supporters (Chotiner 1984: 179–181). These reorganization schemes seemed to be efforts to make the party apparatus more responsive to the will of the first secretary. All these reforms were dismantled by Brezhnev, and the central apparatus returned to the basic organizational structure of 1948.

The central apparatus controls the flow of information into the Politburo and may make recommendations. But the Politburo is the decisionmaker, and it is not dependent on the apparatus alone for information. The government can also provide information and policy recommendations for Politburo consideration. This is especially the case with ministries directly represented in the Politburo, such as the ministries of foreign affairs, culture, and the KGB.

Political Departments. Two departments of the Central Committee are essentially political: Party and Organizational Work, and Administrative Organs. The first is responsible for internal party affairs, and appointments at the territorial level must be cleared with this department. The department maintains dossiers on every member of the party who might be a candidate for a political appointment. The department also processes appointments in the Komsomol and in the trade unions. Among its other functions, the department is responsible for keeping current statistics on party membership, and this information is available to the Politburo in deciding about recruitment policy. The director of this department occupies one of the most sensitive positions in the political system and ordinarily is also a member of the Secretariat.

The Department of Administrative Organs has a similar responsibility with respect to some of the more sensitive agencies of the government. It has jurisdiction over the courts, the police and the KGB, and the party apparatus in the armed forces (Mironov 1962: 233; *Pravda*, Dec. 20, 1984). Thus the department has acquired some of the responsibilities of Stalin's chancellery. The department, however, is not a police or judicial agency: It does not conduct investigations or hold trials, but it keeps the police under surveillance and informs the Politburo about police operations.

Economic Departments. At least ten different departments share responsibility for the management of economic affairs. These departments enjoy the right of control and have nomenklatura over important appointments within the ministries. Individual departments are responsible for the following sectors of the economy: construction, defense industry, heavy industry, machine building, planning and financial agencies, trade and consumer services, agriculture, light and food industry, transportation and communications, and the chemical industry. Under Andropov a new economic department of the Central Committee was created, but its precise responsibilities are not known.

Although the economic departments do not actually manage the economy, they have a right to be informed. In addition to the nomenklatura function, these departments advise the Politburo on economic policy. Probably the government is the best source of information about the economy because it controls the planning agencies and the statistical service. But the Central Committee's economic departments have access to the reports of thousands of primary party organizations at every level of the economy; they receive reports from every industrial enterprise and almost every collective farm in the country. These reports, which are carefully studied and collated, are part of the input into the process of economic decisionmaking.

All heads of the economic departments have had dual careers: They typically were trained as industrial engineers and served in management, and then at some point in their careers they transferred from industry to the party apparatus. The directors of these departments are not ideologues; they are probably as competent and as well informed as the ministers whose work they supervise.

Foreign Departments. Four departments manage the party's international operations (Teague 1980; Kitrinos 1984). The International Department, headed for more than thirty years by Ponomarev, is responsible for monitoring Soviet relations with the non-Communist world: Primarily it conducts relations between the CPSU and Communist or pro-Communist political parties not in power. The International Department has a special responsibility for Soviet relations with the Third World. Whereas the Foreign Ministry manages relations at the diplomatic level, the International Department maintains contacts with radical and Marxist organizations in underdeveloped countries. A former Soviet diplomat has reported instances of disagreements between the Foreign Ministry and the International Department (Shevchenko 1985: 190, 206), which resulted from their different responsibilities and different outlooks.

A separate department, the Department for Relations with Communist and Workers' Parties of the Socialist Countries, is responsible for relations between the CPSU and the other ruling Communist parties. Iurii Andropov became the first director of this department in 1957 and headed it for more than ten years. A third department, Cadres Abroad, has responsibility for Soviet citizens traveling outside the USSR. The Department for International Information, created in 1978, is responsible for maintaining the Soviet Union's image in foreign countries and supervises Radio Moscow and Soviet publications intended for a foreign audience. Its director, L. M. Zamiatin, has some of the functions of a press secretary. Zamiatin served as the principal Soviet press spokesman at the Geneva summit in November 1985.

Like the directors of the economic departments, the leading officials of the international departments seem to be competent and experienced persons. Vadim Zagladin, deputy to Ponomarev in the International Department, was trained at the Soviet foreign service institute (the Institute for International Relations) and then worked as a journalist specializing in foreign affairs. He entered the central apparatus in 1964 and became first deputy director of the department in 1975. Oleg Rakhmanin, first deputy director of the Socialist Countries Department, served in the Ministry of Foreign Affairs for eighteen years and is a graduate of the USSR's Higher Diplomatic School.

Ideological Departments. Three departments share the responsibility for ideological work. The Department of Science and Educational Institutions monitors the work of the education ministries and the Academy of Sciences, which are the parts of the government that manage education and science. The Department of Culture supervises literature, art, and the entertainment industry. The Department of Propaganda manages the party's extensive internal propaganda operations; it supervises the Soviet press and such organizations as the Znanie Society, as well as the party's own network of politinformators.

The first two departments are responsible for supervising the activities of the scientific and intellectual elites in Soviet society. Unlike the directors of the economic and international departments, the leading officials of the ideological departments have not had dual careers and seem poorly prepared for the task. They are usually the product of teacher-training schools that, rightly or wrongly, are ranked near the bottom of Soviet vuzes. Their lack of sophistication accounts in part for the image of the apparatchik as an unskilled ideologue. S. P. Trapeznikov, Brezhnev's choice to head the Department of Science and Educational Institutions, had served as an ideological specialist in Moldavia. He was an object of open contempt among intellectuals in Moscow, and, according to Sakharov (1974: 85), the USSR Academy of Sciences resisted party pressure to make Trapeznikov an academician. Eventually, in 1976, Trapeznikov was given the less glamorous rank of corresponding member of the academy.

During his brief tenure as general secretary, Andropov made some effort to upgrade the qualifications of the officials in the ideological departments. In 1983, he replaced Trapeznikov with Vadim Medvedev, a professional economist and a former professor at a Leningrad technical institute. Medvedev has served in the party apparatus, first in Leningrad and later at the center, since 1968, so he is not an outsider. Nonetheless he brought to this position far better credentials than did Trapeznikov.

Administrative Departments. The Directorate of Services (Upravlenie delami) is the housekeeping agency of the apparatus. Among its activities, the department manages the apartments and houses maintained in and around Moscow for party leaders and officials of the apparatus (RSFSR Decree of Jan. 12, 1956). The General Department is reported to be responsible for secret communications and internal security within the apparatus (Schapiro 1975). In addition to these departments, the Main Political Directorate of the armed forces, which is part of the Ministry of Defense, also has the status of a department of the Central Committee. Its functions are discussed in Chapter 10.

TERRITORIAL APPARATUS

Every party organization has its own apparatus. At the republic or regional level, the party has much the same concerns as it does at the national level (except for foreign relations and military matters). The republic or regional organization is served by a professional staff similar to that of the central apparatus in Moscow. Once again, the key department is the one responsible for party and organizational work, for here the cadres of the apparatus are mobilized. The typical organization of the republic party apparatus is shown in Figure 5.1. The apparatus at the regional level will have much the same structure.

The regional first secretary has a broader and more general sphere of responsibility than does the regional head of government, as illustrated in the structure of the regional apparatus. The regional government is

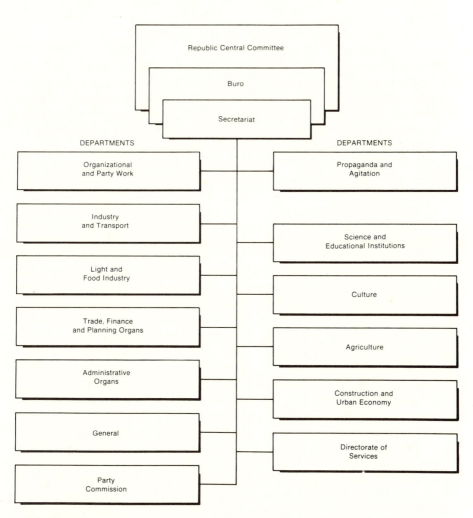

FIGURE 5.1

CPSU Apparatus in a Union Republic. This apparatus structure is typical, but it may vary in different republics. For example, the Azerbaidzhan party organization has a department for the oil industry.

Source: *Partiinoe stroitelstvo*, 5th ed., Moscow: Politicheskaia literatura, p. 167.

responsible for elementary and secondary education but not for higher education or scientific research. The regional apparatus, on the other hand, takes an interest in education at all levels, and it will often have a department of science and educational institutions.

Even at the lowest level in the territorial organization (the district or the small city), the secretary is a fulltime party official and is assisted by a fulltime staff. Moreover, the relationship between the territorial party secretary and the corresponding head of the government administration is considerably different from the relationship between the factory secretary and the factory director. In any Soviet city, there is little question about the political dominance of the party's first secretary over the mayor.

PARTY OFFICIALS

Too little is known about the careers or social background of those who serve in the lower levels of the apparatus. Information is available on the higher-ranking officials of the apparatus: the national party secretaries, directors of Central Committee departments, and the first secretaries of most of the regions and republics. These biographic data reveal that most of the higher-ranking officials are products of the apparatus. Consequently some tentative conclusions may be drawn about the apparatus by studying the careers of these people at the top.

Many apparatus officials got their start by serving as partkom secretaries. Brezhnev received an engineering degree, then went to work in a steel mill, and in a short time was the mill's party secretary. Many of the people in Brezhnev's generation received a technical education, but soon transferred into the apparatus, usually at the partkom level. A few years later such people were more likely to start in the Komsomol. A career in the apparatus is especially tempting to young people with poor backgrounds, a worker's or peasant's child who faces restricted educational and career opportunities. According to their official biographies, most of the present leaders came from just such backgrounds. The apparatus appears to have functioned as a channel of upward mobility. But a career in the apparatus means hard work: The life of the apparatchik, even more than that of the ordinary party member, is at the party's disposal. A career in the apparatus probably is not very attractive to a young person of middle-class background who has other, less risky opportunities.

As a general rule, successful political careers begin in the apparatus. Not very much is known about the process by which some young party members are singled out for further advancement into the apparatus. Self-recruitment is probably the most important factor. At present, the process appears to work like this. Most young apparatchiks get their start in the Komsomol. Every Komsomol organization operates under direct party supervision (Party Statute, art. 65). Therefore party secretaries must be knowledgeable about the work of their counterparts in the Komsomol. Thus, the young activists may begin by serving political apprenticeships in the Komsomol apparatus. If they show promise during terms as local or district Komsomol secretaries, they may become party secretaries.

An individual may be drawn into party work within an appropriate professional field; for example, an engineer in a factory may be elected to the bureau of the primary organization and asked to serve a term as secretary. Once installed in this position, the person may decide to stay in party work. Apparently, a large number of professional people— teachers, engineers, and managers—pass through the lowest level of the apparatus in precisely this way. How many of them remain is unknown.

The party has an extensive system of schools for training apparatchiks, the most important of which is the Higher Party School in Moscow. This school offers a three-year course of study equivalent to a university degree in social science, which is open to journalists and government officials as well as party workers. The curriculum includes courses on practical problems of management and economic planning, but most are oriented toward ideological indoctrination. The fact that the maximum age limit for admission to the Higher Party School is forty suggests that the school offers a special educational opportunity to people who somehow did not have that opportunity in their youth. Similar party schools exist in the republics or in the larger regions. These, too, are organized to train apparatchiks, journalists, and managers. At the top of the party's educational system is the Academy of Social Sciences, which offers postgraduate study leading to an advanced degree.

Careers in the apparatus fall into four categories. First are the line officers, or generalists (Armstrong 1959). They are concerned with overall direction of the apparatus. Second are the economic specialists, responsible for party supervision of industry and agriculture. Third is a category of ideological specialists, and finally come the apparatchiks who specialize in foreign affairs. These groups have different career expectations. The apparatchiks with the best political prospects traditionally have been the organizational specialists. This specialty is more likely to lead to appointment as a regional first secretary and therefore to membership in the Central Committee, with the prospect of ultimate advancement to the toplevel leadership. The election of Andropov (a foreign affairs specialist) and then Chernenko (an ideologist) to the office of general secretary violated this pattern. However, the election of

Gorbachev, a generalist who had served as a regional first secretary, was a return to the earlier tradition.

REFERENCES

Armstrong, John A. 1959. *The Soviet Bureaucratic Elite.* New York: Praeger.

Bakhshiev, D. 1954. *Partiinoe stroitelstvo v usloviiakh pobedy sotsializma v SSSR.* Moscow: Politizdat.

Brown, Archie. 1980. The Power of the General Secretary of the CPSU. In *Authority, Power and Policy in the USSR,* edited by T. H. Rigby, Archie Brown, and Peter Reddaway. New York: St. Martin's Press, pp. 135–157.

Chotiner, Barbara Ann. 1984. *Khrushchev's Party Reform: Coalition Building and Institutional Innovation.* Westport, Conn.: Greenwood Press.

XXIII sezd KPSS: stenograficheskii otchet. 1966. 3 vols. Moscow: Politizdat.

Fainsod, Merle. 1953. *How Russia Is Ruled.* Cambridge: Harvard University Press.

Hammer, Darrell P. 1971. The Dilemma of Party Growth. *Problems of Communism* 20 (July-August): 16–21.

―――. 1984. Brezhnev and the Communist Party. In *The Soviet Polity in the Modern Era,* edited by Erik P. Hoffmann and Robin Laird. New York: Aldine, pp. 193–217.

Harasymiw, Bogdan. 1984. *Political Elite Recruitment in the Soviet Union.* New York: St. Martin's Press.

Hill, Ronald J., and Peter Frank. 1983. *The Soviet Communist Party.* 2d ed. London: Allen & Unwin.

Hough, Jerry F. 1969. *The Soviet Prefects.* Cambridge: Harvard University Press.

―――. 1976. Party "Saturation" in the Soviet Union. In *The Dynamics of Soviet Politics,* edited by Paul Cocks, Robert V. Daniels, and Nancy Whittier Heer. Cambridge: Harvard University Press, pp. 117–133.

Jozsa, Gyula. Die Herrschaftsfunktion des Parteiapparats der KPdSU. In *Einparteisystem und bürokratische Herrschaft in der Sowjetunion,* edited by Boris Meissner, George Brunner, and Richard Löwenthal. Köln: Markus Verlag, n.d., pp. 171–197.

Kapitonov, I. V. 1982. Osnova partii, politicheskoe iadro trudovogo kollektiva. *Kommunist* 7: 4–17.

Kirstein, Tatjana. Das sowjetische Parteischulsystem. In *Einparteisystem und bürokratische Herrschaft in der Sowjetunion,* 199–230.

Kitrinos, Robert W. 1984. International Department of the CPSU. *Problems of Communism* 33 (September-October): 47–75.

Kochetov, Vsevolod. 1962. *Sekretar obkoma.* Moscow: Molodaia gvardiia.

KPSS v tsifrakh (k 60-i godovshchine Velikoi Oktiabrskoi sotsialisticheskoi revoliutsii). 1977. *Partiinaia zhizn* 21: 20–43.

KPSS v tsifrakh (k 80-letiiu vtorogo sezda RSDRP). 1983. *Kommunist* 15: 14–32.

KPSS v tsifrakh: nekotorye dannye o razvitii partii v period mezdhu XXV i XXVI sezdami KPSS. 1981. *Partiinaia zhizn* 14: 13–26.

Lenin, V. I. 1920. *"Leftwing" Communism, an Infantile Disorder*. In *Selected Works*, vol. 2, pt. 2. Moscow: Foreign Languages Publishing House, 1952, pp. 341–447.

Löwenhardt, John. 1982. *The Soviet Politburo*. New York: St. Martin's Press.

Mironov, N. R. 1962. Borba s antiobshchestvennymi iavleniiami—vazhneishaia zadacha. In *XXII sezd KPSS i voprosy ideologicheskoi raboty*. Moscow: Politizdat, p. 233.

Partiinoe stroitelstvo. 1970. Moscow: Politicheskaia literatura.

Partiinoe stroitelstvo. 1978. 5th ed. Moscow: Politicheskaia literatura.

Pervichnaia partiinaia organizatsiia: dokumenty KPSS. 1974. Moscow: Politizdat.

Rigby, T. H. 1968. *Communist Party Membership in the U.S.S.R. 1917–1967*. Princeton, N.J.: Princeton University Press.

———. 1976. Communist Party Membership Under Brezhnev. *Soviet Studies* 38: 317–337.

Rodionov, P. A. 1967. *Kollektivnost-Vysshii printsip partiinogo rukovodstva*. Moscow: Politizdat.

Rosenfeldt, Niels Erik. 1978. *Knowledge and Power: The Role of Stalin's Secret Chancellery in the Soviet System of Government*. Copenhagen: Rosenkilde and Bagger.

Sakharov, A. D. 1974. *Sakharov Speaks*. New York: Random House.

Schapiro, Leonard. 1960. *The Communist Party of the Soviet Union*. New York: Random House.

———. 1975. The General Department of the CC of the CPSU. *Survey* 21: 53–65.

Shevchenko, Arkady. 1985. *Breaking with Moscow*. New York: Knopf.

Shevtsov, Ivan. 1970. *Vo imia ottsa i syna*. Moscow: Moskovskii rabochii.

Stewart, Philip D. 1968. *Political Power in the Soviet Union: A Study of Decision-Making in Stalingrad*. Indianapolis: Bobbs-Merril.

Teague, Elizabeth. 1980. *The Foreign Departments of the Central Committee of the CPSU*. Supplement to the Radio Liberty Research Bulletin, Oct. 17.

Unger, Aryeh L. 1977. Soviet Communist Party Membership Under Brezhnev: A Comment. *Soviet Studies* 29: 306–316.

Voprosy raboty KPSS s kadrami na sovremennom etape. 1976. Moscow: Politizdat.

Weber, Max. 1964. *The Theory of Social and Economic Organization*, translated by A. M. Henderson and Talcott Parsons. New York: Free Press.

6
The All-Union Government

The Communist party rules, but it does not govern. Important political decisions are made by the Politburo and are sometimes publicized in the form of Central Committee decrees. However, the task of carrying out these decisions is usually left to the government, which operates under the party's guidance and control. Lenin's promise that the state and the government that serves it would wither away with the achievement of socialism has not yet been fulfilled.

According to the constitution, the USSR seems to have a parliamentary system, and the structure of the Soviet state has many features that should remind the student of Western European systems. As in most European countries, the constitution does not recognize the concept of separation of powers. According to the 1977 constitution (art. 108), all the power of government is legally concentrated in the Supreme Soviet of the USSR. The government of the USSR (that is, the Council of Ministers), is elected by the Supreme Soviet and legally accountable to it. In addition, the central judicial agencies are elected by the Supreme Soviet: These include the USSR Supreme Court and the General Procurator of the USSR. In this chapter, the Supreme Soviet, its Presidium, and the Council of Ministers and the administrative system will be examined. All references to the constitution and its articles in this chapter are to the constitution of 1977.

THE SUPREME SOVIET

The function of the Supreme Soviet is not to deliberate over issues but to serve as a ceremonial forum where the regime can announce its programs. The Supreme Soviet is a legitimizing body whose powers, in practice, are delegated to other agencies. In theory the Council of Ministers and the Presidium are accountable to the Supreme Soviet, but the soviet has no practical way of controlling them. The Supreme Soviet meets too rarely and its sessions are too short for it to exercise real power. It does provide an additional tool for monitoring the operations of the Soviet bureaucracy, which is perhaps its most important function. Indeed Peter Vanneman (1977: 101) has suggested that the Supreme Soviet might be called an administrative agency rather than a legislature.

Members of the Supreme Soviet are elected for five-year terms. Normally, it meets twice a year, and the sessions run for two or three days. In the first session of the year, usually held in the spring, the Supreme Soviet enacts legislation. In the second session, usually in December, it approves the budget for the following year. At each session, the Supreme Soviet hears a report from the government and the Presidium and gives approval to what has been done in its name.

Unlike the regional and republic soviets, the USSR Supreme Soviet is a bicameral body. One chamber, the Soviet of the Union, consists of deputies elected from single-member constituencies that are equal in population size throughout the USSR. The Soviet of Nationalities consists of deputies elected in the republics and the national regions according to a complicated formula (art. 110): union republic, 32; autonomous republic, 11; autonomous region, 5; and autonomous district, 1. This formula may lead to double representation. A resident of the Tatar autonomous republic, which is within the Russian republic, would vote for a deputy representing the autonomous republic and also for a representative from the Russian republic. On the other hand, a resident of the Estonian republic, which does not contain any national subunits, would vote for only one representative in the Soviet of Nationalities. Deputies to the Soviet of Nationalities are not required to be members of the nationality they are supposed to represent. For example, Marshal Nikolai Ogarkov, the former chief of staff (and an ethnic Russian), was elected to the Soviet of Nationalities as a representative from Lithuania.

The Supreme Soviet has 1,500 deputies, and the constitution requires that the two houses have the same number of members. These deputies are generally representative of the population of the USSR. The houses have a high proportion of women: nearly 30 percent. In the tenth Supreme Soviet, 50.3 percent of the deputies had a higher education (Zlatopolskii 1982: 55), compared with 17.9 in the first Supreme Soviet. Over the years the percentage of intelligentsia has grown (from 28.2 to 45.2 percent). Nonetheless the Supreme Soviet has a higher proportion of working class people than any national legislature in the Western world.

The Supreme Soviet also has a higher turnover rate than most national legislatures, and in each Supreme Soviet more than half the deputies are newcomers. The deputies who get reelected include most of the political elite. Members of the Central Committee (except for ambassadors) are elected almost as a matter of course, although there are some exceptions. The members of the government (ministers), the regional first secretaries, and a rather large contingent of generals, admirals, and marshals serve in the Supreme Soviet. The deputies also include some prominent writers, artists, and scientists.

The remaining seats go to workers and peasants or to local notables. Typically, deputies from this local elite serve only one term, whereas the political leaders may be reelected. Thus, one district in Irkutsk has been represented in successive terms by a physician, a kolkhoz peasant, and a kolkhoz chairman. The first two were not party members. The first secretary of the Irkutsk obkom, on the other hand, always seems entitled to a seat.

Party Control

The party maintains effective control over the Supreme Soviet, and occasionally this control can be documented. The Supreme Soviet over-represents the party: Since the first Supreme Soviet was elected, about 75 percent of the deputies have consistently been either party members or candidates for membership. For the tenth Supreme Soviet, the figure was 71.7 percent (Zlatopolskii 1982: 49). Like other public organizations, the Supreme Soviet has a party group, and in this case the party group is directly subordinate to the Central Committee. The party is thus assured of effective control over the Supreme Soviet.

When the eleventh Supreme Soviet convened for the first time in April 1984, it elected a president and a Council of Ministers in the following way (as shown in the official text of the proceedings).

1. M. S. Gorbachev, party secretary and member of the Politburo, went to the speaker's stand to nominate Konstantin Chernenko for the office of president, to succeed Iurii Andropov (who had died two months earlier). Chernenko was unanimously elected.
2. Chernenko then was recognized to propose that N. A. Tikhonov be elected to a new term as premier.
3. On the following day Tikhonov proposed a list of ministers. The premier and the entire council of ministers were elected without a dissenting vote.

Both Gorbachev and Chernenko used the same formula. They said that they were acting "on instructions of the Central Committee," and their proposals had been "approved by the party group" of the Supreme Soviet (*Izvestiia*, Apr. 11 and 12, 1984).

To further reinforce this control, the constitution (art. 107) explicitly gives the Communist party the right to call for a special election to recall a deputy. This power of recall is seldom used, since the party maintains close control over the nomination of candidates to the Supreme Soviet and the elections are not contested. To become a candidate, one must be nominated by a party organization, a public organization such as a labor union, or a general meeting in a factory or on a kolkhoz. Clearly the party has a dominant voice in all such public organizations.

The law on elections specifically gives the central organs, such as the Central Committee, the right to suggest candidates (Statute on Elections to the USSR Supreme Soviet 1950: 131). The candidates thus nominated are officially registered by district election commissions, and their names are put on the ballot. In practice there is no opposition to the official slate of candidates, although the constitution does not forbid contested elections and in theory more than one candidate could seek a seat. So the Soviet voter has no choice at election time. For anyone brought up in the Western political tradition, the obvious question is, Why even bother with elections in the USSR? There is no clear answer to this question. The regime wants to maintain the appearance that the Supreme Soviet is freely elected, and the election campaigns are taken seriously. The election thus offers an opportunity for the regime to show that it has mass support and an opportunity for the average citizen to demonstrate this support. The law gives every citizen the right to campaign for an official candidate once the nomination process is complete. But the right to campaign for a candidate's nomination is not guaranteed. (For a detailed description of the election process, see Friedgut 1979: ch. 2.)

Standing Committees

The influence of the party can also be seen in the work of the standing committees. Under Stalin, the two chambers had only four committees each, and the committees played no significant role in policymaking. Since the Stalin era, a conscious effort has been made to use the committees more and to give more publicity to their activities. The committees oversee a wide range of activities, although some important areas of government policy are excluded from their oversight. The Supreme Soviet has no committees responsible for defense and military affairs or for law enforcement.

The standing committees have the following functions: (1) working out proposals for consideration by the appropriate chamber or the Presidium of the Supreme Soviet; (2) preparing resolutions on questions submitted for the consideration of the Supreme Soviet or the Presidium; and (3) monitoring the work of the ministries and other agencies of the

TABLE 6.1
Foreign Affairs Committees of the Supreme Soviet
(elected in 1984-1985)

Soviet of the Union

Chairman: E. K. Ligachev (party secretary and Politburo member)

Deputy Chairman: O. V. Rakhmanin (first deputy director of the
    Socialist Countries Department)

Secretary: V. V. Zagladin (first deputy chairman of the Inter-
    national Department)

Soviet of Nationalities

Chairman: B. N. Ponomarev (party secretary, candidate member of
    the Politburo, director of the International Department)

Deputy Chairman: M. V. Zimianin (party secretary)

Secretary: L. M. Zamiatin (director of the International Infor-
    mation Department)

Sources: Vedomosti verkhovnogo soveta SSSR 16 (1984): 403;
Izvestiia, July 3, 1985.

government, as well as agencies of republic and local government (Statute
on Standing Committees of the Soviet of the Union and the Soviet of
Nationalities of the USSR Supreme Soviet 1967: 162).

The committees are developing not into independent decisionmaking
bodies but into another party instrument for maintaining surveillance
over the bureaucracies. As R. W. Siegler (1982) pointed out, a close
functional link exists between the committees of the Supreme Soviet
and the party apparatus. Judging from the membership of the committees,
one of their real functions appears to be to bring together party leaders
and responsible people at the working level in various fields for consultation and discussion. For example, in the foreign relations committees
the top posts are all occupied by officials from the central committee
apparatus (see Table 6.1). The other committees, too, tend to be dominated
by officials from the central apparatus of the party.

This arrangement allows top-ranking party officials, who may hold
no post in the government, to step out of their party roles when dealing
with non-Communist countries. Late in 1984, Mikhail Gorbachev paid
an official visit to England, traveling in his capacity as a Supreme Soviet

deputy and committee chairman. Ponomarev has occasionally met with Western, non-Communist visitors in his capacity as a committee chairman.

Officials of the central government are not members of the committees, although they may speak at committee meetings. The committees also include some experienced deputies from the operational level. In the Soviet of the Union, the Committee on Education, Science and Culture includes several regional secretaries and several other deputies knowledgeable in this field: an actress, a theater director, a composer, school teachers, and working scientists. The committee clearly provides an official forum or an independent channel of communication between the party leadership and an important part of the Soviet system, a channel that avoids the intervening filter of the bureaucracy. In the Soviet of Nationalities, the Committee on Agriculture is headed by V. A. Karlov, director of the Agriculture Department in the Central Committee. Karlov's committee includes several regional secretaries, a large number of agricultural workers such as kolkhoz chairmen, and some officials of local government in important agricultural areas.

The committees do not meet in public, but certain conclusions can be drawn about their functions in the system. First, as already suggested, they provide an additional channel of communication between the central party apparatus and the public. Second, although legislation originates in the government, the committees have a role to play in the law-making process. The committee members have a great deal of expertise, based on practical experience, that can be brought to bear on an issue. Third, the committees do have the legal right to exercise control over the ministries. And finally, they provide a legal platform where officials of the party apparatus can step out of their party roles and speak in their capacity as elected deputies.

Presidium

The Presidium of the Supreme Soviet has extraordinary powers (art. 121). With two exceptions, the Presidium can exercise any of the functions of the Supreme Soviet during the long period when the latter body is not in session. Thus the Presidium functions as a law-making body, and most Soviet legislation actually originates here. Second, the Presidium exercises functions usually regarded as executive: It issues pardons and amnesties, ratifies treaties, receives ambassadors, appoints the high command of the armed forces, and confers titles, medals, and other awards. The Presidium appoints the premier, deputies, and ministers who make up the government, although no doubt the actual decision is made by the Politburo. Third, the Presidium has the function of interpreting the laws. In exercising this function, the Presidium occasionally issues edicts that contain instructions on how a particular law is to be enforced. The two exceptions mentioned above are, first, that the Presidium may not amend the constitution, and second, that it does not elect the president. When the president dies in office, the presidency remains vacant until the next session of the Supreme Soviet.

The Presidium exercises an important additional function not mentioned in article 121: It hears and investigates complaints by citizens. To carry out this function, the Presidium maintains a reception office in central Moscow near the Kremlin. Anyone who has a grievance can visit the reception office and file an appeal with the Presidium. The right to complain about the actions of officials or agencies of the government is protected by article 58 of the 1977 constitution, although no such right was mentioned in the constitution of 1936.

As T. H. Friedgut (1979: 228) pointed out, this procedure for reviewing citizens' complaints is an important mechanism for information flow in the Soviet system. In a highly bureaucratized society, the regime requires channels of communication that can bypass the official bureaucracy and provide information about shortcomings or violations of the law at the operational level. If the experience of local soviets is an indication, then most of the complaints filed with the Presidium concern two matters: pension rights and housing.

The Presidium of the Supreme Soviet has thirty-nine members: a chairman (the Soviet president), a first deputy chairman (the vice-president), fifteen deputy chairmen, a secretary, and twenty-one regular members. A number of traditions have developed about the composition of the Presidium. The fifteen deputy chairmen are to be chosen from the fifteen republics. In practice (although not a requirement of the constitution) the deputy chairmen are the fifteen republic presidents. The secretary's post seems to be reserved for a Georgian. The Presidium usually includes one distinguished deputy who is not a party member. The additional members include several regional first secretaries and other notables. Some high-ranking party officials who are not members of the government are elected to the Presidium as a symbol of authority and an additional assurance of party control over the legal institutions of government. In 1985 Gorbachev, the new general secretary, was elected to the Presidium.

Traditionally, the office of president (chairman of the Presidium) has not been of great political importance. In 1977, Brezhnev took the title of president for a second time. Both Andropov and Chernenko, after assuming the office of general secretary, were also elected president. However, the pattern changed again in 1985, when the veteran foreign minister, A. A. Gromyko, was elected president instead of Gorbachev.

The office of vice-president was created in the 1977 constitution, when Brezhnev assumed the office of president. It was an open secret in Moscow that the job of the vice-president was formed to relieve the ailing president of some ceremonial duties. The first incumbent of this new office, V. V. Kuznetsov, managed to outlive Brezhnev, Andropov, and Chernenko (though he was older than any of them). Following their deaths, when the office of president was vacant, the duties were performed by Vice-President Kuznetsov.

Usually, the Presidium meets in formal sessions once every two months. Only a few members are regularly resident in Moscow, and yet the Presidium issues enactments almost daily. This fact suggests that like the Supreme Soviet, the Presidium functions as a certifying and legitimating body for decisions made somewhere else. Of course, the president is a full member of the Politburo and may have had a voice in a decision at that level. Acts of the Presidium are generally issued over the signature of the president and the secretary. The president, the secretary, and the vice-president are the only officials who devote their full time to the Presidium's work.

Legislative Process

The legislative procedure is extremely simple. Usually, the two chambers meet together, although they vote separately. Voting is by a show of hands and is always unanimous. The discussion of even the most important matters tends to be short and limited to hearing an outline of the proposed legislation. The deputies sometimes devote their speeches to advertising local accomplishments rather than to the business at hand. Western observers who have seen the Supreme Soviet in operation have little doubt that the leadership is in full control of the proceedings.

The Supreme Soviet only enacts two or three statutes a year. Usually these statutes are short documents (fundamental principles) laying down general policies to be followed by the government. For example, the criminal law of the USSR is based on a statute, the "Fundamental Principles of Criminal Law of the USSR and the Union Republics," enacted in 1958, which is only twelve pages long. The actual criminal law is contained in the criminal codes of the fifteen republics, which are much longer documents. In recent years the Supreme Soviet has enacted other legislation setting down fundamental principles of education, health care, family law, and conservation of natural resources. In all these policy areas, after the Supreme Soviet enacted the fundamentals into law, the details had to be filled in by administrative decrees. This practice of confining the Supreme Soviet's legislative activity to writing fundamental principles increases the power of the bureaucracy that has to administer the law.

A law passed by the Presidium is referred to as an edict (*ukaz*) distinguishing it from a statute (*zakon*) of the Supreme Soviet. An edict can legislate on any topic, and in fact most Soviet legislation originates in this form. At each session of the Supreme Soviet, a statute is enacted ratifying edicts issued by the Presidium in the period since the previous session met. The laws and decrees enacted by the Supreme Soviet and its Presidium are published in a weekly bulletin (*Vedomosti verkhovnogo soveta SSSR*).

COUNCIL OF MINISTERS

The Soviet government, in the narrow sense, is the USSR Council of Ministers. The chairman of the council is legally the head of government, or premier. The council includes officials who run the familiar departments of modern government: finance, foreign affairs, and defense. But in the Soviet socialist state, the government also runs the economy, and the Council of Ministers includes some officials who have no counterparts outside the Communist-ruled countries.

The Premier

When Lenin was premier, that office was the most important position in the political system. After Lenin's death, however, the premier was clearly subordinate to the party leadership and later to Stalin personally. The position became that of an administrator rather than a policymaker, a pattern that has generally held true. On the other hand, the premier is always a member of the Politburo and thus has a voice in political decisionmaking at the highest level. As an administrator, the premier is responsible for managing the Soviet economy. At least in noneconomic matters, the premier will defer to the general secretary. In official Soviet protocol, the premier is generally ranked third, after the general secretary and the president. However, in terms of real political influence, the premier probably ranks after the party secretaries who are Politburo members.

In 1941, Stalin suddenly assumed the office of premier while continuing to be general secretary, and he held both offices until his death. The next men to serve as premier again seemed to function primarily as administrators. Then Khrushchev held the premiership for six years, combining it (as Stalin had done) with the office of head of the party. Since the departure of Khrushchev, the office of premier has been held by experienced industrial administrators: Alexei N. Kosygin (1964–1980), Nikolai A. Tikhonov (1980–1985), and Nikolai I. Ryzhkov (1985–). Although the premier is an administrator rather than a political decisionmaker, political connections do affect his career. Kosygin's career was advanced by A. A. Zhdanov, the head of the Leningrad party organization, who was once regarded as a likely successor to Stalin.

After Zhdanov died in 1948, a number of his protégés disappeared in the so-called "Leningrad affair." Kosygin's career seemed to go into decline, but under Khrushchev's administration he again rose within the leadership and eventually succeeded Khrushchev as premier. Tikhonov was also a professional administrator who had no experience in the party apparatus. He was an ethnic Ukrainian from Dnepropetrovsk, and he seems to be one of the Dnepropetrovsk officials who owed their careers to Brezhnev. He retired in 1985 at the age of eighty.

Ryzhkov was born in 1929 and spent most of his career in the industrial city of Sverdlovsk in the Urals. Although Ryzhkov served for nearly three years in the Secretariat, he is not a product of the party apparatus. He was trained as an engineer at the Ural Polytechnical Institute in Sverdlovsk, and he rose through the managerial bureaucracy to become director of Uralmash, one of the country's largest industrial firms. In 1975 he was transferred to Moscow as first deputy minister of machine construction for heavy industry and transport. From this position he was promoted, in 1979, to be first deputy chairman of the state planning agency (Gosplan). This position entitled him to a seat on the Central Committee, to which he was elected in 1981. His ethnic background is somewhat mysterious. In 1974 the directory of Supreme Soviet deputies listed him as Ukrainian; however, later Soviet sources identify Ryzhkov as a Russian. In 1982, in one of the first appointments by Andropov, Ryzhkov was transferred to the party secretariat and given the job of overseeing the Soviet economy. In 1985 the new general secretary, Gorbachev, promoted Ryzhkov to full membership in the Politburo and later appointed him to the office of premier.

The Council and Its Presidium

The constitution (art. 128) describes the Council of Ministers as "the highest executive and administrative" body in the country. As already noted, the Presidium of the Supreme Soviet appoints the premier, deputies, and ministers. The Council of Ministers itself appoints deputy ministers and the heads of departments within ministries. The major function of the Council of Ministers is to coordinate the management of the national economy (Statute on the USSR Council of Ministers, art. 6). Some of the ministries seem to operate more or less independently of the council's control. A. N. Shevchenko (1985: 187) reported that the Ministry of Foreign Affairs is not responsible to the council but on most questions reports directly to the Politburo.

The council is authorized to issue decrees (*postanovleniia*) that have the force of law. It also issues orders (*rasporiazheniia*) on current questions, which are binding on the ministries but do not have the force of law. Decrees that have legal force are published in a periodical gazette

(*Sobranie postanovlenii Pravitelstva SSSR*), but this publication appears to carry only about 10 percent of the government's decrees. Many of the decrees thus remain unpublished. Although the Presidium of the Supreme Soviet theoretically has the right to annul a decree if it violates a statute or the constitution, no such act of annulment has ever been made public.

As presently constituted, the Council of Ministers is an unwieldy body with more than 100 members. In addition to the premier and deputies, the council includes more than fifty ministers, the heads of agencies like the state bank and Gosplan, and the fifteen premiers of the union republics. Thus the Council of Ministers, too, is forced to delegate much of its authority. On most policy questions a smaller body, the Presidium of the Council of Ministers, acts in the council's name. This body (not to be confused with the Presidium of the Supreme Soviet) consists of about fifteen members: the premier, the vice premiers (first deputy chairmen), and the deputy premiers (deputy chairmen). The decrees of the Council of Ministers simply ratify the decisions of the Presidium, and it is doubtful if these decrees are actually discussed by the council in full session. The Presidium of the Council of Ministers probably meets once a week.

Most of the members of the Presidium of the Council of Ministers are industrial administrators and managers. This suggests that in questions of economic policy, the Presidium of the Council of Ministers is the central decisionmaker, under the general supervision of the Politburo. The Presidium controls the State Planning Committee (Gosplan). In practice, the chairman of Gosplan is regularly appointed as a deputy premier and thus sits on the Presidium.

The agencies that are formally subordinate to the Council of Ministers fall into three categories. First, there are the ministries themselves. Then there are about fifteen other agencies, called committees or state committees, whose chairmen belong to the council. These committees include some powerful agencies, such as the KGB (security police) and Gosplan. The exact difference between committee and ministry is largely a matter of nomenclature, since committees are sometimes converted to ministries and vice versa. Finally, the heads of several agencies do not sit on the Council of Ministers but are subject to the council's instructions. These include the Soviet news agency TASS (Telegrafnoe agenstvo Sovetskogo Soiuza), the USSR Academy of Sciences, and Glavlit (the censorship agency).

The Ministries

After the revolution, the term "ministry" was abandoned because it reminded people of the Tsarist regime, and each department of government became a people's commissariat. Each commissariat, in turn, was placed under the control of a committee, or collegium (*kollegiia*). However, this experiment with collegial management did not work and the commissar soon emerged as the official in charge. The principle of one-man management (*edinonachalie*) became the rule in government, as well as in industry. In 1946 the term "ministry" was restored. The collegium still exists but only as an advisory committee to the minister, and the minister is chairman. The collegium has the right to discuss the minister's decisions, but it cannot overrule him. Although any member of the collegium theoretically can appeal to the Council of Ministers, this is not a frequent occurrence, if it happens at all. Even with this restriction, a collegium is a useful body, because it provides a means of consultation outside the top-level management of the ministry. In an industrial ministry, for example, the collegium may include not only the minister and deputies, but also one or two plant managers or other officials from the operating level. Thus the collegium seems to be another device for assuring a full information flow within the ministry (Tomson 1980: 202).

Ministries are of two types: all-union and union-republic. An all-union ministry is a completely centralized bureaucracy not represented in the governments of the union republics. A union-republic ministry, on the other hand, has counterpart ministries (of the same name) in the republics. The republic ministries function under the general supervision of the central ministry in Moscow. The ministries that manage Soviet industry are generally organized according to the all-union scheme. Ministries that carry out more traditional governmental responsibilities have the union-republic organization. The all-union Ministry of the Automobile Industry manages the manufacture of automobiles and trucks throughout the USSR. There are no counterpart ministries in the union republics, and the union republic governments have no voice in the affairs of the automobile industry. On the other hand, the Ministry of Finance, a union-republic ministry, supervises a financial system that includes a ministry of finance in each union republic and a department of finance at the regional and local level.

Union-republic ministries and their subordinate agencies follow the principle of dual subordination (*dvoinoe podchinenie*). According to this principle, a republic ministry is accountable to both the republic government and the counterpart ministry in the central government. Similarly, a local department is responsible to both the local government and the ministry above. Dual subordination is regarded as an application of democratic centralism in public administration (Vishniakov 1965: 49). In practice, dual subordination is not as confusing as it appears. The principle means is that the ministries lay down general policies and regulations, but republic or local agencies have the responsibility for carrying out policy and in the course of doing so they can take account of local conditions. The basic principle of dual subordination is depicted in Figure 6.1, using the example of the Ministry of Finance.

In the actual operations of the union-republic ministries, only some of their functions are delegated to their republic counterparts. The union-republic ministries also may be quite centralized. Thus, within the Ministry of Internal Affairs the supervision of the regular police force is a delegated responsibility and is shared with the republics. Some of the other functions of the Ministry of Internal Affairs, such as the administration of prisons, are strictly under central control.

Whether organized as a committee or a ministry, a government agency is typically divided into a central apparatus (or headquarters office) and subordinate agencies outside of Moscow. The whole network of subordinate agencies is called the system of the ministry. The central apparatus is divided into a number of departments (*otdely*) or directorates (*upravleniia*); the larger or more important ones may be called chief directorates (*glavnye upravleniia*). The functional directorates of a ministry carry out operations common to most agencies of government: planning, finance, construction, personnel (cadres, in Soviet terminology).

The directorate of services (sometimes called the economic department) is a housekeeping office not only responsible for managing the ministry's own building but for providing housing for many of the ministry's employees. This directorate may also provide a variety of other services to the ministry staff: special stores, health services, day-care centers, and even resort areas. The first department (*pervyi otdel*) of the ministry is responsible for internal security and may be staffed by KGB personnel. Finally, many ministries have a department of foreign relations that monitors all foreign contacts.

Every ministry has a primary party organization, organized according to the principles described in Chapter 5. The secretary of the ministry's party organization is an important functionary, although he is always subordinate to the minister. The primary party organization is organized within the central apparatus of the ministry. Subordinate agencies within the ministry system have their own party organizations. Since 1971 the primary party organization within the central office of a ministry has enjoyed the right of monitoring the ministry's operations. This internal party organization, like the organization throughout the Soviet system, provides the party leadership with a direct source of information about the activities of the government.

The minister has the authority by law to issue orders and instructions that govern the activities of the ministry (General Statute on USSR Ministries 1967). In addition, some ministries exercise the authority to

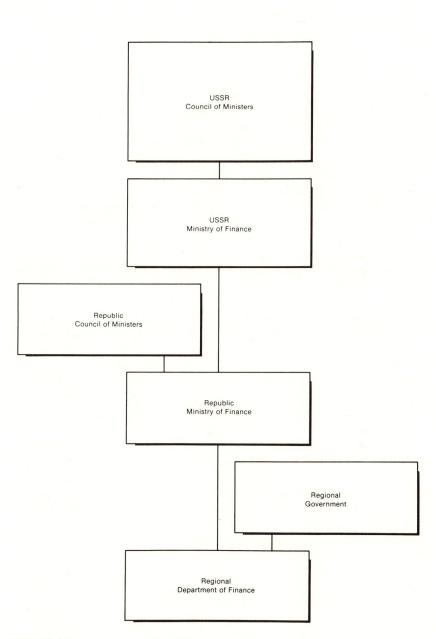

FIGURE 6.1
Dual Subordination in the Soviet Administrative System

issue regulations that have general legal force. For example, the Ministry of Finance has issued regulations governing the import and export of currency.

A Soviet ministry is a highly professionalized bureaucracy where most employees spend their whole careers within the organization. With certain exceptions, a ministry has no political appointees brought in from outside. The minister and his deputies are usually career officials who have worked their way to the top through the ministry's system. This pattern is so widespread that the occasional exceptions are worth special attention. The state security police (KGB) has usually been headed by an official from the party apparatus. Iurii Andropov, for example, was a party secretary when he was appointed KGB chairman in 1967 and had no previous experience in state security. Andropov's successor, Vitalii Fedorchuk, was a career KGB official, but he served in this post barely six months. His successor, Viktor Chebrikov, was a product of the party apparatus (although he spent several years in the KGB as a deputy to Andropov, Chebrikov did not come up through the KGB system). The Ministry of Culture is another agency where the minister has always been appointed from the party apparatus. In the post-Stalin era, the minister of defense has usually been a career officer. Dimitry Ustinov, minister of defense from 1976 to 1984, was an exception to this rule. Ustinov's career was spent in industrial management and later in the party secretariat, and he had no military experience. When Ustinov died in 1984, he was succeeded by a career officer. On the other hand, when A. A. Gromyko, a career diplomat, left the foreign ministry in 1985, his successor was Eduard Shevardnadze, the former Georgian first secretary, who had had no experience in foreign affairs.

The typical minister had a specialized education, worked for a time at the lower administrative level, and then joined the ministry's central establishment. He joined the party along the way, and after reaching the top as a minister, he was elected to the Central Committee. In a capitalist society, such an individual would be expected to be a strong company man. Clearly, political changes within the party leadership have much less impact on the government and economic bureaucracies than on the party's own apparatus.

On the other hand, there is no reason to suppose that officials who serve in the ministries have political ambitions. The career patterns of Soviet officials show that a party career is much riskier than a bureaucratic career. Obkom secretaries can think of themselves potentially as Central Committee secretaries and perhaps as members of the Politburo. Inevitably, the secretaries are drawn into leadership politics, and their own fates may be in the hands of others. The ministries to some extent seem to have insulated themselves against the vagaries of apparatus politics.

Consequently, the bureaucratic career is much more secure than a career in the party apparatus. Some of the present ministers have held office continuously for the past fifteen or twenty years.

PARTY AND BUREAUCRACY

Some agencies of government operate with little evidence of party interference and control; yet the ultimate authority of the party leadership cannot be denied. Without question, the party's Politburo is the supreme decisionmaker and the final arbiter of disputes within the government bureaucracy.

The relationship between the party and the government is not easy for Westerners to understand; indeed it is not always clear to Soviet citizens who live in the system. When the new constitution was adopted in 1977, there was some discussion of transferring governmental functions directly to the party, thus allowing the Politburo or the Central Committee to exercise legislative and executive functions directly. General Secretary Brezhnev, in reporting on this discussion, insisted that such proposals were "profoundly mistaken," that the party must continue to realize its program by operating through the agencies of the state (1977: 526).

In trying to define their own role in the decisionmaking process, the party leaders have been torn between two objectives. On the one hand, they want to place competent persons at all levels, people who are capable of taking the initiative on matters within their sphere of competence. If the people who administer the system are too dependent on the party for guidance, the party leadership will be swamped with requests for instructions. On the other hand, the party wants to be free to intervene at all levels to ensure that its program is being carried out. To maintain its power, the party has created a complex system of processing information, and it has access to much information that does not pass through the normal bureaucratic machinery.

The party directs the work of the government bureaucracy in many ways. The most important means of control is nomenklatura, whereby the party in effect appoints the ministers and their chief deputies. The party also enjoys the right to monitor the ministries' work through the primary party organizations. Finally, the central party organs give instructions to the ministries "while not restricting their operational independence" (Ananov 1960: 23). The second part of this statement may be only a pious hope.

The general rules governing the relationship between party and government are contained in two principles. The first principle, laid down by Lenin (1920: 371), is that the government is subordinate to the general line of the party. According to one authoritative text: "No important decision is ever taken by an organ of government, or by an administrative organ, without corresponding instructions from the Party" (Vlasov 1959: 361). In the same vein, a leading Soviet scholar (Lepeshkin 1962, 2: 450) wrote that all important political questions requiring a decision by the government are examined in the Central Committee (Politburo). The second principle is that, although the party gives guidance and instructions, it does not take the government's place. Not unexpectedly, this question arose early in the history of Soviet regime. In 1919 the 8th Party Congress took up the problem and issued a formulation still widely quoted:

> In any case there should be no confusion between the functions of the Party collectives and the functions of state organizations such as the Soviets. Such a confusion could lead to disastrous results, especially in military affairs. The Party must carry out its functions through the Soviet organs and *within the framework of the Soviet Constitution.* The Party strives to *direct* the activity of the Soviets, but not to take their place. (Emphasis in original.) (*KPSS v rezoliutsiiakh* 1953, 1: 446)

This decree is still on the books and is frequently cited to justify a measure of self-restraint by the party. In particular, the last sentence is quoted to prevent local party organizations from interfering unduly with agencies of local government. Sometimes the party has given extensive publicity to cases of too much interference. Local party officials who thus interfere in the operations of government agencies are accused of petty tutelage, which, where it occurs, sows the seeds of irresponsibility in government. Of course, there is also this point to be considered: The party leaders believe that if local party functionaries get too deeply involved in administrative matters that are not their proper concern, they will lose their overall perspective and will not carry out their own functions.

The party is supposed to make policy, not carry it out. This formula is very convenient because it leaves the leadership free to blame its mistakes on faulty execution. Problems can be blamed on those who have to conform to the party's policies. In particular, failures can be charged to bureaucrats and bureaucracy, sometimes but not always anonymously. Bureaucracy means breakdown in government, organizational inertia, lack of initiative, but not on the part of the CPSU. Bureaucracy with all its shortcomings is a familiar target in the Soviet press: It is found in government, in the economy, and sometimes in the labor unions—but never in the party.

REFERENCES

Ananov, I. N. 1960. *Ministerstva v SSSR.* Moscow: Iurizdat.

Brezhnev, L. I. 1977. O proekte konstitutsii (osnovnogo zakona) Soiuza Sovetskikh Sotsialisticheskikh Respublik i itogakh ego vsenarodnogo obsuzhdeniia. *Leninskim kursom,* vol. 6. Moscow: Politicheskaia literatura, pp. 517–538.

Friedgut, Theodore H. 1979. *Political Participation in the USSR.* Princeton, N.J.: Princeton University Press.

General Statute on USSR Ministries. July 10, 1967. In *Basic Laws on the Structure of the Soviet State,* edited and translated by Harold J. Berman and John B. Quigley, Jr. Cambridge: Harvard University Press, 1969, pp. 82–97.

KPSS v rezoliutsiiakh i resheniiakh sezdov, konferentsii i plenumov TsK. 1953. 7th ed. 2 vols. Moscow: Politizdat.

Lenin, V. I. 1918. *State and Revolution.* In *Selected Works,* vol. 2, pt. 1. Moscow: Foreign Languages Publishing House, 1953, pp. 199–325.

———. 1920. *"Left-Wing" Communism, an Infantile Disorder.* In *Selected Works,* vol. 2, pt. 2. pp. 341–447.

Lepeshkin, A. I. 1961–1962. *Kurs sovetskogo gosudarstvennogo prava.* Moscow: Iurizdat.

Little, D. Richard. 1972. Soviet Parliamentary Committees After Khrushchev: Obstacles and Opportunities. *Soviet Studies* 24: 41–60.

Shevchenko, Arkady N. 1985. *Breaking with Moscow.* New York: Knopf.

Siegler, Robert W. 1982. *The Standing Committees of the Supreme Soviet: Effective Co-optation.* New York: Praeger.

Stalin, J. V. 1936. On the Draft Constitution of the USSR. In *Problems of Leninism,* 11th ed. Moscow: Foreign Languages Publishing House, 1953, pp. 679–712.

———. 1939. Report to the Eighteenth Congress of the C.P.S.U.(B.) on the Work of the Central Committee. In *Problems of Leninism,* pp. 746–803.

Statute on Elections to the USSR Supreme Soviet. January 9, 1950. *Sbornik zakonov SSSR i ukazov Prezidiuma Verkhovnogo Soveta SSSR 1938–1975,* vol. 1. Moscow: Izdatelstvo Izvestiia sovetov deputatov trudiaschchikhsia, 1975, p. 131.

Statute on Standing Committees of the Soviet of the Union and the Soviet of Nationalities of the USSR Supreme Soviet. October 12, 1967. *Sbornik zakonov SSSR i ukazov Prezidiuma Verkhovnogo Soveta SSSR,* vol. 1, p. 162.

Statute on the Procedure for Recall of a Deputy of the USSR Supreme Soviet. October 30, 1959. *Sbornik zakonov SSSR i ukazov Prezidiuma Verkhovnogo Soveta SSSR 1938–1975,* vol. 6, p. 352.

Statute on the USSR Council of Ministers. July 5, 1978. *Vedomosti verkhovnogo soveta SSSR* 28, item 436.

Tomson, Edgar. 1980. *Der Ministerrat der UdSSR.* Berlin: Berlin-Verlag.

Vanneman, Peter. 1977. *The Supreme Soviet: Politics and the Legislative Process in the Soviet Political System.* Durham, N.C.: Duke University Press.

Vishniakov, V. G. 1965. O dvoinom podchinenii organov sovetskogo gosudar-
    stvennogo upravleniia. *Pravovedenie* 2: 46–54.
Vlasov, V. A. 1959. *Sovetskii gosudarsvennyi apparat.* Moscow: Iurizdat.
Zlatopolskii, D. L. 1982. *Verkhovnyi sovet SSSR—vyrazitel voli sovetskogo naroda.*
    Moscow: Iuridicheskaia literatura.

7
Government
and Administration
in the Provinces

Soviets sometimes describe their country as divided into two parts, the center and the periphery. The center means Moscow, although by courtesy the old imperial capital at Leningrad is sometimes included. Moscow is the cultural, political, economic, and administrative center of the country. The periphery includes more than 250 million people who live in different national republics within the USSR and in hundreds of smaller units of government. For this reason, this study of the Soviet political system would be incomplete if it concentrated exclusively on the national government.

A discussion of the regional political systems is important at this point in the study of Soviet politics for several reasons. First, about 150 regional political systems are present in the USSR, and they are quite diverse in their cultural and historical backgrounds. They also vary considerably in size, geographic location, and level of economic development. The regions vary from Murmansk in the far north, where the population is almost entirely Russian, to Azerbaidzhan in the south, where the people are Islamic in religion and Turkic in nationality and where Russians make up only a small minority. The regions include Catholic Lithuania in the west as well as sparsely settled areas in Siberia where the people are akin to the Alaskan Eskimos in language and culture. All these regions share a common political culture, and of course all are ruled by the Communist party. The comparative study of regional political patterns allows us to generalize about Soviet behavior while reducing the influence of such confounding variables as nationality and cultural background.

A second reason for studying regional government is that most of the recent members of the Soviet leadership spent the formative years of their political careers working at the regional level. The highest ranking national leaders tend to be former first secretaries from regional party organizations. In fact, a careful study of the career backgrounds of Soviet officials shows that people who made their political careers in the central government or the central party apparatus in Moscow are not likely to rise to the top. The elevation of Mikhail Gorbachev to the office of general secretary confirms this general rule. Consequently, a partial answer to the question, "Where do the leaders come from?" is that they come from the periphery.

Third, this study of the regional political systems reaches one of the central issues of Soviet policymaking—nationalities policy. In Chapter 3 the great ethnic and cultural diversity of the USSR was described. Nationalities policy is composed of the programs that the regime has used to cope with this diversity and to prevent ethnic or nationalist issues from becoming a threat to the stability of the regime.

One elementary but important fact should be remembered in reading this chapter. The structure of the Communist party organization seems to parallel the structure of the state, but there are some crucial differences. At least in theory, the state is organized according to the federal principle, and in fact a certain amount of federalism (decentralization of authority) exists within the formal structure of the state. By contrast, the Communist party is not federal, not even in theory. The party is a highly centralized political organization where power is concentrated in Moscow.

NATIONALITIES POLICY

The constitution (art. 70) describes the USSR as a federal and multinational state. The system is federal in the sense that the territory of the country is divided into a number of constituent units and each unit has its own government. Just as the United States is divided into fifty states, the USSR is divided into fifteen Soviet socialist republics. However, U.S. and Soviet federalism are very different because each Soviet republic represents a distinct nationality with its own language and its own ethnic identity.

The federal system evolved in response to two needs: (1) to hold together the disparate nationalities of the old Russian Empire, while allowing the various nationalities to maintain some sense of ethnic identity, and (2) to promote rapid economic development throughout the country, including the areas of non-Russian nationality. The federal system allowed the regime to exploit nationalism for its own interests, so that instead of being a divisive force, nationalism could become a force for political integration. This system was largely the work of Stalin, who was the party's chief expert on nationalities before the revolution and became minister for nationalities in the Soviet government. Before 1917 the party confronted a growing wave of nationalism, and both Stalin and Lenin looked on nationalism as a dangerous ideology that could turn the minds of the workers away from Marxism and socialism. Stalin (1913: 301) warned of an "epidemic" of nationalism.

Lenin had a more visionary view of the future than Stalin did, at least before the revolution. Lenin's proposals for a Bolshevik nationalities policy were set down in a short pamphlet written in 1916, in which he stated that the revolution would give to all peoples the right of national self-determination. This meant, in particular, that small nationalities had the right to demand their independence from great empires such as Russia or Austria-Hungary. Lenin here seemed to be supporting the traditional demand of nationalists: political independence and the creation of a sovereign nation-state. He described the Russian Empire as a "prison of nations" and suggested that after the revolution each nationality would acquire the right to secede if it chose. However, Lenin also expected that national differences would disappear after the revolution. Just as he predicted a new society without classes and without a state, he also anticipated the disappearance of nationalities. When this happened, hostility among nations would disappear, and the smaller nationalities would lose both the desire and the need for independence.

In the long run, according to Lenin (1916: 160), the aim of the revolution was not merely to draw nations together (*sblizhenie*) but to bring about their merger (*sliianie*). This distinction is of great importance in understanding the later course of Soviet nationality policy. Drawing together means that hostility between nations is overcome, and nations can live together in harmony. Merger means the complete disappearance of national differences.

Once again, a sharp contrast can be seen between Lenin's visionary view of the future and the reality of Soviet policy. After the revolution, Lenin (1920: 420) dismissed as a "foolish dream" the idea that national differences would be abolished. Ultimately Lenin accepted the idea of federation, which he had rejected before the revolution.

Stalin was determined to hold intact the multinational state that the Bolsheviks had inherited from the empire. To accomplish this overriding objective, Stalin was prepared to enter into some accommodation with the national minorities. Soviet nationality theory today generally accepts a definition of nation developed by Stalin before the revolution. A nation is defined as a community of people who share a common language, a common territory, and a common economic life and have a distinctive culture. In practice, the emphasis is on language: The various nationalities are defined primarily on the basis of their distinct languages.

Stalin's basic nationalities policy was laid down in a little-known memorandum that he wrote in 1929, although it remained unpublished for twenty years. In this note, Stalin (1929: 349) flatly rejected the slogan of "national self-determination," which had been the basis of Lenin's prerevolutionary platform. The creation of a sovereign nation-state, as a goal for an oppressed nationality, was now an outdated idea. Second, Stalin rejected the visionary idea of a merger of nations. He insisted that the revolution had not eliminated national differences. On the contrary, as a result of the revolution the number of languages (and hence the number of nationalities) had actually increased. The revolution had created the conditions for a "flourishing" of national culture that had not existed before.

> It would be incorrect to think that after the defeat of world imperialism national differences will be abolished and national languages will die away immediately, at one stroke, by decree from above, so to speak. Nothing is more erroneous than this view. To attempt to bring about the merging [*sliianie*] of nations by decree from above, by compulsion, would be playing into the hands of the imperialists, it would spell disaster to the cause of the liberation of nations, and be fatal to the cause of organizing co-operation and fraternity among nations. (Stalin 1929: 362)

Stalin then made some specific proposals that were to be the basis for nationalities policy.

1. Schools should be developed in all the republics, with instruction in the national language, and illiteracy eliminated among the national minorities.
2. The regime should create a local elite in each national republic to staff both the party and the government apparatus.
3. There should be widespread development of the press, theater, movies, and other cultural institutions in each national language.

"Why in the national languages?" Stalin asked. "Because only in their national, native languages can the vast masses of the people be successful in cultural, political and economic development" (1929: 370). Stalin was not willing to grant political independence to the Soviet nationalities, but his policy did allow some autonomy to the national republics in carrying out cultural and educational programs. All nationalities could find full scope for the development and flourishing of their own national culture within the multinational Soviet state. This culture, Stalin said, was to be "national in form and socialist in content" (1936: 687).

Stalin was very shrewd in perceiving the threat of nationalism as a potentially disruptive force in a modernizing country and in formulating a policy to neutralize the threat. At one point he (1936: 687) said that one of his objectives was to avoid the mistakes of Austro-Hungary, which had tried and failed to create a viable multinational state. Measured by this standard, Soviet nationalities policy has been a success. Although the emphases have changed, the main principles of Stalin's nationalities policy remain in effect today: Lenin's idea of the merging of nations has been postponed indefinitely; the policy aims at an accommodation of the interests of the non-Russian nationalities, by encouraging a flourishing of national cultures, but any idea of separatism or achieving political independence is absolutely ruled out.

The Khrushchev era was generally marked by an enthusiasm for Lenin and an effort to bring back Lenin's original vision about the future socialist society. In the field of nationalities policy, this tendency led to a new interest in the idea of a merging of nations. Khrushchev himself threw cold water on this idea in his speech to the 22d Party Congress. He said that the process of drawing together (*sblizhenie*) was proceeding as planned. Then he warned that "even after the achievement of Communism, it would be premature to make declarations about the merger [*sliianie*] of nations. As is known, Lenin stated that . . . national differences will continue to exist long after the victory of socialism in all countries" (*XXII sezd KPSS* 1: 217). Actually, it was Stalin who said this.

FEDERAL SYSTEM IN PRACTICE

Both the United States and the Soviet Union are multinational states, and in each country the diversity of ethnic and cultural backgrounds has been a cause of social pressures and political problems. The United States, in contrast to the USSR, has taken pride in being a melting pot society. The various immigrant groups that came to the United States have gradually been assimilated, and national differences have tended to disappear. The obvious mark of this assimilation of nationalities is language. Although the original immigrant families tended to cluster into ethnic neighborhoods in the cities, their children learned English in school and grew up as Italian-Americans, Polish-Americans, or Japanese-Americans. Even the Americans who have not been so successfully assimilated (black Americans, for example) have grown up in an English-speaking culture.

The Soviet Union has a different tradition. It has no hyphenated nationalities. Far from assimilating or trying to Russify the different nationalities, the Soviet policy has been to preserve and even to encourage differences of language and culture. Instead of becoming a melting pot, the USSR has remained a multinational state. This diversity of culture, language, and historical tradition is the basis for Soviet federalism. The fifteen union republics are not quite analogous to the U.S. states, and the administrative subdivisions within the republics are much more complicated than the division of the states into counties.

What makes the Soviet territorial-administrative structure so complicated is that administrative regions are organized along two different, and to some extent conflicting, principles. First, administrative divisions and subdivisions are primarily territorial, and their boundaries geographic. Superimposed over this territorial-administrative system are divisions organized around distinct nationalities, and their boundaries are ethnic or linguistic. Therefore, the student of political geography in the USSR finds a rather bewildering arrangement of regions, territories, and districts. To add to the confusion, there are two different kinds of republics. To minimize this confusion, the discussion that follows has been somewhat simplified.

Territorial-Administrative Organization

The larger union republics are divided into territorial units called *oblasti,* or regions. More than 100 oblasts are present throughout the USSR, and in size and population they are generally comparable to the U.S. states. The smaller republics are not divided into oblasts, which leads to a somewhat curious situation. In a small republic like Estonia, the republic is the only administrative level between a city and the central government. In a larger republic, however, one or two levels of administration may intervene.

Sometimes a region is designated a *krai* rather than an oblast. Unlike an oblast, a krai normally includes a subdivision in which the population is from a national minority.

The oblasts or smaller republics are divided into cities and rural districts (*raiony*). The larger cities are in turn subdivided into urban districts (*gorodskie raiony*), or boroughs. Within the rural districts, there are villages (*sela*). Altogether, the USSR contains 3,000 raions (including 40,000 villages) and about 2,000 cities. These various administrative levels have basically the same structure of government, simpler at the local level and more complex at the level of the republic. At each level, widespread use of the principle of delegation of authority takes place. The executive at all levels has wide powers to act in the name of the elected soviet, and in practice, no real distinction exists between executive and legislative power. Each of these regional or local governments functions under the supervision of the Communist party.

Because of this basic similarity in structure, a general description can be given of regional administration, a term referring to the administration of territories and republics as well as of those units of government officially called regions (oblasts). First, however, the structure of the national republic must be examined more closely.

The Republics

Great disparity among the union republics can be seen in size and in social and economic development. The largest, the Russian Soviet Federative Socialist Republic (RSFSR), has 75 percent of the territory and more than 50 percent of the total population. The RSFSR is about 100 times the size of Estonia, which has the smallest population of the union republics. Since the RSFSR has no separate CPSU organization, the affairs of the Russian republic are managed by the central party apparatus. In certain respects the administrative organization of the state also ignores the existence of the RSFSR. Soviet federalism is further complicated by the existence of the smaller nationalities, which do not have the status of Soviet socialist republics but are still organized as separate territorial units.

Within the RSFSR alone, thirty organized nationalities are represented in addition to the Russians. These nationalities are organized into three different types of national-administrative units. The most important of these—just a step below the level of the union republic—is the autonomous Soviet socialist republic (ASSR). There are twenty ASSRs, sixteen of which are within the Russian federation.

Some of the autonomous republics are larger in size than the smaller union republics. The Bashkir ASSR, for example, has a population of 4 million. However, the constitution (art. 72) gives a union republic the right to secede, a right that an autonomous republic does not have. This right has never been exercised, and, in practice, the right to secede from the USSR appears to be meaningless. Still, Stalin (1936: 705) once pointed out that if the right to secede were to be used, the republic that was withdrawing from the union ought to border on the outside world. This argument has some logic, so nationalities located in the interior part of the country (such as the Bashkirs) are entitled only to an autonomous republic.

The next lower level is the autonomous oblast (AO), of which five are in the RSFSR and three in other republics. The largest of the AOs, the Khakassian oblast in central Siberia, has a population of less than half a million. Most of the autonomous oblasts are much smaller. The typical AO is made up of a backward people living in a remote and economically underdeveloped region. The Jewish AO, located in the Soviet Far East, is a curious exception. It was created in 1934 to attract

Soviet Jews and to serve as an alternative to the Jewish homeland. Few Jews have settled there. The Jewish AO has a total population of 175,000, including only 20,000 Jews.

The lowest level of national-administrative unit is the autonomous district. All ten of these are located within the Russian federation. The autonomous districts represent primitive peoples and are all quite small in population, such as the Chukchi people who have a national district in the easternmost reaches of the country. The total Chukchi population is only 14,000, and the Chukchi people were so backward that their language had never been written down until a Chukchi alphabet was devised by Soviet scholars in 1930.

Thus, the USSR has a national-administrative structure that includes fifty-three national units of various sizes at various levels of cultural and economic development. Even so, some nationalities do not have their own republic or region; some of these nonterritorial nationalities are too widely scattered. Another criterion for a republic, as laid down by Stalin, was that the nationality should be located in one more or less compact geographic area. Two of the geographically scattered nationalities are of special interest. More than 1.5 million Germans live in the USSR. Before the war, many of these lived in the Volga-German Autonomous Republic. The Volga-German Republic was dissolved in 1941 after the Nazi invasion, and the Germans in the area were forcibly resettled in the east. This policy was instituted in a moment of temporary panic, as was the detention and relocation of Japanese-Americans after Pearl Harbor. The Soviet government now acknowledges that the forced resettlement of the Germans was a mistake and that the Germans in the republic were loyal (or no less disloyal than other Soviet citizens). However, the Germans have not been allowed to return to their original homes along the Volga or to reestablish a German republic elsewhere in the USSR.

The Poles, whose number is only slightly smaller than that of the Germans, represent an equally sensitive group, although the government has less reason to be vengeful toward the Poles as a nationality. A deep-rooted anti-German sentiment prevails in the USSR, especially among the Russians, and the government would not win any plaudits by a gesture toward the Germans. The policy toward the Poles is dictated by other considerations. Most of the Poles in the USSR live, or did live, in the western territories annexed in 1939. To create a Polish administrative unit here might raise the question of why the territory was not simply returned to the Polish state.

Table 7.1 provides a statistical profile of the major nationalities and reveals some significant patterns. The table lists nationalities that have at least 1 million population. The first item that the reader may notice

TABLE 7.1
Major Nationalities: A Statistical Profile

	Population (millions)			1979 Population as % of 1959 Population	Native Language Factor*
	1959	1970	1979		
Union-republic nationalities					
Russians	114.1	129.0	137.4	120.4	99.8
Ukrainians	37.3	40.8	42.3	113.7	85.7
Uzbeks	6.0	9.2	12.5	207.1	98.6
Belorussians	7.9	9.1	9.5	119.6	80.6
Kazakhs	3.6	5.3	6.6	181.0	98.0
Azeri	3.9	4.4	5.5	186.3	98.2
Armenians	2.8	3.6	4.2	148.9	91.4
Georgians	2.7	3.2	3.6	132.7	98.4
Moldavians	2.2	2.7	3.0	134.1	95.0
Lithuanians	2.3	2.7	2.9	122.6	97.9
Tadzhiks	1.4	2.1	2.9	207.4	98.5
Turkmen	1.0	1.5	2.0	202.4	98.9
Kirgiz	1.0	1.5	1.9	196.7	98.8
Latvians	1.4	1.4	1.4	102.8	95.2
Estonians	1.0	1.0	1.0	103.1	95.5
RSFSR nationalities					
Tatars	5.0	5.9	6.3	127.2	89.2
Chuvash	1.5	1.7	1.8	119.1	86.9
Dagestan peoples	.9	1.4	1.7	175.3	96.5
Mordovians	1.3	1.3	1.2	92.8	77.8
Bashkirs	1.0	1.2	1.4	138.6	66.2
Other nationalities					
Jews	2.3	2.2	1.8	79.9	17.7
Germans	1.6	1.8	1.9	119.5	66.8
Poles	1.4	1.2	1.2	83.4	32.5

Source: *Pravda*, April 17, 1971; *Istoriia SSSR* 5 (1980): 24-47.

*In the census, all persons were asked to identify their native
languages. The column headed "native language factor" gives the
percent of each nationality that claimed the language of that
nationality as native. For example, 85.7 percent of the Ukrainians
identified Ukrainian as their native language.

is the disparity in population growth among the nationalities (this
demographic problem will be discussed in Chapter 11). The native
language factor in Table 7.1 can be used as an indicator of the degree
of russianization. By this standard, the other East Slavic peoples (Ukrainians and Belorussians), whose languages are close to Russian, are much
more russianized, when compared with the other union-republic nationalities. The russianization of the Ukrainians may also be explained
by the fact that Ukrainians are widely distributed throughout the territory

TABLE 7.2
Nationalities in the Union Republics
(as a percent of total population)

Republic	Indigenous Nationality	Russians
RSFSR	82.6	---
Ukraine	73.6	21.1
Belorussia	79.4	11.9
Uzbekistan	68.7	10.8
Kazakhstan	36.0	40.8
Georgia	68.8	7.4
Azerbaidzhan	78.1	7.9
Lithuania	80.0	8.9
Moldavia	63.9	12.8
Latvia	53.7	32.8
Kirgizistan	47.9	25.9
Tadzhikistan	58.8	10.4
Armenia	89.7	2.3
Turkmenia	68.4	12.6
Estonia	64.7	27.9

Source: Istoriia SSSR 5 (1980): 24-47.

of the USSR, so that many Ukrainians have grown up in a Russian-speaking culture outside the Ukraine. The table also reveals that the status of a union republic provides a high degree of protection against russianization. The nationalities within the RSFSR that have only ASSR status tend to be more russianized. The nonterritorial nationalities and the Jews are, by this measure, even more russianized. Nationalities like the Germans and the Poles do not have the cultural institutions, found in all the republics, that would help to preserve their language and their ethnic identity.

Table 7.2 shows the distribution of Russians in the USSR. Ethnic Russians are found throughout the country, but their distribution is uneven. At one extreme is Armenia in which the population is over-whelmingly Armenian and the Russians are a tiny minority. At the other extreme, in Kazakhstan the Kazakhs are actually outnumbered by Russians.

Russian, the language of the largest nationality, is understood through-out the USSR, although a sizable minority of Soviet citizens still do not speak the language at all or speak it badly. Russian is the common language of the educated elite and of the higher-level bureaucracy, and Russian is also the language of that great assimilator, the Soviet Army.

Still, the use of other languages is not only tolerated but fostered, to encourage the flourishing of different national cultures.

The aim of the regime's language policy is complete bilingualism, so that all Soviet citizens who are non-Russian would have a command of Russian in addition to their native languages. In recent years, efforts to spread knowledge of Russian have increased, including the introduction of Russian language classes at an earlier age in the non-Russian schools. Some Western commentators perceive this policy as one of intensified "russianization" (Bilinsky 1981; Solchanyk 1982). However, the increased use of Russian can also be seen as an instrument of sovietization rather than russification. As A. Shtromas pointed out, "national oppression under the Soviet regime is, as a matter of fact, the lot of all nations without exception—Russians and non-Russians alike" (1978: 269). The use of Russian as a tool of sovietization does not put the ethnic Russians in a privileged position. Some Russians quietly complain that as Russian becomes the universal language, migration increases from the republics into the RSFSR, and the republic loses its traditionally Russian character. It is true that the widespread use of Russian enables Russians to serve in any part of the USSR. However, on the other side of the coin, a command of Russian also allows non-Russians to hold important jobs in the Russian republic, as well as in the central government.

Another crucial variable related to nationalities is the proportion of party members. Table 7.3 shows the number of party members for the major nationalities, together with the party saturation statistic.

Republic Government

The general characteristics of governmental administration were described in Chapter 6. These operating characteristics can be summed up as follows:

1. All legal authority is vested in a representative assembly consisting of party members and nonparty members.
2. In practice, this authority is exercised by a much smaller executive body.
3. The executive body operates under direct control of the party.
4. The party's authority is assured by the principles of kontrol and nomenklatura.

The formal structure of republic government is uniform throughout the country and is much the same in both union and autonomous republics. In theory, all power belongs to the republic's elected supreme soviet, a single-chamber body elected for a five-year term. Just as at the all-union level, the supreme soviet of the republic delegates its powers to

TABLE 7.3
CPSU Membership by Nationality

Nationality	Members (millions)	As a % of CPSU Membership	Party Saturation*
Russian	10.809	59.7	7.34
Ukrainian	2.899	16.0	6.32
Belorussian	.684	3.8	6.51
Uzbek	.428	2.4	2.92
Kazakh	.355	2.0	4.77
Georgian	.303	1.7	7.78
Azeri	.305	1.7	4.77
Lithuanian	.135	0.7	4.17
Moldavian	.098	0.5	2.73
Latvian	.074	0.4	4.79
Kirgiz	.070	0.4	2.99
Tadzhik	.080	0.4	2.42
Armenian	.273	1.5	6.03
Turkmen	.069	0.4	2.75
Estonian	.058	0.3	5.24
Others	1.476	8.1	---

Source: Kommunist 15 (1983): 23.

*Party saturation has been calculated on the basis of the 1979 census data.

a republic presidium and a republic council of ministers. The presidium is authorized to enact legislation when the supreme soviet is not in session. The chairmanship of the presidium, also called republic president, is a ceremonial office without real power, usually held by an experienced political administrator of the local nationality. The republic council of ministers is the highest administrative body. The chairman of this council (the premier of the republic) is the head of the government but occupies a position subordinate to the head of the republic party organization (first secretary). Under Stalin, these two offices were sometimes held by a single individual; now, however, they are always kept separate.

The members of the council of ministers are the heads of the executive departments, or ministries. The main function of the council, in fact, is to coordinate the ministries' work. Most of the republic ministries operate according to the principle of dual subordination and therefore are subject to the orders of the central authorities. A few ministries, the so-called republic ministries, have no counterpart at the center. These ministries are responsible for public services or light industry. For example, the

RSFSR has republic ministries for social security, consumer services, housing, and the textile industry.

Tadzhik and Georgian Republics

The republic has the responsibility of preserving and protecting the national heritage and maintaining Soviet authority, following the principle that the culture must be "national in form, socialist in content." The basic political structure of the Soviet system is found in each of the republics, but significant differences occur in the level of social and cultural development. Each republic invests part of its resources in the support of national and cultural activities. Every union republic now has its own academy of sciences, which not only promotes research in the pure sciences, but also supports the study of cultural history, linguistics, and folklore, studies that help foster a sense of national identity. Most republics have a national theater devoted to performances in the language of the republic, as well as a republic movie studio. Some local performing groups (the Georgian national dancers, for example) have entertained around the world. And every union republic has at least one university as well as other institutions of higher education, where both Russian and the republic language are used for instruction.

Of necessity, the non-Russian areas maintain a dual school system, one in Russian and a second conducted in the national language of the area. Curriculum and texts for the Russian schools in all the republics are provided by the RSFSR ministry of education, but the republic ministry controls the non-Russian schools. The local political elite is trained and recruited through the school system, the Komsomol organization, and, of course, the party.

Who belongs to this local elite? The pattern varies considerably from one republic to another, depending on the level of development. In the Tadzhik Republic, one of the culturally deprived areas of the country, the revolution found the local population entirely unprepared for the transition to modern society, to say nothing of the introduction to socialism. Before 1917, the Tadzhik population consisted mainly of illiterate peasants. According to all reports, the people had no real sense of national identity. The native elite consisted of the Muslim clergy and the officials of the local emir, and the literary language was Arabic. The Tadzhik written language was created after the revolution, first using the Latin alphabet, and then Cyrillic. The first Tadzhik newspaper and the first organized system of Tadzhik schools appeared after the revolution.

The Tadzhik autonomous republic was formed in 1926 and elevated to the status of a union republic three years later. Only gradually were educated and politically reliable Tadzhiks recruited into the government of the republic. In these circumstances, it was inevitable that the Tadzhik government and administration would be in the hands of the Russians after the revolution. Even today, ethnic Russians account for a substantial part of the political leadership in the Tadzhik Republic. In particular, Russians dominate the party organization of the republic, although in the postwar period, the head of the republic party (the first secretary) has invariably been Tadzhik. In the government, a characteristic pattern is to have a Tadzhik at the head of a department and a Russian as the principal deputy (Rakowska-Harmstone 1970).

Georgia, the homeland of Stalin, presents a remarkable contrast to the Central Asian republics such as Tadzhikistan. It was the homeland of an ancient civilization; the kingdom of Georgia engaged in active trading with the Greeks several centuries before Christ. Georgia was incorporated into the Russian Empire early in the nineteenth century, and although efforts were made at forced russianization, the Georgians developed a strong sense of national identity. Today, they are a compact and comparatively unrussianized people. (About 97 percent of the Georgians in the USSR live in the republic.)

By Soviet standards, the Georgian republic is prosperous, and Western visitors are usually impressed by the high standard of living. The economy remains basically agricultural, but Georgia delivers products like tea, fruit, and wine, which bring a high income to the republic. Georgia is also the center of the Soviet tobacco industry. Georgia ranks first in the USSR in the level of education and in the incidence of Communist party membership. The Georgians, unlike the Tadzhiks, played an active role in the revolutionary movement and were among the leaders of the Petrograd Soviet in 1917. Georgia was under Menshevik rule until 1921 when it was conquered by Bolshevik forces. Since then, a loyal and competent Georgian party elite has developed, and during most of their history as a Soviet republic, the Georgians appear to have managed their own affairs. The power structure of the republic is primarily Georgian, although (as in other union republics) the second secretary of the party organization is usually a Russian. The political stability is suggested by the long tenure of the head of the republic KGB, General A. N. Inauri, an ethnic Georgian, who has served continuously in that post since 1954. According to Teresa Rakowska-Harmstone (1970: 114), the police in Tadzhikistan have always been under Russian control.

The experience of Georgia would suggest that a republic can achieve a certain amount of national autonomy within the framework of Soviet federalism. To accomplish this requires the presence of an educated local elite that is technically competent and politically reliable. In the case of Georgia, it is not certain that the republic would be a viable state if it were to become independent. Some educated Georgians believe that they are really better off within the Soviet Union: Certainly in the economic sphere, the USSR provides a huge and almost insatiable market for the republic's produce.

In today's Tadzhik Republic, a pattern is discernible that is similar to that of other colonial societies during the postwar era. The republic is in a period of transition, moving "from dependence and economic backwardness to limited self-government and a developing economy." To some extent, the management of the republic's affairs is still in the hands of Russians. But the most visible posts—republic president, premier, and party first secretary—are held by Tadzhiks. There is a growing Tadzhik elite, who are trained in modern skills of technology and management (Rakowska-Harmstone 1970: 140).

This comparison of two republics illustrates the disparity in political, cultural, and social development within the USSR. The regime has committed great resources to the development of the more backward regions of the country. Indeed some Russians quietly complain that the resources all flow outward from the RSFSR to the periphery; there is some truth in this complaint. This effort has paid off: If the Tadzhik republic is compared, not with Georgia, but with neighboring Afghanistan, the results of the Soviet development program are quite impressive. Nonetheless the Central Asian republics continue to lag behind in the development of Soviet society. This is particularly visible in the status of women in these republics, even though the women there are much more liberated than those in some other Islamic societies. All the union-republic constitutions have a provision (art. 33) promising equal rights for women. In the constitutions of the five Central Asian republics, an additional provision makes it a punishable offense to violate women's rights.

REGIONAL AND LOCAL GOVERNMENT

The regional soviet manages all the affairs of government within the region, but it does so under the general direction of the regional party organization. At least that is what is written in a Soviet text on regional (oblast) government (Azovkin 1962: 20). In fact, the authority of regional and local government is quite weak. As E. M. Jacobs (1983a) pointed out, local government is an integral part of the giant bureaucracy that runs the Soviet Union. The integration of local government into the bureaucracy is assured by the rule of dual subordination.

The formal structure of the government is fairly simple. Legislative authority resides in the regional or local soviet, a single-chamber body of deputies elected for a term of two and one-half years. (Thus two terms of a local soviet correspond to one term of the republic soviet.)

The soviet itself usually meets four times a year in sessions lasting only one day. The management of the region's affairs is then delegated to the regional executive committee, or *ispolkom* (for *ispolnitelnyi komitet*). The ispolkom combines the functions performed at the republic level by the presidium and the council of ministers. The chief executive is the chairman of the ispolkom and has a job in some ways analogous to that of a U.S. governor (in the case of a regional ispolkom) or mayor (for a city ispolkom). In addition to the chairman and deputies, the members of the ispolkom are the heads of local government departments (*otdely*), such as finance, culture, education, health, and social security.

The main function of regional and local government is to provide goods and services to the population. Some of these can be categorized as public goods: goods and services available to all at government expense. Such public goods include parks, streets, and the school system. In the socialist state, the regional government also provides many goods and services on a commercial basis. Most retail stores, restaurants, public transportation, and miscellaneous services like laundries and barber shops are state-owned enterprises and are managed by the regional government.

The regional authorities are also responsible for what Soviet practice calls cultural services. This broad category includes most forms of entertainment: Movie theaters and the circus are considered to be cultural services along with art museums and public libraries. Another function of local government is to provide housing, and a large part of the housing in all Soviet cities is municipally owned and operated. Thus, in addition to the departments listed, local government typically has departments for trade, consumer services (*bytovoe obsluzhivanie*), cinema, and food service.

Important areas of government activity, however, are not under the authority of the regional administration. The management of industry generally belongs in this category. The regional government does have direct control over certain industries that produce goods for the consumer sector of the economy. The furniture industry, for example, is largely managed by local authorities. But all economic decisionmaking is centralized in Moscow, and all heavy industry is controlled by all-union ministries. Therefore, the major industries of the area are free from regional control.

A second area from which regional government is largely excluded is the administration of law. According to the constitution, the regional soviet elects a regional court for a five-year term. However, the work of the judiciary is supervised by the higher courts. Criminal prosecutions are the responsibility of the procuracy, another agency of the central government free of local control. The local authorities do have some limited powers over the regular police, but they have none over the security police.

The USSR's centralized budget system also imposes limits on the power of local government. The national budget makes allocation of resources for local government, and local agencies have little discretion over how these resources are used (Lewis 1983: 51). Although the local budget must be approved by the soviet, this approval is a formality, as is the case with the Supreme Soviet and the national budget. The local budget is formulated by the local department of finance, and under the rule of dual subordination, this department is ultimately controlled by the USSR Ministry of Finance.

The weakness and limited power of regional government is a source of some confusion and inefficiency. The regional government has a general responsibility for education and housing, but it is hampered by the central agencies that operate some of the schools and own some of the apartment buildings. A substantial amount of urban housing is owned and maintained by industrial plants for their employees, since the managers have found that it is important to have housing and other amenities available in order to attract workers. Many other institutions provide housing for their staff. And for various reasons, some schools remain outside the regional government's jurisdiction. One Soviet study found that in an oblast that had 800 schools, 100 of them were operated by the ministry of railroad transportation and hence were not under regional control (Azovkin 1962: 24).

In every city, the presence of large and economically powerful industries is a further limitation on regional government. A U.S. study of Leningrad uncovered a serious conflict between the local authorities and heavy industry on the problem of water pollution. Some large enterprises were dumping industrial waste into the Neva river and even into the canals that crisscross the city. Since the industrial plants were under the control of central ministries, Leningrad officials had little power either to stop or to control the pollution. Finally, the city government appealed for criminal prosecution of the plant directors who were responsible. This appeal seemed to help, but it did not finally solve the problem (Cattell 1968: 97).

The typical regional soviet has about 200 deputies. However, the electoral districts are kept small, and larger regions have much larger soviets. The Moscow city soviet, for example, has had more than 1,000 deputies in recent years.

The government has published detailed statistics on the composition of local soviets, so that these bodies can be compared with the USSR Supreme Soviet (Jacobs 1983b). The local soviets have a somewhat higher proportion of workers and peasants and considerably more women.

In 1980 (the last year for which the data are available) 49.5 percent of local soviet deputies were women. Party saturation is less than at the national level: In 1980 it was 43.1 percent. Just as in the USSR Supreme Soviet, Russians are slightly underrepresented in the local soviets. As in the Supreme Soviet, turnover tends to be high: At the oblast and city level turnover has been almost 60 percent. The village soviets were somewhat more stable: Their turnover rate is less than 50 percent.

The decisionmaking power of the regional soviet is limited by the constitutional structure, by the fact that the soviet only meets a few days a year, and by the reality of party control. But the soviet does perform a certain representative function in the Soviet system. It is not representative in the sense that it allows the people to share power, but it does give them a sense of participation in the affairs of government and some limited experience in administrative matters. No doubt the local soviet also serves as a recruiting ground for political leaders. Certainly, participation is very widespread. If the cited figures on turnover are projected, it could be conservatively estimated that over a ten-year period about 6 million persons will be elected to regional or local soviets.

REGIONAL POWER STRUCTURE

The true power center is the regional or local party buro. The chairman of the local ispolkom is invariably a member of the party buro, but the buro is dominated by the party secretaries. In the relationship between the party and the government the party leader has the predominant role. The regional first secretary is not only the political boss of the area but is often a member of the CPSU Central Committee and thus belongs to the national political elite. The first secretary also has political prospects and can rise higher in the system. In the RSFSR oblasts, the first secretary usually holds office for only a few years in any one place. This policy of rotation and reassignment helps to ensure that the secretary's loyalty is to the party and not to the region.

In the national republics, the first secretary may hold office for much longer. In the Tadzhik republic the first secretary, Dzhabar Rasulov, has occupied this post for twenty-five years. The long tenure of party leaders in the outlying republics results because these people typically have no place else to go; their prospects for promotion are not very good because promotion would mean transfer outside the republic. There have been occasional exceptions. N. A. Mukhitdinov, the first secretary in the Uzbek republic, was transferred to Moscow during the Khrushchev regime and made a national secretary and member of the Politburo. He was later removed from these high positions, however. In 1982 Gaidar Aliev, the first secretary in Azerbaidzhan, was brought to Moscow, elevated to the Politburo, and appointed vice premier. In 1985 the Georgian first secretary became foreign minister.

Many Soviet specialists have commented on the fact that the second secretary in a national republic is usually an ethnic Russian and often an outsider. For example Iu. I. Polukarpov, second secretary in Tadzhikistan, had not served in the republic until his appointment to this position. Previously he had been an obkom first secretary in the RSFSR and an official of the central party apparatus. The second secretary is not invariably a Russian, but the practice is becoming more common (Miller 1977). The second secretary usually is in charge of cadres, or nomenklatura appointments, and thus is in a strategic position to supervise both the republic party organization and the republic government. For this reason many of the Russian second secretaries, like Polukarpov, had previous experience in the cadres department in the central party apparatus. Since in most of the republics the Russians represent the second largest ethnic group, it is not surprising that they should also be represented in the republic's party leadership.

The regional party secretary has far greater responsibilities than his counterpart, the head of the regional government. Although the regional government's responsibilities are limited to supervising public services and local industry, the party secretary is accountable to Moscow for everything that goes on in the region. Heavy industry, higher education, ideological questions, even military affairs—all outside the jurisdiction of the regional government—are among the party secretary's concerns.

The regional first secretary has a dual role: representing the national leadership that appointed him, but also speaking for the interests of the region at the center. The center makes certain basic demands on the region, which are defined in the national economic plan. Every region must meet the center's targets for the production of agricultural and manufactured goods. The region, in turn, must be given the resources to meet the planners' production targets. The first secretary must obtain sufficient resources for the region. Thus the first secretary's success or failure as political boss of the region depends not only on the ability to lead at home but also on contacts in Moscow.

FUTURE OF SOVIET FEDERALISM

Soviet policy aims at instilling a sense of Soviet patriotism in all the citizens of the country. Patriotism in the Soviet definition is not nationalism; it is understood to be loyalty to the state. Although national loyalty is not excluded (provided that it is socialist in content), Soviet patriotism is assumed to be a higher form of loyalty than loyalty to a

particular nationality. Along with Soviet patriotism comes the development of a common Soviet culture. This common culture will not
sweep away the separate national cultures, which are still supposed to
flourish.

These concepts are embodied in the idea of "the Soviet people as a
new historical community," which provided the framework for nationalities policy in the Brezhnev period. In 1982, shortly after his election
as general secretary, Andropov unexpectedly revived the idea of merger.
In a December speech, he quoted from Lenin's 1916 pamphlet and
reminded his audience that the ultimate goal was the disappearance of
national differences (*Pravda*, Dec. 22, 1982). This idea, however, was
not repeated. Andropov's speech, it appeared, did not represent any
change of policy.

Reports sometimes published in the West about growing national
conflict in the USSR or about the possible revolt among the republics
clearly are exaggerated. The regime seems to have been basically successful in creating a stable multinational state and in reducing tensions
among the nationalities. There are still problems with which the regime
must cope. One is the difference in population growth rate; another is
the growing defensive nationalism of the Russians, who fear that their
own interests are being sacrificed to support the development and
integration of the minority nationalities. However, although nationalist
sentiments occasionally break into the open, no evidence indicates that
a nationalist movement threatens the breakup of the USSR.

The most restive nationalities are perhaps the Lithuanians and the
western Ukrainians. Anti-Soviet dissent among these two ethnic groups
is probably related more to religious oppression than to pure nationalism.
(One of the best-established samizdat journals in the USSR is the
Chronicle of the Lithuanian Catholic Church.) Occasionally outbursts of
nationalist sentiment occur elsewhere.

Among the Caucasian republics, and especially in Georgia, language
policy has been a sensitive issue. In 1976 a leading Georgian writer
openly complained that Georgian was being suppressed in favor of
Russian. In particular, he protested against plans to increase the use of
Russian at the University of Tbilisi. His speech (Dzhaparadze 1976)
circulated in samizdat and eventually reached the West. In 1978, the
proposed constitution for the Georgian republic omitted the statement
about language contained in the previous constitution. In April 1978,
while the draft constitution was under discussion by the republic central
committee, a protest demonstration broke out among university students
and apparently spread to other parts of the city. The draft was quickly
amended to include a formal statement that Georgian was the official
language of the republic, although Russians living in Georgia were

guaranteed the right to use their language as well (Constitution of the Georgian SSR, art. 75). Similar statements were included in the constitutions of Armenia and Azerbaidzhan but not in the other republic constitutions. This incident is a good illustration of the established policy of accommodating the interests of the minority nationalities. The official objective is to encourage use of Russian, but the regime is not prepared to press this policy to a point where it will provoke a nationalist reaction.

The new historical community is the Soviet people. This community is described as a multinational people (*narod*) and not a nation (*natsiia*). It is a community in the ideological, political, and economic sense but not in the sense of language or ethnic identity (Kulichenko 1981). In introducing this concept, Brezhnev said: "In speaking of a new historical community of men, we do not at all mean that national differences are disappearing, much less that a merger [*sliianie*] of nations has taken place" (1973: 243). All the nationalities retain their national character and language. The new community concept does not abolish nationality. It says that nationality is less important than common ideological, political, and economic ties.

In discussing the new constitution of 1977, Brezhnev disclosed that some disagreement existed about the future of the federal system. Some critics of the constitution, he said, wanted to introduce the idea of a Soviet nation (*natsiia*) instead of the new historical community. They wanted to reduce the powers of the union republics and autonomous republics or even abolish them, and proposals had been made to abolish the Soviet of Nationalities (Brezhnev 1977: 525). He repeated that national differences had not disappeared, but he also said that the national question, in the main, had been resolved in the USSR. "The friendship of the Soviet peoples is unbreakable, and their drawing together [*sblizhenie*] is proceeding in the process of Communist construction. . . . But we would start out on a dangerous path if we began artificially to force this objective process of the drawing together of nations" (Brezhnev 1977: 525).

REFERENCES

Azovkin, A. I. 1962. *Oblastnoi (kraevoi) sovet deputatov trudiashchikhsia.* Moscow: Gosiurizdat.

Bennigsen, Alexandre, and Marie Broxup. 1983. *The Islamic Threat to the Soviet State.* New York: St. Martin's Press.

Bilinsky, Yaroslav. 1981. Expanding the Use of Russian or Russification? *Russian Review* 40: 317–332.

Brezhnev, L. I. 1973. V splochennom stroiu sovetskikh respublik. *Leninskim kursom,* vol. 4. Moscow: Politicheskaia literatura, pp. 237–256.

————. 1977. O proekte konstitutsii (osnovnogo zakona) Soiuza Sovetskikh Sotsialisticheskikh Respublik i itogakh ego vsenarodnogo obsuzhdeniia. *Leninskim kursom* 6: 517–538.

Carrère d'Encausse, Hélène. 1979. *Decline of an Empire: The Soviet Socialist Republics in Revolt*, translated by Martin Sokolinsky and Henry A. LaFarge. New York: Newsweek Books.

Cattell, David T. 1968. *Leningrad: A Case Study in Soviet Urban Government*. New York: Praeger.

XXII sezd KPSS. 1962. 3 vols. Moscow: Politicheskaia literatura.

Dzhaparadze, R. 1976. Speech of April 4 to the Eighth Georgian Writers' Congress. AS no. 2583.

Friedgut, Theodore. 1979. *Political Participation in the USSR*. Princeton, N.J.: Princeton University Press.

Jacobs, Everett M. 1983a. Introduction: The Organizational Framework of Soviet Local Government. In *Soviet Local Government and Politics*, edited by Everett M. Jacobs. London: Allen & Unwin, pp. 3–17.

————. 1983b. Norms of Representation and the Composition of Local Soviets. In *Soviet Local Government and Politics*, pp. 69–77.

Kulichenko, M. I. 1981. *Rastsvet i sblizhenie natsii v SSSR*. Moscow: Mysl.

Lapidus, Gail Warshofsky. 1984. Ethnonationalism and Political Stability: The Soviet Case. *World Politics* 36: 555–580.

Lenin, V. I. 1916. The Socialist Revolution and the Right of Nations to Self-Determination. In *Selected Works*. New York: International Publishers, 1971, pp. 157–168.

————. 1920. *"Left-Wing" Communism, An Infantile Disorder*. In *Selected Works*, vol. 2, pt. 2. Moscow: Foreign Languages Publishing House, 1952, pp. 341–447.

Lewis, Carol W. 1983. The Economic Functions of Local Soviets. In *Soviet Local Government and Politics*, pp. 48–66.

Miller, John H. 1977. Cadres Policy in National Areas—Recruitment of CPSU First and Second Secretaries in Non-Russian Republics of the USSR. *Soviet Studies* 29: 3–36.

Rakowska-Harmstone, Teresa. 1970. *Russia and Nationalism in Central Asia: The Case of Tadzhikistan*. Baltimore: Johns Hopkins Press.

Shtromas, A. 1978. The Legal Position of Soviet Nationalities and Their Territorial Units According to the 1977 Constitution of the USSR. *Russian Review* 37: 265–272.

Solchanyk, Roman. 1982. Russian Language and Soviet Politics. *Soviet Studies* 34: 23–42.

Stalin, J. V. 1913. Marxism and the National Question. In *Works*, vol. 2. Moscow: Foreign Languages Publishing House, pp. 300–381.

————. 1929. The National Question and Leninism. In *Works*, vol. 11, pp. 348–371.

————. 1936. On the Draft Constitution of the U.S.S.R. In *Problems of Leninism*. 11th ed. Moscow: Foreign Languages Publishing House, 1953, pp. 679–712.

8
From Brezhnev
to Gorbachev

In the Soviet Union, a change of leadership is not a change of government. In the British parliamentary system, a new prime minister has virtually a free hand to appoint a new cabinet and to dismiss cabinet officers. In the United States, a new president not only appoints a new cabinet but several hundred other government officials. This power of appointment is an accepted principle of government in the Western democracies, where no one questions the right of the head of government to select subordinates. It is not an accepted principle of government in Moscow. The Soviet system is a self-perpetuating oligarchy, which puts a high value on stability and where political change comes slowly. A new general secretary does not have a blank check to appoint a new government. With the passage of time, the general secretary can appoint new officials in both the party apparatus and the government, but it may take several years to consolidate power in this way.

This chapter is devoted to a study of elite politics. We will review the process of change in the position of general secretary between 1982, when Leonid Brezhnev died, and 1985, when Mikhail Gorbachev assumed the post. This process was accompanied by changes in several other posts, although the process evolved slowly. The major changes were in party positions, not in the government. It was rare for any officeholder to be dismissed to make room for a new appointee. Important positions usually changed hands because the incumbent died in office or was promoted.

The study of elite politics requires the use of the kremlinological method to analyze the available evidence. Kremlinology can be defined as the use of protocol evidence to determine the relative standing of members of the Politburo and Secretariat. Elite politics is highly ritualized in the USSR, and the protocol in Moscow tends to follow rather rigid rules. For example, when the general secretary dies, the arrangements for the funeral and the election of a successor follow a set pattern. Any deviation from the pattern may be deliberate, in an effort to convey some hidden message. These hidden messages are one example of protocol evidence.

Another type of protocol evidence is found in the Supreme Soviet elections, which are ritualized events. During the three or four weeks before election day, all the leaders make election addresses in their districts. These speeches are reported in reverse order, with the junior members coming first and the general secretary giving the final speech in the series. The order of election speeches and the press coverage given to them form another example of protocol evidence that can be interpreted by the kremlinologist.

SUCCESSION PROCESS

In theory, the general secretary's term coincides with the term of the Central Committee, and each new Central Committee elects the general secretary at its first meeting. In practice, however, the general secretary is appointed for life, and no procedure is regularly established for designating a successor during his lifetime. Some Western observers have seen this lack of a designated successor as a structural weakness in the Soviet system, which could lead to a major political crisis at a time of succession. Michael Voslensky (1984: 356) wrote that the succession always involves a struggle for power that shakes the entire political class. During the post-Stalin period, however, the Soviet regime seems to have been generally able to manage the succession process without a power struggle that would undermine the stability of the political order.

In most political systems, the successor to a political office is not designated in advance. (The United States, where the vice-president automatically succeeds to the presidency, is an exception.) What is important is not having the successor appointed before the office becomes vacant but having an efficient procedure for filling the office, and such a procedure does exist in the USSR. The leadership has now gone through this process three times within three years, and the rules of the game are well known.

When the office of general secretary becomes vacant, the Politburo meets to decide on a new general secretary. Once the Politburo has acted, it convenes the Central Committee to ratify this choice. No effort is made to disguise the Politburo's role. The public reports admit that the Central Committee acts on the recommendation of the Politburo [*Kommunist* 5(1985): 6]. A succession crisis could develop if the Politburo is unable to reach a quick decision. However, the Politburo has only a small number of candidates to choose from. Furthermore, the Politburo has an overriding interest in maintaining unity at the top, so it tries to reach a decision quickly for presentation to the Central Committee.

Second-Ranking Secretary

Under Stalin and Khrushchev, an unofficial heir apparent usually was recognized as the second-ranking party secretary and most likely candidate for the top post. Myron Rush (1965) analyzed the political maneuvering in which an heir was selected and his authority balanced by a counter heir. At the national level, the post of second secretary has never been formalized as an office, so this arrangement was an informal one. (Second secretaries are appointed at the republic level and lower, but not in Moscow.) The position of the second-ranking secretary was sometimes announced in a hidden message. Party protocol usually called for the second-ranking secretary to appear at the national congress and deliver a short speech on changes in the party rules. Under Stalin, A. A. Zhdanov occupied this position from 1939 until his death from a heart attack in 1948. Thereafter, G. M. Malenkov appeared to be the second-ranking secretary, and following Stalin's death, Malenkov for a short time seemed to have the edge over other possible successors. He was appointed to succeed Stalin as premier while remaining a Central Committee secretary, although he did not take the title of general secretary. This arrangement lasted only two weeks. Malenkov resigned from the party Secretariat, and from that point the succession appears to have involved a sharp struggle (Conquest 1961: 195–292). For six months, the party had no clearly recognized head. Then in September 1953, N. S. Khrushchev was named first secretary of the Central Committee. This title has been interpreted as containing a hidden message that, although Khrushchev ranked first in the leadership, he had not inherited Stalin's position or his power (Rush 1959).

The powers of this office (if it was an office) were not defined, and for a time Khrushchev had to share power with Malenkov, who remained premier until 1955. The top political leadership seemed torn by internal strife for four years until the anti-Party crisis of June 1957. At that time a coalition of party leaders, who made up a majority of the Politburo, tried to force Khrushchev to resign. Khrushchev refused and demanded that the issue be decided by a full meeting of the Central Committee, which had elected him first secretary. He had his way, and a Central Committee plenum was convened. The Central Committee supported Khrushchev and denounced the anti-Khrushchev coalition as an anti-Party group. One by one, the members of the anti-Party group were forced out of the Soviet leadership; they were not all removed at once, to conceal the fact that a majority had actually lined up against Khrushchev.

Khrushchev now became the dominant political leader, and in the following year he assumed the office of premier. Although Khrushchev now held two of Stalin's titles, he never acquired Stalin's power. Linden (1965: ch. 3) concluded that Khrushchev achieved only an "incomplete victory" over the opposition. In 1964 Khrushchev was overthrown—the only time in Soviet history when the party's leader was forced out of office.

During most of Khrushchev's period of dominance, there was a general consensus within the leadership about who should be second-ranking secretary and likely successor. Khrushchev himself seemed to make a deliberate effort to groom a successor. No one, however, held the position for very long:

1. A. I. Kirichenko, a Khrushchev protégé, was rather mysteriously removed from the leadership in January 1960.
2. He was succeeded by F. R. Kozlov, who was clearly not Khrushchev's choice. Kozlov became seriously ill in 1963 and was no longer a factor in leadership politics.
3. The vacancy created by Kozlov's illness was filled by L. I. Brezhnev, who managed to succeed Khrushchev in 1964.

Even with this limited number of cases, some generalizations can be made about the position of the second-ranking secretary. First, it is not a very secure position, and no one seems to last very long. On the other hand, the potential successor may become a focus of opposition to the general secretary, and such opposition can develop into a threat to the general secretary's position. Therefore, the general secretary is bound to look on any second-ranking secretary as the leader of a possible opposition movement. This situation certainly arises if the general secretary, like Brezhnev, is a former successor designate who conspired to seize office.

Compromise and Détente

Indeed the entire Brezhnev era was clouded by memories of the coup of 1964. During Brezhnev's long period of dominance (1964–1982) there was no second secretary. Four party congresses were held under Brezhnev's leadership, and on each occasion the agenda did not call for a speech on the party rules. Brezhnev probably prevented anyone from acquiring this unofficial position precisely because he wanted to avoid Khrushchev's fate. Political leaders who might have challenged Brezhnev were eased out of office, and he never was threatened with serious opposition.

Khrushchev was overthrown because his policies threatened too many bureaucratic interests—in particular, the interests of the party apparatus. Brezhnev was careful not to threaten these interests, and the hallmark of his regime was compromise and accommodation. Unlike Khrushchev, who was attacked for adventurism and hare-brained schemes, Brezhnev was a very cautious leader, and in particular he was careful not to take personal responsibility for controversial policies. He was extravagantly praised for his personal contribution to Soviet policymaking, but it is hard to find any major policy innovations of this period that were in fact Brezhnev's own. One of the most significant decisions of the period was to enter into a detente relationship with the United States. However, Brezhnev seemed to take care not to be too closely identified with this policy. President Nixon visited the USSR in 1972; the first Strategic Arms Limitation Talks (SALT) agreement was signed; and Brezhnev paid a return visit in 1973. On the Soviet side, the negotiations were carefully orchestrated so that detente was not closely and personally connected with Brezhnev. Soviet officials who might possibly have opposed detente were brought into the Politburo in 1973: Gromyko, the foreign minister; Andropov, head of the KGB; and Marshal Grechko, the minister of defense. The national security bureaucracies thus were made responsible for the policy.

Aside from foreign policy, the important decisions of the Brezhnev regime were often nondecisions: decisions to compromise or to put off crucial issues. The most important area left unattended was the country's economic policy. Although various projects for reform in both industry and agriculture were discussed extensively, the reforms attempted were only incremental. Several Western observers have pointed out that the discussion of policy issues was much freer under Brezhnev than under Khrushchev. However, discussion is not the same thing as innovation. The cautious and conservative Brezhnev did not embark on genuine economic reform.

Cadres Policy

Another area in which the regime was marked by extreme caution was cadres policy, especially at the top level. Brezhnev's goal was stability in cadres. He came into office with an explicit promise to put an end to the organizational reforms that Khrushchev had introduced, and that promise was kept. Stability, especially at the Politburo level, was marked during the entire Brezhnev period. T. J. Colton (1984: 101) calculated that turnover in the Politburo (measured in terms of dismissals) was three times as great under Khrushchev as under Brezhnev. Even the party congresses, which had always been occasions for policy pronouncements and leadership change, offered little that was new. In fact, Brezhnev stretched out the period between congresses (from four years to five). In 1981 the Brezhnev regime achieved the ultimate in political stability. At the 26th Party Congress the entire leadership (Politburo and Secretariat) was reelected with no changes (see Table 8.1).

Brezhnev brought Soviet society a certain amount of tranquillity, which may have been precisely what was needed after the tumult of the Khrushchev years. Toward the end of his regime, Brezhnev was frequently ill and not able to devote full time to his office. Western visitors reported that he was sometimes unfamiliar with the details of foreign policy. This has been confirmed by a former Soviet diplomat (Shevchenko 1985: 302) who attended meetings in which Brezhnev was present. In this situation, much of the day-to-day management of the general secretary's office fell to his personal staff, which included Aleksandr Aleksandrov-Agentov (for foreign policy) and Georgii Tsukanov (his personal assistant), as well as Konstantin Chernenko. Decisions were made when necessary, and the staff tried to project an image of a healthy and active president. Brezhnev's staff was able to handle the routine business of government in this way, but the situation did not encourage innovation in policy. Everyone in the leadership understood that sooner or later the succession problem would have to be resolved.

Generational Change

Succession involves more than the choice of a general secretary, although that choice is the most dramatic part of the process. Succession also involves *generational change:* A generation of leaders is replaced by younger men. Thus the succession process involves a transformation of the entire political elite: the Politburo, Secretariat, the directors of the central party apparatus, and the regional secretaries. It is a slow, almost glacial process for two reasons. First, the pool from which the leaders can be drawn is limited. Politburo members and national secretaries come from the Central Committee, and the Central Committee membership is renewed only once in five years. Second, the older generation has shown an obvious reluctance to surrender power. Sometimes during the Brezhnev period, important posts changed hands without changing generation. For example, when Premier Kosygin left office at age seventy-six, he was replaced by Tikhonov, who was then seventy-five.

The stability of the political system depends on its ability to cope with the problem of generational change. Seweryn Bialer (1980: 76–77) concluded that Brezhnev had given no thought to grooming a new general secretary and had not tried to prepare a younger generation of leaders to assume office. As the Tikhonov example shows, he preferred

TABLE 8.1
Soviet Leadership in January 1982

Name*	Year of Birth	Year Elected**	Position
Members of Politburo			
L. I. Brezhnev	1906	1957	General secretary and president
Iu. V. Andropov	1914	1973	Chairman of KGB
M. S. Gorbachev	1931	1980	Central Committee secretary
V. V. Grishin	1914	1971	First secretary, city of Moscow
A. A. Gromyko	1909	1973	Minister of foreign affairs
A. P. Kirilenko	1906	1962	Central Committee secretary
D. A. Kunaev	1912	1971	First secretary, Kazakh republic
A. Ia. Pelshe	1899	1966	Chairman, Party Control Committee
G. V. Romanov	1923	1976	First secretary, Leningrad
M. A. Suslov	1902	1955	Central Committee secretary
N. A. Tikhonov	1905	1979	Premier
D. F. Ustinov	1908	1976	Minister of defense
K. U. Chernenko	1911	1978	Central Committee secretary, Director, General Department
V. V. Shcherbitskii	1918	1971	First secretary, Ukrainian republic
Candidate Members of Politburo			
G. A. Aliev	1923	1976	First secretary, Azerbaidzhan republic
P. N. Demichev	1918	1964	Minister of culture
T. Ia. Kiselev	1917	1980	First secretary, Belorussian republic
V. V. Kuznetsov	1901	1977	Vice-president
B. N. Ponomarev	1905	1972	Central Committee secretary, Director, International Department
Sh. R. Rashidov	1917	1966	First secretary, Uzbek republic
M. S. Solomentsev	1913	1971	RSFSR premier
E. A. Shevardnadze	1928	1978	First secretary, Georgian republic
Other Members of Central Committee Secretariat			
I. V. Kapitonov	1915	1965	Director, Department of Party and Organizational Work
V. I. Dolgikh	1924	1972	
M. V. Zimianin	1914	1976	
K. V. Rusakov	1909	1977	Director, Socialist Countries Department

Source: XXVI sezd KPSS 2: 244.

*Except for Brezhnev, Politburo members listed in Russian alphabetical order in each category. The secretaries were apparently listed by seniority.

**"Year elected" means the year entered current status in the Politburo or Secretariat.

people of his own generation. Most of the Politburo members purged during the Brezhnev years were younger men (younger, that is, than Brezhnev) who presumably represented a threat to the general secretary. The rather surprising rise of Mikhail Gorbachev at the end of the Brezhnev era runs counter to this general pattern.

RISE OF GORBACHEV

Mikhail Sergeevich Gorbachev was born in 1931 in a village in Stavropol province, one of the most important grain-growing regions in the USSR. His official biography, released after his election as general secretary, states that he was born into a peasant family [*Kommunist* 5(1985): 12]. However, biographies published prior to 1985 do not mention his family background. They do say that Gorbachev began his working career at the age of 16, when he was employed as a combine operator. In 1950 at the age of 19, Gorbachev enrolled in the law school at Moscow University. This was the turning point in his career. An American who was at the Moscow law school a few years later (Osborn 1970: 134) recalled that it had a high proportion of students from farming regions because, compared with other university disciplines, law ranks close to the bottom in terms of prestige and the difficulty of getting admitted. A large number of law graduates in fact do not practice law but become administrators. At the university Gorbachev took an active role in the Komsomol organization, and in 1952 he joined the party. This date is important because it means that Gorbachev's political career began, and his early political values were formed, while Stalin was still alive. As a Komsomol leader, Gorbachev was responsible for supervising other students. A contemporary now living in the West has recalled that in his Komsomol activities, Gorbachev always took an "extremely orthodox position" (Rar 1985).

In 1955, after completing the five-year law course, Gorbachev returned to Stavropol but not to work as a lawyer. In fact he never practiced the profession for which he had been trained. He became a fulltime Komsomol official and thus began his career in the apparatus. From this point, his career record sounds much like that of thousands of other young, ambitious apparatchiks except that he rose more rapidly than his contemporaries. In 1956 he was first secretary of the Komsomol organization for the city of Stavropol. Two years later he had risen to become Komsomol secretary for Stavropol krai, and then was promoted to first secretary. In March 1962, he left this post and worked for a brief time in agricultural management, but by the end of the year he received an important post in the regional party apparatus. The first secretary in Stavropol was then Fedor Kulakov, and Gorbachev became director of the department of party organs. At the young age of thirty-one he was an important apparatus operative, managing cadres policy for Kulakov.

After Brezhnev became head of the party, Kulakov's career flourished: He was called to Moscow to become director of the Central Committee department for agriculture, then advanced to be a party secretary (with responsibility for agriculture) and Politburo member. Gorbachev was to follow much the same path. In 1968, Gorbachev became second secretary of the Stavropol party organization, and in 1970 he was promoted to the office of first secretary. At the next party congress in 1971 he was automatically elected to the Central Committee.

In 1978, Kulakov died, creating an opening in the national Secretariat. At the end of the year, Gorbachev was made a Central Committee secretary and took over the job of supervising Soviet agriculture. He was then forty-seven, still considerably younger than all other members of the central leadership.

There has been much speculation about the choice of Gorbachev as Kulakov's successor in the Secretariat. One rumor circulating in Moscow was that Gorbachev was the choice of Andropov. According to this story, Andropov took his vacations in Kislovodsk, a watering place in Stavropol krai. Gorbachev, as first secretary, was responsible for seeing to the personal comfort of the vacationing KGB chairman. A more likely explanation is that the Stavropol first secretary is bound to have considerable experience with agriculture and thus is a leading candidate for the job of supervising agriculture.

Speculation has also centered around Gorbachev's possible connection with M. A. Suslov, who had been first secretary in Stavropol between 1939 and 1944. However, Suslov left the region when Gorbachev was only thirteen years old, so it is not likely that there was a Suslov connection that advanced his career. Other speculation has linked Gorbachev with various members of the leadership, but no reliable evidence supports any of these versions of Gorbachev's rise.

In 1979 Gorbachev became a candidate member of the Politburo, and in October 1980 he was promoted to full membership. He had thus arrived, at the relatively young age of forty-nine, at the top level of the Soviet oligarchy. He was the youngest member of the Politburo and the only person of his generation to rise to such prominence under Brezhnev. He remained in the background, avoiding publicity and not associating himself with any policy issues. This reticence is reflected in the fact that, at the time he became general secretary, the party press had still not published a volume of his collected speeches—something rather unusual for a Politburo member.

Later, when he had become general secretary, much was made of Gorbachev's relative youth and the fact that he represented a new generation of leadership. However, except for his rapid rise to the top, Gorbachev had a typical apparatus career that spanned thirty years. Gorbachev's career prospered under Stalin, under Khrushchev, and under Brezhnev.

BEGINNING OF TRANSITION

The succession process was set in motion with the death of Suslov at the age of seventy-nine, in January 1982. Suslov had been the senior member of the oligarchy: He actually outranked Brezhnev within both the Secretariat and the Politburo. Suslov was usually described as the chief ideologist of the regime, and he did seem to have supreme authority in this sphere. His responsibilities, however, were much broader. Although in official protocol he ranked in the middle of the Politburo, in terms of real authority in some respects he outranked all his colleagues (Avtorkhanov 1979: 94). Suslov was not a candidate for the office of general secretary, and no evidence exists that he ever sought the office. However, his seniority and his unrivaled prestige within the apparatus could have given him the role of kingmaker. Had Brezhnev died earlier, Suslov might have designated his successor as general secretary, and the other members of the Politburo would have accepted this choice.

Who were the contenders? Western analysts agree on the basic characteristics of a candidate for the office of general secretary (Donaldson 1985: 8). First, he is a full member of the Politburo and a member of the Secretariat. The Politburo makes the decision, and it seems inconceivable that its members would choose someone from outside their own ranks. Promoting the general secretary from within the Secretariat ensures continuity in managing the internal affairs of the party. These basic requirements—membership in both Politburo and Secretariat—mean that the choice usually is narrowed to two or three candidates. In addition to the basic requirements, the candidate is almost certain to be a career apparatus official, who probably got his start in the Komsomol organization. He is most likely to be an ethnic Russian (or at least a Slav) and to have some experience as first secretary of an important region in the USSR. In fact, service as a regional first secretary is probably the best preparation for being general secretary. Like the general secretary, the regional first secretary is a political executive who supervises both the government and the party and bears the total responsibility for the region entrusted to him. He should have some experience in managing industry or agriculture—and preferably both.

To these qualifications, J. F. Hough (1980: 65) added one more. He pointed out that the office of general secretary had always gone to the candidate with the most experience in dealing with the national minorities. (Stalin had been commissar for nationalities. Both Khrushchev and Brezhnev had served as first secretary in non-Russian republics.)

Given these constraints on the choice of a general secretary, identifying the contenders is not difficult. As of January 1982, the possible candidates were A. P. Kirilenko, K. U. Chernenko, and Gorbachev. Kirilenko was an experienced party secretary who ranked just after Brezhnev in seniority. However, he was actually older (by a few months) than Brezhnev, and had he become general secretary he obviously would have been only a transitional leader.

Brezhnev himself seemed to favor Chernenko. But Chernenko was not a likely candidate because he lacked most of the qualifications for the job: He had no experience in economic management, and he had never served as first secretary of a region or a republic. Gorbachev, although he had the qualifications, was still too young to be a serious contender.

After the death of Suslov, the Soviet leadership seemed ready for the first time to deal with the succession problem. In May, Andropov left the KGB to return to the Secretariat (where he had served until 1967), and in retrospect, that move seems to have been decisive. Andropov quickly assumed the role of unofficial second secretary and most likely successor. Two other appointments came in May that also seemed connected with the succession process. V. I. Dolgikh, a party secretary who had extensive experience as an industrial manager, was promoted to candidate membership in the Politburo. This appointment provided the leadership with additional expertise in economic policy, an area where Andropov was totally lacking in experience. It also brought to the Politburo a party official who could have supervised a program of economic reform. Andropov's post at the KGB went to Vitalii Fedorchuk, a career KGB official without political connections who was not even a member of the party's Central Committee. Not surprisingly, in a period of political transition the KGB was entrusted to a career officer. This appointment would ensure that the KGB would be loyal to the party leadership as a whole and not to any individual. The same thing had happened during the political transition after Stalin.

In studying the events of 1981-1982, some Western analysts have concluded that Andropov, though still KGB chairman, was engaged in intrigues to undermine Brezhnev (Medvedev 1983: 61–70). Several incidents seemed calculated to undermine Brezhnev's authority. At the end of 1981 a literary magazine [*Avrora* 12(1981): 75] published a thinly disguised spoof on Brezhnev's pretensions as a writer. (Brezhnev had won a Lenin prize for his war memoirs.) Early in 1982 a complicated scandal came to light that involved the Soviet circus, bribery, diamond smuggling—and Brezhnev's daughter, Galina Churbanova. A figure from the entertainment world known as Boris the Gypsy, rumored to be a close friend of Churbanova, was arrested. Later the first secretary in Krasnodar krai, Sergei Medunov, was dismissed amid rumors of a scandal, and this event was also interpreted as a concealed attack on Brezhnev.

In October, Kirilenko was dropped from the leadership, without explanation. (Here we have to rely on kremlinological evidence. On October 3, *Pravda* published an obituary of a republic party secretary signed in the usual protocol by all members of the Politburo. On October 5, *Pravda* published another obituary signed by all Politburo members except Kirilenko. We can infer that Kirilenko was ousted on October 4.) Probably Kirilenko had challenged Andropov's claims to the position of second secretary but was outvoted and then forced out. In November, Brezhnev died. Andropov was announced as chairman of the commission to arrange the funeral, and kremlinologists recognized this as a signal that Andropov would be the successor. (In 1924, Stalin was in charge of Lenin's funeral.) One day after the announcement of Brezhnev's demise, the Central Committee unanimously elected Andropov as general secretary. At the Central Committee meeting Chernenko spoke in the name of the Politburo and recommended the election of Andropov [*Kommunist* 17(1982): 9].

ANDROPOV AND CHERNENKO

Neither Andropov nor his apparent rival, Chernenko, fits the described pattern. Neither had served as a regional first secretary. Andropov had at one time been second secretary in the Karelian republic, but Chernenko had not risen even this high in the territorial hierarchy. Both men were products of the regional apparatus, but they had spent most of their careers at the center in Moscow, rather than on the periphery. Furthermore, neither of the two had any experience in managing economic affairs. On the other hand, both had had some experience in governing national minorities—Andropov in Karelia and Chernenko in Moldavia.

Andropov disappeared from view in August 1983 and was never seen again in public. We now know that he was critically ill and probably played no significant role in policymaking during the last five months of his life. His personal staff tried to project an image of an active leader by publishing letters and interviews that had allegedly taken place. Once again, the regime seemed to lack policy coordination and seemed able to deal only with routine business. This failing is reflected in the tragic incident of September 1983, when a Korean Air Lines plane was shot down after it penetrated Soviet air space in the Far East, apparently by accident. The Kremlin issued several conflicting statements, and more than a week passed before it provided a consistent explanation of what had happened.

Andropov thus had only nine months in office, far too little time to institute a program of change and reform. The difference between Andropov and Brezhnev was more in the style of leadership than in the substance of policy. The outlines of an Andropov program are evident from this short period but not his real accomplishments. In his first major speech as general secretary, Andropov admitted that he had no "readymade recipes" for economic reform (*Pravda*, Nov. 23, 1982), although he clearly believed that the economy was the country's number one problem. Nine months later in his last speech, Andropov said that there was a need for a basic change in the economic mechanism (*Pravda*, Aug. 16, 1983), but again he made no specific proposals.

The first solution that Andropov chose to emphasize was a crackdown on corruption and an increase in labor discipline. *Pravda* (Dec. 11, 1982) announced that the Politburo was acting in response to many letters from workers complaining about violations of the law. In Andropov's first months in office, a strident public campaign was waged against shirkers, against absenteeism, and against drunkenness on the job. This campaign, however, did not last long enough to have any visible economic effect.

In December, Andropov hinted at possible changes in nationalities policy (*Pravda*, Dec. 22, 1982). We have already noted his sudden revival of the idea of the merger of nationalities, which was quickly forgotten again. Andropov also called for an intensified effort to appoint national minorities to leading posts in the republics. In all the republics, most of these posts are now held by members of the nationality that gives the republic its name. Ethnic Russians—an important minority in all the republics—are also found in positions of responsibility. Thus, as Z. A. Medvedev (1983: 149) argued, Andropov must have been referring to other nationalities often excluded from important positions, such as the large number of Armenians in the Georgian republic. This policy, if carried out, would have broken down some barriers and encouraged the merger of nationalities. Again, however, Andropov did not live long enough to effect a significant change.

The personnel decisions that Andropov presided over may have been the most important ones of his brief administration. The general secretary does not have a free hand to make appointments, although he has somewhat greater freedom in the party apparatus than in the government. All important appointments are discussed and approved by the Politburo. Thus major personnel changes are like moves on a chessboard: They appear to be carefully thought out and are made as part of some overall political strategy. During his short tenure as general secretary, Andropov seemed to have a plan for changes in the leadership, and he made the following significant appointments.

Vitalii Vorotnikov. Vorotnikov was an apparatus official who had been a regional first secretary and vice premier of the RSFSR. In 1979, Brezhnev had exiled him to the post of ambassador to Cuba. Andropov made him premier of the Russian republic and a Politburo member.

Nikolai Ryzhkov. Ryzhkov was an industrial engineer and experienced manager who had been deputy chairman of Gosplan. In November 1982, Andropov appointed him to the Central Committee Secretariat and director of the Central Committee's economic department.

Gaidar Aliev. In one of his more surprising appointments, Andropov brought Gaidar Aliev to Moscow and made him a full member of the Politburo and vice premier. Aliev is an ethnic Azeri who had spent his entire career in the Azerbaidzhan republic. Most of this career was in the political police, and Aliev rose to head of the republic KGB. In 1969 he became first secretary of the republic party. His appointment as a vice premier brought an official of Muslim origin into the central leadership for the first time since the Khrushchev era.

Viktor Chebrikov. Chebrikov was an experienced party official who entered the KGB in the same year as Andropov (1967) and had served as one of Andropov's chief deputies for fifteen years. In December 1982, Chebrikov replaced Fedorchuk as chairman of the KGB, and a year later he was promoted to a candidate member of the Politburo.

Egor Ligachev. Ligachev had served for many years as a regional party secretary. Prior to that he was an official in the central apparatus, where he served in the party organs department. Andropov brought him to Moscow to take charge of cadres policy and subsequently promoted him to the party Secretariat.

At the beginning of 1982, the median age of Politburo members was seventy-three. During the period being reviewed, the median age dropped markedly primarily because six of the original thirteen members died between January 1982 and March 1985: Suslov, Brezhnev, Arvid Pelshe, Andropov, Ustinov, and Chernenko. Andropov was bringing younger people into the leadership, but they were not raw youths. In 1983 the median age of the five newcomers listed was sixty.

In one other important change, G. V. Romanov was transferred from Leningrad, where he served as first secretary, into the national Secretariat in Moscow. This reassignment, of course, made Romanov a potential candidate for general secretary.

In addition to these major appointments, changes were made in the central apparatus of the party, but no massive influx of newcomers occurred. Of twenty-three departments of the Central Committee, at least eight had new directors in 1982-1983. Andropov appeared to be making an effort to bring more competent people into the departments with ideological responsibilities, as is shown by the appointment of Medvedev (see Chapter 5). The most significant of these appointments in the apparatus was the selection of Ligachev to be director of the Department of Party and Organizational Work, replacing I. V. Kapitonov who, however, remained a member of the Secretariat.

Significant changes also were made in the regional secretaries, although these might have come anyway. About 20 percent of the regional first secretaries were replaced. However, this rate of turnover is not exceptionally high, and some changes were inevitable. The regional party secretaries are elected every two and one-half years. There had been elections at the end of 1980 and beginning of 1981, in preparation for the 26th Party Congress. Under the statutes, therefore, elections were due in mid-1983, and they took place as scheduled.

In February 1984, after a long and debilitating illness Andropov died. The choice of a successor was not made as swiftly as in 1982, leading to speculation that the Politburo was unable to agree on a name. However, Chernenko had immediately been appointed chairman of the funeral commission, so he appeared to be the Politburo's choice for general secretary.

Andropov, despite his poor health, had tried to project an image of a vigorous and innovative leader. Chernenko seemed to represent a return to the slower pace of the Brezhnev regime. Chernenko was not personally associated with any new policies, although Moscow did agree to return to arms negotiations with the United States, which the Soviet Union had broken off. "Stability in cadres" was again the rule, and under Chernenko no new appointments were made in the Politburo, the Secretariat, or among the directors of the Central Committee apparatus. Chernenko, even more than Andropov, led a caretaker administration. After he died, it was revealed that Gorbachev had in fact taken charge of the Secretariat and presided at Politburo meetings in the absence of Chernenko.

The relative political standing of the members of the leadership during the Chernenko administration is shown in Table 8.2. As noted earlier in this chapter, the election speeches of the party leaders are a ritualistic event. This table is based on the reports about the election to the USSR Supreme Soviet (1984) and the elections to republic supreme soviets (1985). From the order in which the speeches are published, the kremlinologist can calculate the relative standing of individuals within the

TABLE 8.2
Political Standing of Soviet Leadership in 1984 and 1985

1984*	1985*
Chernenko	Chernenko
Tikhonov	Tikhonov
Gorbachev	Gorbachev
Ustinov	Gromyko
Gromyko	Grishin
Grishin/Romanov	Kuznetsov
Solomentsev/Shcherbitskii	Solomentsev
Ponomarev	Romanov
Aliev/Kunaev	Aliev
Vorotnikov	Shcherbitskii
Kuznetsov	Kunaev
Dolgikh/Shevardnadze	Vorotnikov
Demichev/Chebrikov	Ponomarev/Shevardnadze
Zimianin/Kapitonov/Ryzhkov	Dolgikh/Chebrikov
Ligachev	Demichev/Rusakov
Rusakov	Zimianin/Kapitonov
	Ligachev/Ryzhkov

Source: Compiled by the author from reports on the election
speeches, Pravda, February–March 1984 (USSR Supreme Soviet)
and February 1985 (republic supreme soviets).

*A slash indicates that two or three men received equal
coverage in the same issue of Pravda.

hierarchy. There was only one change in the composition of the leadership
(the death of Ustinov), so the table shows the relative standing of the
entire leadership at two points in time. According to the table, Gorbachev
ranked third, after General Secretary Chernenko and Premier Tikhonov
at both times. That position is a clear indication that Gorbachev had
won recognition as a second-ranking secretary and was the logical
candidate for the succession. In contrast, Romanov, Gorbachev's only
serious rival, fell in the rankings between 1984 and 1985.

GORBACHEV AS GENERAL SECRETARY

The succession process that had begun in 1982 ended in 1985 with
the election of Gorbachev to the office of general secretary. Chernenko
died March 10. The Central Committee met the following day to elect
a successor, thus acting much more swiftly than in the past. The speed
of the transition suggested that the choice had been made earlier, an
inference confirmed by the speech that Foreign Minister Gromyko,
speaking on behalf of the Politburo, made nominating the new general
secretary:

First of all let me emphasize that all the activity of Mikhail Sergeevich in carrying out our domestic and foreign policy affirms that he is worthy of election as General Secretary of the CC CPSU. It should be emphasized that he has great experience in party work. First at the level of a krai, and then here, at the center, in the Central Committee: first as a secretary, then as a member of the Politburo. He has directed the Secretariat, as is known. He also presided at meetings of the Politburo in the absence of Konstantin Ustinovich [Chernenko]. [*Kommunist* 5(1985): 6–7]

Like Andropov in 1982, Gorbachev seemed to be a vigorous new leader ready to take the country in a new direction. The first important steps were appointments. Under Andropov, three new full members had entered the Politburo—two of them promoted from the status of candidate member. During Chernenko's tenure as general secretary, no new appointments were made either to the Politburo or to the Secretariat. On the other hand, shortly after Gorbachev's election, several important appointments were made. Some Western commentators saw this as a move by Gorbachev to put his political friends into the leadership. However, a detailed review of the changes made under Gorbachev suggests that a different explanation can be made:

1. Four new Politburo members were appointed: KGB chairman Chebrikov (who was promoted from candidate member) and Ryzhkov and Ligachev, the two newest party secretaries, who were promoted directly to full membership; Shevardnadze, the Georgian first secretary who was slated to become foreign minister, was promoted to full membership in July.

2. The Minister of Defense, Marshal Sergei Sokolov, was made a candidate member of the Politburo, as was Nikolai Talyzin, head of Gosplan.

3. Three appointments were made to the Secretariat: (1) V. P. Nikonov, an experienced regional secretary who had been deputy minister of agriculture; (2) B. N. Eltsin, an industrial engineer and former first secretary in Sverdlovsk; and (3) L. N. Zaikov, an industrial engineer and former mayor of Leningrad who had succeeded Romanov there as first secretary.

4. Undoubtedly the most important change was the dismissal of Romanov, who was allowed to resign from the leadership for reasons of "health" (*Pravda*, July 2, 1985). The aging premier, Tikhonov, retired in October 1985 (*Pravda*, Oct. 16, 1985).

The composition of the leadership after these changes is recapitulated in Table 8.3. None of the new appointees had any past link with Gorbachev, and there is no reason to believe that they were his clients. The members of the Politburo were now somewhat younger than they

TABLE 8.3
Soviet Leadership in November 1985

Name*	Year of Birth	Year Elected	Position
Members of Politburo			
M. S. Gorbachev	1931	1980	General secretary
G. A. Aliev	1923	1982	Vice premier
V. I. Vorotnikov	1926	1983	RSFSR premier
V. V. Grishin	1914	1972	First secretary, city of Moscow
A. A. Gromyko	1909	1973	President
D. A. Kunaev	1912	1971	First secretary, Kazakh republic
E. K. Ligachev	1920	1985	Central Committee secretary
N. I. Ryzhkov	1929	1985	Premier
M. S. Solomentsev	1913	1983	Chairman, Party Control Committee
V. M. Chebrikov	1923	1985	Chairman of KGB
E. A. Shevardnadze	1928	1985	Minister of foreign affairs
V. V. Shcherbitskii	1918	1971	First secretary, Ukrainian republic
Candidate Members of Politburo			
P. N. Demichev	1918	1964	Minister of culture
V. I. Dolgikh	1924	1982	Central Committee secretary
V. V. Kuznetsov	1901	1977	Vice-president
B. N. Ponomarev	1905	1972	Central Committee secretary, Director, International Department
S. L. Sokolov	1911	1985	Minister of defense
N. V. Talyzin	1929	1985	Chairman of Gosplan
Other Members of Central Committee Secretariat			
B. N. Eltsin	1931	1985	Director, Construction Department
L. N. Zaikov	1923	1985	
M. V. Zimianin	1914	1976	
I. V. Kapitonov	1915	1965	
V. P. Nikonov	1929	1985	
K. V. Rusakov	1909	1977	Director, Socialist Countries Department

Source: Soviet press reports, 1982-1985.

*Except for Gorbachev, listed in Russian alphabetical order within each category.

had been at the end of the Brezhnev era: The median age was about sixty-five. The new appointments did restore to the Politburo some of the balance that existed at the end of the Brezhnev period—in particular a balance between government officials and party secretaries. The KGB and the Ministry of Defense were represented (the ministry, however, only by a candidate member). The promotion of Ryzhkov, an Andropov appointee and a newcomer to the party apparatus, prepared the way for his selection a few months later as USSR premier. His appointment passed over V. I. Dolgikh, a party secretary (since 1972) and candidate member (since 1982), who had been the chief specialist on industry within the leadership. The sudden elevation of Ligachev and Ryzhkov also shows a weakness of the kremlinological method, for by the usual indicators (see Table 8.2) they were ranked lowest in the leadership.

At the end of 1985, the Politburo thus consisted of five holdovers from the Brezhnev period, three men appointed by Andropov, and four by Gorbachev. It appeared that the three top-ranking leaders, after Gorbachev himself, included two of his appointees:

Gromyko, the president, who still seemed to have special authority in foreign affairs, although he did not attend the Geneva summit.

Ryzhkov, the premier, in overall charge of economic policy.

Ligachev, the only other party secretary who was a full Politburo member; he has special responsibility for ideological questions and internal party affairs.

Gorbachev discussed cadres policy in his first major speech as general secretary (*Pravda*, April 24, 1985) and seemed to be cautiously calling for a greater turnover in personnel. On the one hand, he promised to continue the line of "stability in the party leadership," but said that this would be guaranteed by a "proper mix" of both young and experienced officials. He also promised to avoid "stagnation" in the movement of cadres. "In their letters to the Central Committee, Communists draw our attention to the fact that certain leaders, after occupying the same post for a long time, cease to see anything new, and accept shortcomings." He called for appointing more women and more "young, far-sighted" people.

At the time of Gorbachev's election, much was made of his relative youth, his vigor, and his supposed interest in reform. We should not, however, overlook the powerful constraints that limit the power of the general secretary. The 27th Party Congress was scheduled to meet during Gorbachev's first year in office. The congress and the preparatory period of elections to the regional and republic party organizations provide opportunities for political change at this level. In announcing plans for the congress, Gorbachev made a point of stating that the congress would not hear a speech on changing the Party Statute, suggesting that the general secretary was not ready to designate a second-ranking secretary and possible successor.

Gorbachev may indeed be the harbinger of a new sort of Soviet politician. His legal training is unique among members of the Soviet leadership. Most of the leaders of Brezhnev's generation were trained as industrial engineers. In addition to studying law, Gorbachev spent twenty-five years as an official of the party apparatus, an experience that has no doubt shaped his ideas, his values, and his style.

Gorbachev has made clear that his principal concern is economic policy. Any serious attack on the economic problems of the country will require a review of national priorities and in particular reconsideration of the vast resources spent on the Soviet military. Gorbachev also faces serious challenges in Soviet social policy. Finally, he has indicated an interest in continuing Andropov's campaign against corruption and for strengthening labor discipline.

REFERENCES

Avtorkhanov, A. 1979. *Sila i bessilie Brezhneva*. Frankfurt: Posev.

Bialer, Seweryn. 1980. *Stalin's Successors: Leadership, Stability, and Change in the Soviet Union*. Cambridge: Cambridge University Press.

Breslauer, George. 1982. *Khrushchev and Brezhnev as Leaders: Building Authority in Soviet Politics*. London: Allen & Unwin.

Colton, Timothy J. 1984. *The Dilemma of Reform in the Soviet Union*. New York: Council on Foreign Relations.

Conquest, Robert. 1961. *Power and Policy in the U.S.S.R.* London: Macmillan.

Donaldson, Robert H. 1985. Political Leadership and Succession: The Passing of the Brezhnev Generation. In *Soviet Politics: Russia After Brezhnev*, edited by Joseph L. Nogee. New York: Praeger, pp. 1–14.

XXVI sezd KPSS—stenograficheskii otchet. 1981. 3 vols. Moscow: Politizdat.

Hough, Jerry F. 1980. *Soviet Leadership in Transition*. Washington, D.C.: Brookings Institution.

Linden, Carl A. 1965. *Khrushchev and the Soviet Leadership 1957–1964*. Baltimore: Johns Hopkins Press.

Medvedev, Zhores A. 1983. *Andropov*. New York: Norton.

Osborn, Robert J. 1970. *Soviet Social Policies: Welfare, Equality, and Community*. Homewood, Ill.: Dorsey Press.

Rar, Aleksandr. 1985. "Liubimets partii": kto takoi Mikhail Gorbachev? *Russkaia mysl*, April 18.

Rush, Myron. 1959. Esoteric Communications in Soviet Politics. *World Politics* 11: 614–620.

———. 1965. *Political Succession in the USSR*. New York: Columbia University Press.

Shevchenko, Arkady. 1985. *Breaking with Moscow*. New York: Knopf.

Voslensky, Michael. 1984. *Nomenklatura: The Soviet Ruling Class*. Garden City, N.Y.: Doubleday.

9
Law Enforcement and Human Rights

The dictatorship of the proletariat was to be the first step toward a stateless society. Every state is "organized force," according to Lenin, and this organized force would still be necessary after the revolution. Gradually the need for the state would disappear. People would grow accustomed to obeying society's rules without the fear of punishment (Lenin 1918a: 285, 292). When this last happens, the state would begin to wither away. During the transitional period, the foundations of the new order would be built: a new order without government, courts, jails, or police. Disputes between citizens would be settled by comradely agreement. Crime, supposedly a disease of the old society, would be only a memory. Occasional violations of public morality would be dealt with by the community acting together without the formality of police or trial. The party program of 1919 called for the elimination of all courts, judges, and prisons.

Lenin's vision turned out to be unworkable. The Soviet government, as any other modern government, needs order and stability, and it needs law as a guarantor of order and stability. In Soviet terminology, law and order became socialist legality. Socialist legality is based on the belief that some minimum of order, security, and predictability must be maintained in the political system. In one sense, these are restraints on the government. At the same time legality makes the central government more secure. By ensuring uniformity in law and administration, socialist legality tries to prevent petty dictators at the lower levels of the system.

In practice, socialist legality was a difficult concept to enforce. Russian society lacked any strong tradition of rule of law, although it had a long tradition of authoritarian government. Furthermore, Lenin had openly proclaimed that the regime was a dictatorship, and the very idea of dictatorship seems to deny the concept of legality. During the new economic policy (NEP) period a serious effort was made to enforce legality as part of the general effort to restore order and rebuild the economy. The dictatorship of Stalin, however, brought an end to this striving toward legality. Stalin himself (1926: 162) defined dictatorship as rule based on force and unlimited by law. Stalin increasingly relied on the criminal law—not only against his political opposition but to deal with peasants who hoarded grain or workers who shirked their duty (Juviler 1976: 48).

After 1953 a serious effort was undertaken to restore socialist legality and to undo the worst features of the Stalin dictatorship. During the Khrushchev regime the power of the political police was reduced, and criminal law was reformed. Khrushchev also wanted to restore Leninism, and for him this meant returning to the original vision of the withering away of the law. In the late 1950s, Khrushchev introduced several new social institutions, such as the "parasite" law. This law provided a procedure whereby individuals who were social parasites could be sent off to the provinces and forced to work. Parasites (that is, individuals who seemed to have unearned income) could be punished by a meeting of their neighbors or fellow workers. Here was Lenin's vision in practice: The courts played no role in the parasite procedure, and the community took action as conscience dictated.

The parasite laws, and other institutions such as the comrades' courts, threatened to undermine socialist legality, and the new institutions were opposed by the legal profession. The continued existence of a political police system, even though its power was curtailed, also was a challenge to socialist legality.

SECURITY POLICE

The first secret police organization was established six weeks after the Bolsheviks seized power. The name of the organization, Extraordinary Commission for Struggle with Counterrevolution and Sabotage, defined its functions. From the Russian initials for Extraordinary Commission (Ch. K.) came the name of Cheka.

Cheka

The dangers that the Cheka was supposed to ward off were not imagined. The young Bolshevik regime held only a tenuous grip on power. From 1918–1920, the regime was constantly confronted with civil war, foreign intervention, and the danger of secret agents in the rear. The regime also faced a danger from the Left, from the other revolutionary parties that refused to accept Bolshevik rule. In 1918, a series of assassinations took place, including an attempt on Lenin's life.

The Bolsheviks' response was spelled out in the decree of September 5, 1918, on the "red terror": "In the present situation protection of the rear by means of terror is a direct necessity . . . it is necessary to protect the Soviet Republic from class enemies by isolating them in concentration camps . . . that all persons involved in White Guard organizations, conspiracies, and uprisings are subject to shooting." Lenin argued, in defense of the Cheka, that the regime had no choice but to use force (1918b: 174).

The early experience of the Cheka established two principles that governed the operations of the political police. First, the Cheka was an instrument of the revolutionary dictatorship, unrestricted by law. The initial conflict was between the Cheka and the ministry of justice, as the ministry tried to supervise the Cheka's activities (Leggett 1981: 45–49). This conflict was quickly resolved, however, when the Cheka established its power as unrestricted by law. Second, although the Cheka was a part of the state apparatus, it was controlled directly by the party leadership and took its orders from the Politburo.

The GPU, OGPU, and NKVD

The end of the civil war and the beginning of NEP led to changes in the organization of the security police. In 1922 the functions of the Cheka were transferred to the State Political Directorate, or GPU (Gosudarstvennoe politicheskoe upravlenie). The GPU was supposed to operate within the law. The decree establishing the GPU specifically provided that in the future, its cases were to be turned over to the courts for trial. No more summary executions like those carried out by the Cheka took place. However, the establishment of the federal system at the end of 1922 had the effect of removing the political police from legal control. A new, all-union organization, OGPU (for united GPU), was created, and like the Cheka, it was responsible directly to the party leadership. Furthermore, the development of OGPU was influenced by the succession struggle and the rise of the Stalinist autocracy. The Cheka had not interfered with party members who might have opposed Lenin's policies, such as the Workers' Opposition group. The OGPU did not have this restraint, and the police gradually were transformed from an instrument of the party into an instrument of Stalin's autocracy. In 1934 OGPU was abolished, and its functions were assigned to a new ministry, the USSR People's Commissariat of Internal Affairs, or NKVD (Narodnyi komissariat vnutrennikh del). Much more important than this change of name was the creation of a special board (*osoboe soveshchanie*) in the NKVD with extraordinary powers. The special board had the authority to imprison or exile, for a term up to five years, anyone who was thought to be socially dangerous. The board was not required to follow any legal procedure, and a person sentenced in this way could not appeal the verdict.

The security police under Stalin steadily expanded its powers. Thousands, perhaps hundreds of thousands, of peasants were forcibly removed from their homes and taken to corrective labor camps. These camps had existed since 1918, but they had not been economically important. Now, however, the security police had a sizable labor force under its control. The prisoners were put to work on large-scale construction projects, such as the White Sea canal or the Moscow-Volga canal. With the beginning of the great purges, many thousands of new prisoners were sent to the camps. NKVD agencies such as Dalstroi (Far Eastern Construction Trust) became major economic enterprises.

Operating through his own personal secretariat and through the special sector, Stalin managed to keep the police under his own control. But he seemed to realize that the police apparatus represented a serious threat to his own power. In the last ten years of Stalin's rule, the police were under the control of two separate agencies, the Ministerstvo vnutrennikh del (ministry of internal affairs) (MVD) and the Ministerstvo gosudarstvennoi bezopasnosti (ministry of state security) (MGB). After Stalin died the security police were reorganized as the KGB. The economic empire of the security police was broken up, and the enterprises were assigned to various ministries. The secret board was abolished (Vlasov and Studenikin 1959: 263). Lavrentii Beria, who had headed the police under Stalin, was charged with conspiracy against the regime, and he and several other police officials were executed. The new KGB did not function as an agent of the dictator; like the Cheka, its loyalty was to the party leadership as a group.

The KGB

The KGB is a highly secretive organization, and much of our knowledge about its operations is based on fragmentary information. According to one Soviet source from the 1960s (Kozlov 1968: 523ff), the KGB was responsible for four areas: (1) protecting the Soviet border, (2) exposing and rendering harmless foreign agents, (3) investigating political crimes, and (4) protecting state secrets. A more recent source added a new function to the list: protecting the country against "ideological sabotage" (Lunev 1979: 67). To carry out these functions the KGB is vested with extraordinary powers, but it is also supposed to rely on preventive and educational measures, especially in dealing with ideological sabotage. Although little is published about the KGB's organization, it can be reconstructed from the testimony of defectors (Barron 1983). The division of the KGB most directly involved in law enforcement is the second main directorate, which is charged with internal security. A new fifth main directorate was created in the 1970s and given responsibility for dealing with political dissent.

In addition to these police functions, the KGB also operates the USSR's secret intelligence service (first main directorate). Another directorate maintains a special military force that protects the Soviet border. Among other duties, the Border Guards check the passports of individuals entering and leaving the country. The KGB's other functions include the personal protection of Soviet leaders, communications security, and military counterintelligence. Thus, the KGB combines functions performed in the United States by several agencies: the Central Intelligence Agency (CIA), the Federal Bureau of Investigation (FBI), the Coast Guard and the Border Patrol, military counterintelligence, and the National Security Agency.

The KGB is organized as a union-republic ministry, and the chairman is a member of the Council of Ministers. In fact the KGB is highly centralized, and the union republic KGBs have limited powers. There is no KGB for the RSFSR, and state security for the Russian republic is the responsibility of the USSR KGB. Regional directorates of state security do not observe the principle of dual subordination but are responsible to the union republic KGB (or in the RSFSR, to the USSR KGB).

LAW AND COURTS

Three agencies are concerned with law enforcement in the USSR: the courts, the procuracy, and the police. All are supposed to be governed by law. Ultimately, of course, the party leadership determines what the law is. But the regime has usually refrained from direct interference in the job of law enforcement, at least with respect to civil (that is, noncriminal) matters or to criminal cases that do not have political overtones. Thus the procuracy, the courts, and the regular police are institutions of socialist legality.

The law is enforced by a system of courts with a hierarchical structure similar to that of Western judicial systems. In every district in the USSR, a people's (district) court has original jurisdiction in most cases arising under civil or criminal law. The court is presided over by a judge elected for a five-year term. As in the case of other elections in the USSR, nominations in the judicial elections are controlled by the party, and the elections themselves are uncontested. Nearly all judges have professional legal training, and most (but not all) are members of the party.

Alongside the presiding judge in the people's court sit two lay judges, or people's assessors (*narodnye zasedateli*). The assessors are elected for terms of two and one-half years. In practice, they sit on the court for only about two weeks each year and then are replaced.

Although the assessors take the place of the jury in the U.S. system, they are not a jury, and legally, no distinction exists between the functions of the assessors and the professional judge. The three decide all questions before the court—including that of guilt or innocence in criminal cases—by majority vote.

Despite its federal structure, the USSR has a uniform system of courts. Above the people's court in the judicial hierarchy stand the appeals courts: the regional (oblast) court and the supreme court of the republic. Cases decided in the people's court may be reviewed by these higher courts. (In the smaller union republics that do not have the regional division, an appeal may go from the people's court directly to the supreme court of the republic.) An appeal from a lower court is decided by a panel of professional judges.

The supreme court of the republic is the highest court to which one can carry an appeal. The USSR Supreme Court does not accept appeals from the republic courts, but it does review cases from the lower courts—usually at the request of the procuracy. The USSR Supreme Court is a much less powerful body than the Supreme Court of the United States. As already explained, Soviet legal theory does not recognize the principle of separation of powers. The court has never claimed the right to annul acts of the legislature or to review the actions of administrative agencies. In fact, the Supreme Court is not even supposed to interpret the law. That function (described in Chapter 6) is reserved for the Presidium of the Supreme Soviet.

Despite these limitations, the Supreme Court has some influence over the development of Soviet law. The court's decisions in particular cases are published regularly for the guidance of the lower courts. Moreover, the Supreme Court has the authority to issue decrees that are binding on the other courts. These decrees usually deal with technical legal questions. But they do affect the way in which the law is interpreted in judicial practice and may fill in gaps in the statutory law.

Alongside the court system stand the military tribunals, which are organized within military commands. These tribunals have jurisdiction over all military personnel and also over civilians accused of espionage. Cases can be appealed through the hierarchy of military tribunals up to the military division of the USSR Supreme Court. Although they have a specialized jurisdiction, the military tribunals are part of the regular Soviet judiciary: They must follow the same rules of procedure and apply the same rules of evidence as the civilian courts.

According to the constitution (art. 155), judges are independent and subject only to the law. Although they are not free to ignore the party's general policies, local party agencies are not to interfere in the work of the judiciary. One rather widely publicized case can serve to illustrate this point. In Tula, Judge N. Ia. Tarakanova was formally reprimanded by the local party organization because, it was charged, she had "ignored" the local officials of the party and had been "nonobjective" in certain of her decisions. Apparently a local party official had tried to influence her, and she had insisted on being independent. After Tarakanova had been reprimanded, the central party leadership stepped into the affair and denounced the local party authorities. The Central Committee issued a decree that warned against such illegal interference in the work of the judiciary and reminded the party that judges were subject to control by the procuracy and the higher courts in accordance with the law [*Kommunist* 1(1963): 57]. The fact that the case was made public shows that the regime wished to teach an important lesson to local party organizations throughout the country.

THE PROCURACY

Many functions that are judicial in the United States are performed in the USSR by the procuracy (*prokuratura*), which has no real counterpart in the United States. It is responsible for criminal prosecutions, and for this reason, prokuratura is sometimes translated to mean prosecutor's office. Criminal prosecutions, however, are only one of the procuracy's functions.

Lenin decided that the procuracy should not follow the principle of dual subordination like other agencies of the central government. He wanted the law to be uniform throughout the country and to prevent localism in the interpretation and enforcement of law. The procuracy was to ensure uniformity of the law throughout the country. Thus it became one of the most highly centralized agencies in the country. Its head, the procurator general of the USSR, is elected by the Supreme Soviet for a seven-year term and in turn appoints the subordinate procurators in the republics and the regions. Thus the subordinate procurators are not in any way accountable to the republic or regional government.

The legal functions of the procuracy can be considered under three headings: (1) criminal prosecutions, (2) judicial supervision, and (3) general supervision. In criminal prosecutions, the procuracy is responsible for investigations, carrying out the prosecution, and reviewing the decisions of the courts.

Judicial supervision means that all court decisions in both criminal and civil cases are subject to review by the procuracy. A local procurator who feels that a court has reached a wrong decision has a right to file a protest with a higher court. The procurator can act either because he believes that a decision was illegal or because the verdict was based on insufficient evidence. If the court agrees with the procuracy, it will reverse the decision of the original court. According to G. B. Smith (1978: 19), the procuracy is successful in about 80 percent of these protests. Why should a procurator protest a criminal verdict when the procuracy was responsible for the prosecution in the first place? The answer is that prosecutions and judicial supervision are handled in different agencies within the procuracy. It is, in fact, not at all uncommon for the procuracy to file a protest against a criminal conviction and for the conviction then to be invalidated by a higher court.

General supervision refers to the procuracy's authority to watch over all administrative agencies and to ensure strict observance of the law by all Soviet officials. In performing the function of general supervision, the procurator is really acting as the central government's agent in watching over the lower levels of the administration (Smith 1978: 29). To carry out this function, the procuracy is supposed to have access to all the files of government agencies. A procurator who considers an administrative act illegal has the right to file a protest. The agency concerned has ten days to respond—either by withdrawing the act in question or by providing legal justification.

General supervision includes the responsibility of seeing that strict legality is observed in all places of confinement—jails, prisons, and labor camps. A representative of the procuracy is to visit all such institutions to make certain that no one is illegally held in custody. Any prisoner has a right to submit a complaint, and the prison or camp administration is legally obliged to send such a complaint to the procuracy for review.

In general, procurators do not have the authority to issue direct orders to an administrative agency—even when they believe that it is acting illegally. There are, however, some important exceptions to this general rule. Procurators have the authority to give binding instructions to the investigators in a criminal case. This authority, at least in theory, includes directing the KGB's investigators. A procurator who files a protest against a judgment by the court may also order a stay of execution until a higher court has disposed of the case. And finally, the procuracy may order the release of any person held under arrest in prison or in a camp, if the person is being held illegally.

An agency with the powers of the procuracy should have a key role in the development of rule of law. But N. R. Mironov (1962: 233), once the head of the party's Administrative Organs Department, admitted that under Stalin most procurators were afraid of the NKVD organs. Many of the operations of the political police were simply outside the law rather than technically illegal. Where the police were clearly acting illegally, some judicial agencies did try to protest. In 1939, the USSR Supreme Court sent a letter to Stalin in which it reported that many cases of counterrevolutionary crimes had been rushed through the courts in violation of proper judicial procedure. The Supreme Court recommended that all cases in question be reviewed. The court's letter was never answered (*Izvestiia*, April 19, 1964).

THE MVD

In theory the KGB is responsible for state security, including the investigation of political crimes. The MVD, or Ministry of Internal Affairs, is responsible for the regular police, and its scope includes investigations of nonpolitical crimes. The MVD also carries out other internal-affairs functions. The all-union MVD has departments that carry out police functions: the criminal police (*ugolovny rozysk*), investigation of economic crimes (OBKhSS), the state traffic police (GAI), and the regular city police patrols. The MVD also is responsible for fire protection. Penal institutions are managed by the MVD's Main Directorate of Camps (Glavnoe upravlenie lagerei), the infamous GULAG. In addition, the MVD controls a paramilitary organization in its internal troops, which can be called on to deal with serious public disorders. The convoy troops are used to guard prisoners.

Like the KGB, the all-union MVD is directly responsible for the Russian republic, and there is no RSFSR MVD. On the other hand, the principle of dual subordination operates in the local departments of internal affairs, which are thus accountable to both local government and the union republic MVD. The director of a local department for internal affairs also has the title of chief of police (*nachalnik militsii*).

Among other responsibilities, the MVD is supposed to control firearms, dangerous drugs, and the manufacture of rubber stamps. Internal passports are required for all Soviet citizens, beginning at age sixteen, if they live in cities or state farms. Before the 1974 statute was adopted, persons living on collective farms were not given passports and thus were effectively denied the right to leave without special permission. Under the new rules, persons living on collective farms may be given passports if they leave the area for an extended period of time. If they leave for less than six weeks, they receive temporary travel documents. All citizens are required to have their places of residence registered with the local MVD agency. This regulation gives the MVD a tool for controlling the movement of the citizenry and for keeping people out of cities (such as Moscow and Leningrad) that might otherwise become overpopulated.

CPSU AND LAW ENFORCEMENT

The strengthening of socialist legality was a significant improvement in Soviet life. The atmosphere of terror that Stalin had created gradually subsided, and Soviet citizens developed some sense that, if they obeyed the law, the law would leave them alone. However, the main beneficiary of the new legality was the party apparatus. The apparatus had suffered most from the purges and had most to gain from reducing the power of the political police.

The Central Committee's Department of Administrative Organs supervises the MVD and KGB, as well as the courts and the procuracy. Certain particularly sensitive questions, such as the rehabilitation of former political criminals imprisoned under Stalin, were handled within this department. But the main function of the Department of Administrative Organs is nomenklatura within the police apparatus. Another important responsibility of the department is acquiring information to ensure that the will of the central party leadership is not thwarted by the police or the judiciary and also to prevent petty arbitrariness on the part of the local officials.

In the following incident, made public by the head of the Department of Administrative Organs, a local secretary attempted to influence an investigation.

A scandalous incident took place in Tadzhikistan. Comrade Dzhuraev, an investigator in the Kuibyshev district, displayed firmness and stood up against open pressure from the first secretary of the Party raikom, Suleimanov, who demanded that he discontinue the investigation of the rape of two girls by a group of raion officials among whom was a relative of a raikom secretary

Soon after the conviction of the rapists, the investigator, Comrade Dzhuraev, was expelled from the Party on the basis of slanderous charges. It was necessary for the CC of the Communist Party of Tadzhikistan to intervene before the raikom reversed its decision.

Here is what Comrade Dzhuraev wrote in his statement:

After the reversal of his decision Comrade Suleimanov called me to his office and we had a personal conversation, where he said that he had wanted to expel me from the Party because I had not listened to him in the rape case.

Also he told me that I was still a young man and ought not to ignore the raikom first secretary. If I were always to listen to the secretary, then I would become a big and a smart man. The law is the law. But the raikom secretary is the raikom secretary.

The fate of such a raikom secretary reached its logical conclusion. Now it is he who has been expelled from the Party and turned over to the courts. (Mironov 1962: 236–237)

SOVIET CRIMINAL LAW

Soviet criminal law can be divided into three broad categories. First, there are ordinary crimes that would be recognized as such in any society: murder, robbery, assault. Second, a class of economic crimes is created by the nature of the socialist system. Producing substandard goods, falsifying information about plan fulfillment, engaging in private enterprise, and speculation are among the activities punished as economic crimes. Finally, a category of political crimes, which Soviet law calls "crimes against the state," includes espionage, sabotage, and smuggling. However, some political crimes are broadly defined to cover almost any act of dissent against the regime. A Soviet citizen who leaves the country illegally or refuses to return from a foreign country can be charged with treason.

The criminal law is harsh in most of its punishments. The death penalty is applicable to a variety of different crimes, including certain economic ones. The procedure in a criminal trial is simpler than in Western states and seems to favor the prosecution. On the other hand, everyone put on trial is not convicted; Soviet law does provide some procedural safeguards for the individual accused of crime. According to a former Soviet defense attorney (Kaminskaya 1982: 62): "The judicial system in the Soviet Union does work, and not only convictions but verdicts of acquittal have been given. . . ." Even a person accused of a political crime is entitled to a trial in a regular court and is not supposed to be found guilty except on the basis of objective evidence.

Originally, Soviet criminal law contained some provisions that would not have been acceptable to traditional Western jurisprudence. Article 16 (of the RSFSR Criminal Code of 1926) provided that if a "socially dangerous act" was not specifically defined as a crime, a court could nonetheless punish an individual "by analogy" with some other article of the code that in the judge's opinion might apply. This provision undermined any notion of rule of law in dealing with misconduct.

A number of special enactments in the 1930s provided criminal sanctions for political acts or other deviant behavior that alarmed the regime. A law of 1932 provided for the death penalty for anyone guilty of stealing state-owned property. Another law of 1934 allowed punishment of persons not guilty of a crime: This law (which became art. 58-1/a of the code) provided that if a person in military service fled abroad, then members of his family, *even if they were not implicated in the crime,* could be punished with a term of internal exile. (Internal exile, or *ssylka*, is a common form of punishment in Soviet law, as it was under the Tsar. A person sentenced to exile is required to remain in a particular locality, often in Siberia, although not actually incarcerated.) These decrees, incorporated as article 58 of the code, defined the punishment for various counterrevolutionary crimes; these crimes included "counterrevolutionary propaganda and agitation" (art. 58-10).

The reform of criminal law set aside most of these special enactments and has been called a "turning point" in Soviet history (Ioffe and Maggs 1983: 287). In 1958, new legislation was passed that set forth the fundamental principles of criminal law and criminal procedure. On the basis of this legislation, each union republic adopted its own codes early in the 1960s. The codes were standard throughout the USSR although there were some regional differences. In the following discussion, reference is made to the criminal code of the RSFSR, which went into effect in 1961. The new code gave the USSR a body of criminal law that in broad outline followed the principles of Western law. The analogy rule, for example, was implicitly rejected: Article 3 defined a crime as a "socially dangerous act *provided by law*" (emphasis added) and not just any act thought to be dangerous. The same article provided that punishment could only be applied by a court. Article 6 stated that a law defining a crime or increasing the punishment for a crime could not be retroactive.

Even under the new law, criminal sanctions can be extremely harsh for crimes that are matters of special concern to the regime. Soviet criminal law retains the death penalty for a variety of different crimes, including failure to respond to an order for mobilization in wartime (art. 81), counterfeiting (art. 87), large-scale theft of state property (art. 93-1), aggravated homicide (art. 102), aggravated rape (art. 117), and taking a bribe (art. 173). The death penalty is also applicable to certain crimes against the state or to crimes committed by those in military service.

On the other hand, the law shows certain surprising gaps. The code does not define prostitution as a crime, although drawing a minor into prostitution is illegal (art. 210). The police sometimes round up prostitutes in the larger cities and send them away, perhaps on charges of parasitism (Ioffe and Maggs 1983: 283). Homosexual acts between two men are severely punished, although the law is silent regarding sexual acts between women. The law is also silent on the censorship system, so evading the censorship is not a crime.

The criminal law is also disturbingly vague on certain points. It is a crime to violate the rules on separation of church and state (art. 142), but the code does not define exactly what actions are covered by this provision. It is also a crime to engage in a "prohibited" trade (art. 162), but the code does not specify what is prohibited.

Furthermore, the government has not always complied with the new criminal laws. Only a few months after the adoption of the RSFSR code, two black-market operators, Rokotov and Faibishenko, were given maximum fifteen-year sentences for illegally dealing in foreign currency. A few weeks later, the law was changed to permit the death penalty for illegal dealings in foreign currency (Edict of July 1, 1961). The republic supreme court then sentenced the two to death (*Pravda,* July 21, 1961), an act that clearly violated article 6.

In 1980 the most famous Soviet dissident, academician Andrei Sakharov, was removed from Moscow and exiled to Gorkii, a city in an area closed to foreigners. Sakharov was never put on trial. His forced exile to Gorkii appears to be a violation of article 3. Furthermore, the maximum term of exile allowed under the law (art. 26) is five years; Sakharov completed five years of exile in January 1985. Nonetheless, as was suggested at the beginning of this discussion, the law does seem to work properly in the case of ordinary crimes. The accused has a right to have a defense lawyer at the trial (though not during the investigation before the trial). When the court errs in reaching a guilty verdict, the procuracy may enter a protest.

A case resolved by the supreme court of the RSFSR can illustrate this procedure. One S. (the name of the defendant is not reported) had been convicted of rape under the following circumstances. S. had seduced a girl, identified as K., after proposing to her. After she became pregnant, he refused to marry her. Upon the complaint of K., S. was tried and convicted of "rape by fraud." However, the criminal division of the supreme court reversed the decision, and it acted on grounds that would probably convince a U.S. court. The supreme court held that what S. did, however reprehensible, was not a crime; that is, it was not specifically prohibited by the criminal code. This opinion is of some interest because the court gave a strict construction to the statute, and it held that S.'s acts did not amount to rape. The conviction was overturned (Case of S. 1960).

FIGHT WITH CORRUPTION

The harsh penalties for economic crimes have not prevented the theft of state property or other forms of corruption. Of course statistics on this point are not published, but there is no reason to believe that less corruption occurs in the USSR than in Western societies; there may be more.

Konstantin Simis (1982) drew a distinction between everyday corruption and official corruption. Everyday corruption involves petty bribery to obtain goods and services and is mostly a result of the chronic shortage of consumer goods. According to Simis's account (1982: 217), most Soviet stores lead a double life. Alongside the regular business there is an illegal operation from which the consumer can buy (at a high price) goods that the store's management has set aside. Simis also cited cases where bribes were paid to get medical attention, to pass a university examination, or to get a cemetery plot. This everyday corruption is so widespread that a second economy has developed around the illegal selling of goods and services (on the second economy, see Bornstein 1981: 61–93). Robert Sharlet (1985: 86) reported that Soviet public opinion polls show a widespread tolerance of the second economy. Most Soviet citizens could not survive without it.

Official corruption involves high-level officials who engage in illegal trade or take bribes. Often large sums of money are involved. Another form of official corruption is false reporting, when, for example, a factory director reports overfulfillment of planning targets when in fact the goals were not met. In a study of official crime in the 1970s, Nick Lampert found that embezzlement and bribery were more severely punished than false reporting; in some cases of bribery or embezzlement, the guilty officials received the death penalty.

Lampert also found that officials with political connections (especially with local party officials) were relatively safe from prosecution. "There is a strong tendency for party organizations to protect the managers of organizations within their domain, a tendency which is likely to be broken only if there is very definite pressure from above to act" (1984: 379). Under Brezhnev, there was little such pressure. The Brezhnev regime, with its emphasis on stability in cadres and security for officials, showed a marked tolerance for corruption. Under Brezhnev, the only publicized case of official corruption came in 1972. The first secretary of the Georgian republic, V. P. Mzhavanadze, was retired, and there were rumors of widespread corruption there. No charges against Mzhavanadze were made public, but soon after his dismissal, the republic press reported investigation into corruption on the part of lower ranking officials (*Zaria vostoka*, June 26, July 31, 1972).

Andropov, during his short tenure as general secretary, was publicly critical of corrupt officials and launched a campaign against violations. Persistent rumors circulated about corruption in the Uzbek republic, possibly involving the first secretary, Sh. Rashidov. In 1984 General Secretary Chernenko, admitted that investigations of corruption were needed in both the Uzbek republic and Krasnodar, as well as in the Rostov oblast [*Kommunist* 18(1984): 17]. Chernenko pointedly noted that cases of corruption in these regions had not been uncovered by the regional party organizations—which suggests that they had been covered up. The anticorruption theme was continued after Chernenko's death (*Izvestiia*, Mar. 22, 1985; *Selskaia zhizn*, March 24, 1985).

Rumors of corruption circulated within the MVD and especially within the OBKhSS. In December 1982 Minister Nikolai Shchelokov was replaced by KGB Chairman Vitalii Fedorchuk, who began a thorough purge of the police apparatus. Both Shchelokov and Medunov (former first secretary in Krasnodar) were expelled from the Central Committee (*Pravda*, June 16, 1983), events that seemed to confirm the rumors. Press reports appeared throughout 1983 on police corruption (*Sovetskaia Rossiia*, Mar. 22; *Pravda*, Aug. 10, Nov. 23), including an admission that local party officials had engaged in a cover-up in Krasnodar krai. A new political administration was created in the MVD, headed by party officials, to improve party control over the police.

As Lampert noted, the spread of corruption is a threat to socialist legality. If people can use their offices for illegal activities, then general respect for the law is diminished. On the other hand, the second economy is so widespread in Soviet society that repressive measures are not likely to stop its operations.

INDIVIDUAL RIGHTS

A superficial reading of the constitution (arts. 34–36, 39–69) suggests that Soviet citizens have a wide range of rights protected by the government. The rights listed in the constitution can be divided into three categories: (1) economic rights specific to the Soviet socialist system, (2) political rights, which in form resemble the rights guaranteed in Western constitutions, and (3) procedural rights. The economic rights in the constitution include the right to a job, rest, health care, support in old age or in the event of disability, housing, education, and access to culture. The political rights include the right to participate in public affairs, the right to criticize agencies of the government, freedom of speech and press, the right to join public organizations, and freedom of conscience (defined as the freedom to profess a religion or to be an atheist). The constitution also forbids discrimination on the basis of sex, nationality, social origin, or religious belief. In addition, it guarantees "inviolability of the person": The police cannot arbitrarily arrest an individual, search a home, or intercept correspondence. The police can make an arrest or conduct a search with a court order or with the sanction of the procuracy.

The rights guaranteed by the constitution are not meaningless. In particular, the economic rights are guaranteed by Soviet legislation that protects the basic welfare of the population. However, a careful reading of the constitution shows that the political rights are all subject to restrictions. The constitution specifically provides (art. 39) that citizens may not exercise their rights in a way that is detrimental to society as a whole or to the state or to the rights of other citizens.

Freedom of Expression

Although the constitution provides for freedom of expression, in practice this freedom is limited in two important ways. First, legal limitations are put on free expression, limitations that do not violate the constitution, as understood in the USSR. Second, effective administrative controls are set over freedom of expression. Article 50 of the constitution, on freedom of expression, provides that these rights are not granted for their own sake but for a higher state interest: "In accordance with the people's interests and for the purpose of strengthening and developing the socialist system, USSR citizens are guaranteed freedom of speech, of the press, of assembly, of mass meetings and of street processions and demonstrations." Thus a law that limits freedom of expression in the interests of the state is not a violation of the constitution. Further, speech or writing that does not strengthen the socialist system is not protected by article 50. The criminal code makes it illegal to engage in anti-Soviet propaganda.

> *Article 70. Anti-Soviet Agitation and Propaganda.* Agitation or propaganda carried on for the purpose of subverting or weakening Soviet authority or of committing particular, especially dangerous crimes against the state, or circulating for the same purpose slanderous fabrications which defame the Soviet state and social system, or circulating or preparing or keeping, for the same purpose, work of such content in written, printed, or other form, shall be punished by deprivation of freedom for a term of six months to seven years, with or without additional exile for a term of two to five years, or by exile for a term of two to five years.
>
> The same actions, committed with the use of monetary resources or other items of value received from foreign organizations or from persons acting in the interests of these organizations, or committed by a person previously convicted of especially dangerous crimes against the state or committed in wartime shall be punished by deprivation of freedom for a term of three to ten years, with or without additional exile for a term of two to five years.

This article has been extensively used against Soviet dissidents, and their underground writing (samizdat) is not protected by the constitution.

The most important administrative control is the censorship system, which has existed since the late 1920s. The censorship is managed by the Main Directorate for the Protection of State Secrets in the press, more commonly known by its former name, Glavlit. With a few exceptions, nothing can be published in the USSR without Glavlit's prior approval.

The censorship process begins when a publishing house or journal submits material for approval. Glavlit maintains a long but secret list of items that cannot be mentioned in publications (Dewhirst and Farrell 1973: 56). The censors sometimes function as editors: Instead of merely suppressing information, they may suggest extensive changes in a text (Golovskoi 1984). If they approve the material for printing, then proof copies are run off and returned to the censors for final approval. The censors check the printed version and approve it for publication. The book or journal can then be printed and put on sale.

One result of Glavlit's operations is self-censorship that influences every writer and editor. Material likely to be forbidden by Glavlit is not submitted and may not even be written. Yet even with Glavlit's rigorous system of control, unacceptable material sometimes is published. The party has, on occasion, publicly reprimanded journals for what they published. The censor who approved the material probably received a private reprimand. In extreme cases a publication may be removed from circulation.

Glavlit also has supervision of material in Soviet libraries (Chalidze 1975: 80–82). Books not wholly approved by Glavlit are kept in a special depository (*spetskran*). Books in this category include the writings of Trotskii and other discredited Communist leaders and a great many foreign publications. Scholars with a legitimate need for such forbidden material may obtain access, but special permission is needed.

Freedom of Conscience

The right to religious freedom is also carefully circumscribed by article 52 of the constitution:

> USSR citizens are guaranteed freedom of conscience, that is, the right to profess any religion or to profess none, to perform religious worship or to conduct atheistic propaganda. The incitement of hostility and hatred in connection with religious beliefs is prohibited.
>
> In the USSR the church is separate from the state and the school is separate from the church.

This article should be read carefully. Although all citizens have the right to engage in atheistic propaganda, the rights of religious believers are limited to conducting worship services. Religious propaganda is not protected by the constitution: The state can and does forbid religious instruction of children or the distribution of religious literature, without violating article 52.

As in the case of freedom of expression, religious freedom is controlled both by law and by administrative means. A special agency, the USSR Council for Religious Affairs, is responsible for monitoring the activity of all religious organizations. Every church must be registered with the committee or its local agents, and a church group that tries to function without this registration is in violation of the law. The committee has registered Orthodox churches, Roman Catholic churches, and a variety of Protestant denominations, as well as non-Christian faiths. But many believers of these officially approved churches have been refused registration, usually on the grounds that no building was available for their use or that another church was not needed in that locality. Some religious faiths have been refused registration. These include the Uniate church (the Roman Catholic Church of the Byzantine rite) and various Pentecostal sects. Some religious sects have refused to register as a matter of principle and operate underground. Individual clergymen of any faith must also be licensed by the Council for Religious Affairs. The threat to withdraw the license, which can be done at any time, gives the Council for Religious Affairs great power over every clergyman.

In the late 1970s a dissident organization, the Christian Committee for Believers' Rights, managed to publicize many instances of violations of religious freedom, including in particular the refusal of the committee to register groups of believers. Many cases were documented where religious believers wished to open a church, sometimes in rural areas with no functioning church, and the Council refused. In 1979 the leader of the Christian Committee, the Orthodox priest Gleb Iakunin, was arrested and tried for anti-Soviet propaganda under article 70. After Iakunin's imprisonment, the Christian Committee virtually ceased to function.

REFERENCES

Barron, John. 1983. *KGB Today: The Hidden Hand*. New York: Reader's Digest Press.

Bornstein, Morris, ed. 1981. *The Soviet Economy: Continuity and Change*. Boulder, Colo.: Westview Press.

Case of S. 1960. *Sbornik postanovlenii Prezidiuma i opredelenii Sudebnoi kollegii po ugolovnym delam Verkhovnogo suda RSFSR 1957–1959 gg*. Moscow: Iurizdat, pp. 16–17.

Chalidze, Valery. 1975. *To Defend These Rights: Human Rights and the Soviet Union*, translated by Guy Daniels. New York: Random House.

Decree of September 5, 1918. *Dekrety sovetskoi vlasti,* vol. 3. Moscow, 1964, pp. 291–292.

Decree of November 6, 1922. *Iz Istorii Vserossiiskoi chrezvychainnoi komissii 1917–1921, sbornik dokumentov.* Moscow, 1958, pp. 471–474.

Dewhirst, Martin, and Robert Farrell, eds. 1973. *The Soviet Censorship.* Metuchen, N.J.: Scarecrow Press.

Golovskoi, Valerii. 1984. Sushchestvuet li tsenzura v Sovetskom Soiuze? *Kontinent* 42: 147–174.

Ioffe, O. S., and Peter B. Maggs. 1983. *Soviet Law in Theory and Practice.* New York: Oceana Publications.

Juviler, Peter. 1976. *Revolutionary Law and Order: Politics and Social Change in the USSR.* New York: Free Press.

Kaminskaya, Dina. 1982. *Final Judgment: My Life as a Soviet Defense Attorney.* New York: Simon and Schuster.

Kozlov, Iu. M. 1968. *Administrativnoe pravo.* Moscow: Iurizdat.

Lampert, Nick. 1984. Law and Order in the USSR: The Case of Economic and Official Crime. *Soviet Studies* 34: 366–385.

Leggett, George. 1981. *The Cheka: Lenin's Political Police.* Oxford: Clarendon Press.

Lenin, V. I. 1918a. *State and Revolution.* In *Selected Works,* vol. 2, pt. 1. Moscow: Foreign Languages Publishing House, 1952, pp. 199–325.

———. 1918b. Speech at a meeting of Cheka officers. In *Polnoe sobranie sochinenii,* vol. 37. Moscow: Politizdat, 1958–1965, pp. 173–174.

———. 1922. "Dual" Subordination and Observation of the Law. In *Selected Works,* vol. 2, pt. 2, pp. 682–687.

Lunev, A. E., A. S. Bakhov, V. M. Bezdenezhnykn et al. 1979. *Sovetskoe administrativnoe pravo—upravlenie v oblasti administrativno-politicheskoi deiatelnosti.* Moscow: Iuridicheskaia literatura.

Mironov, N. R. 1962. Borba s antiobshchestvennymi iavleniiami—vazhneishaia zadacha. In *XXII sezd KPSS i voprosy ideologicheskoi raboty.* Moscow: Politizdat, p. 233.

On Increasing Criminal Liability for Violating the Regulations on Foreign Currency. Edict of July 1, 1961. *Vedomosti verkhovnogo soveta SSSR,* no. 27, item 291.

Sawatsky, Walter, 1976a. The New Soviet Law on Religion. *Religion in Communist Lands* 4, no. 2: 4–10.

———. 1976b. Secret Soviet Lawbook on Religion. *Religion in Communist Lands* 4, no. 4: 24–34.

Shafarevich, I. P. 1973. *Zakonodatelstvo o religii v SSSR.* Paris: YMCA Press.

Sharlet, Robert. 1985. Soviet Legal Policy Under Andropov: Law and Discipline. In *Soviet Politics: Russia After Brezhnev,* edited by Joseph L. Nogee. New York: Praeger, pp. 85–106.

Simis, Konstantin. 1982. *USSR: The Corrupt Society.* New York: Simon and Schuster.

Smith, Gordon B. 1978. *The Soviet Procuracy and the Supervision of Administration.* Alphen, Netherlands: Sijthoff and Noordhoff.

Soviet Criminal Law and Procedure: The RSFSR Codes. 1966. Introduction and analysis by Harold J. Berman. Cambridge: Harvard University Press.

Stalin, J. V. 1926. On the Problems of Leninism. In *Problems of Leninism.* 11th ed. Moscow: Foreign Languages Publishing House, pp. 149–212.

Statute on the Passport System in the USSR. 1974. *Sobranie postanovlenii pravitelstva SSSR,* no. 19, item 109.

Vlasov, V. A., and A. I. Studenikin. 1959. *Sovetskoe administrativenoe pravo.* Moscow: Iurizdat.

Zakonodatelstvo o religioznykh kultakh: sbornik materialov i dokumentov. 1971. [Printed for official use only.] 2d ed. Moscow: Iurizdat; reprint edition, New York: Chalidze Publications, 1981.

10
The Industrial and Military Bureaucracies

According to Lenin (1918: 228) the two most oppressive institutions in the old, bourgeois state were the standing army and the bureaucracy. Lenin promised that in the higher stage of socialism, both of these would disappear. They have, however, not only survived but grown stronger—the bureaucracy, to manage the Soviet economy, and the army, to protect the Soviet state.

For the student of the Soviet political system, the basic issue about the army and the bureaucracy is their influence in the decisionmaking process. They were created to serve the regime. In the ideal case for the political leadership, the Politburo makes defense and economic policies, and the high command and the industrial managers carry them out. Inevitably, however, the industrial and military bureaucracies have developed interests and values of their own. Most Western observers now recognize that, although the party dominates the system, it is by no means the only organization of political importance. A large number of different organizations and institutions seek to represent particular interests and to influence policy. A realistic model of the system must allow for the influence of these special interests. On the other hand, the USSR is not a truly pluralistic system: Interest groups, in the usual U.S. sense of this term, are not found in Moscow.

INTEREST GROUPS AND BUREAUCRACY

Political scientists distinguish between associational interest groups and institutional interest groups. An associational interest group is based on a membership organization such as a labor union or a professional association. In a competitive political system, an associational interest group may wield great influence because of the potential voting power of the membership. A veterans' organization that claims to speak for several million voters will certainly be listened to by the elected representatives of the people. Institutional interest groups are not membership organizations but are typically bureaucratic organizations that are part of the governmental apparatus but have special interests of their own. The military professionals are one example of an institutional interest group.

The USSR does have membership associations, such as the labor unions or the organizations of creative artists. All such organizations are hierarchically structured in the model of the Communist Party of the Soviet Union (CPSU). The real power in the organization is concentrated in a bureaucratic apparatus, and the key positions are subject to the nomenklatura of the party. Thus even membership organizations can be classified as institutional interest groups in the USSR.

Stalin (1953: 164) once described the mass organizations as "transmission belts" or "gears" through which the party ruled Soviet society. He conceived of the party as the guiding force in the system, operating through such driving gears as the labor union organization and the Komsomol. Any gear, however, can run in two directions. An organization can transmit orders, and it can try to educate the people and mobilize support for the party's program. However, the same organizational mechanism can also transmit the ideas, the aspirations, and even the demands of the members to the political leadership.

A Soviet work on the labor unions says that they are supposed to exercise two functions: (1) educating the workers in the spirit of communism, and (2) protecting workers' legal rights (Singireva and Iavich 1967: 107). From the viewpoint of the party leadership, the first function is undoubtedly more important. But the organization's legitimacy in the eyes of the mass membership and its ability to influence the workers requires that the second function not be entirely meaningless.

The Soviet worker does receive some benefits from membership in a union. Of course a Soviet union would not conceivably call a strike for higher wages. But the union organization does have responsibilities in the administration of social insurance, housing, and the organization of leisure. The worker who needs help in applying for disability payments, maternity leave, or housing can get it from the local union. Thus the labor union organization is not just a propaganda instrument, as the term transmission belt would imply. It has a number of important functions to perform, and to carry them out it needs an administrative organization. No doubt the union apparatus is consulted on matters where it has expertise.

The unions have a national congress every four years, consisting of delegates who represent constituent unions and republic union organizations. Like the party congress, the union congress is a ceremonial body with no real power. The congress elects a central council of labor unions, which in turn elects a presidium and a secretariat that actually manage the affairs of the union. In the past the chairman of the central council has been an experienced party official and sometimes a member of the Politburo. In recent years, however, this office seems to have been downgraded.

The most influential special interests are bureaucratic organizations like the unions. Most Soviet bureaucracies enjoy some degree of independence from the party and have identifiable interests of their own on policy issues. A major bureaucratic organization has the following common characteristics.

It is a group of people with some professional identity based on a common background and usually some common specialized training.

It is represented within the political system by a well-established organization, such as the Academy of Sciences or the Union of Soviet Writers. The institution is subject to party supervision and control; yet it has a certain organizational life of its own.

It has its own organ and some form of access to public opinion, which can be used to articulate the bureaucracy's views and interests.

The group has some access to the central political leadership, generally formalized through representation in the Central Committee of the party. In addition, a bureaucratic organization will have informal contact through the central party apparatus.

The central issue in interest-group politics in the USSR is the allocation of resources. Most Western scholars who have studied the subject agree that the objective of the typical bureaucratic organization is to maximize the resources that it obtains from society. In examining the Downs model (see Chapter 1), we saw that bureaucrats usually have multiple goals, such as power, prestige, empire-building, and organizational security. As W. A. Niskanen, Jr. (1971), pointed out, the best way for a bureaucracy to achieve these goals is to maximize its share of society's resources. Of course much less systematic study of Soviet bureaucracy has been made than of bureaucratic behavior in the Western world, and we must be wary of sweeping generalizations. Nonetheless, this seems to be the goal of Soviet bureaucratic organizations, too. We can assume that the industrial managers, the generals, and the managers of the Soviet space program are all interested in getting a large share of the national budget.

The bureaucratic interest group cannot use Western methods of pressure-group politics. No lobbies compete for influence with the Supreme Soviet, and no associations try to mobilize their members in support of a particular piece of legislation. Nonetheless, the bureaucratic groups are not without influence in the political system.

An organization may have an opportunity to influence policy while it is being made through the process of bureaucratic consultation. Knowledge is a powerful political resource, and the bureaucratic professionals have knowledge, experience, and technical skills that the political leadership cannot ignore. The Soviet leadership certainly believes in the old shibboleth that "the experts should be on tap, and not on top." Yet even when this rule is followed, the experts can be a powerful group. The departments of the Central Committee are the principal point of contact between the bureaucratic groups and the party leadership. The primary function of the central apparatus is to protect the interests of the Politburo. Yet most of the departments are headed by people who qualify as professional experts. In some instances the department may represent the special interests of the bureaucracy, too. This is not to suggest that the department would take the side of its external constituency in the case of direct conflict with the Politburo. But in cases where two departments disagree, the Politburo must play the role of power broker among conflicting special interests.

BUREAUCRATIC ECONOMY

In the Soviet command economy, the important economic decisions are made by the political leadership. The Politburo decides what will be produced and how the goods and services that the economy produces are to be distributed. In this type of economy, little room exists for market forces to operate. As in any economic system, what the economy produces must be divided: Some resources will be used for military hardware and some for investment in future economic growth, and some will be allocated to the consumer. The command economy allows the political leadership to make these allocation decisions without being concerned about the market. In the command economy, consumer preferences play only a minor role in the allocation of resources.

The organization of the economy can be considered at three levels: the central planning authority, the ministries, and the individual enterprise. The enterprise can be a coal mine, a factory, a railroad line, or a construction firm. In the command economy the goal of the enterprise is not to make a profit but to achieve production targets that it gets from the government. Enterprises do in fact make profits, but these are not their main goal. In fact profits from the state-owned enterprises are the major source of government revenue. Some profits are left with the enterprise, in an enterprise fund, and can be spent on bonuses, other incentives for workers (profits may be used to build a workers' club, for example), or for investment to improve production.

Above the enterprise is the ministry, which controls the enterprises in a particular sector of the economy. For example, the coal mines are operated by the Ministry of the Coal Industry. The ministry receives its instructions from Gosplan (the state planning committee).

According to a former official of the agency (Kushnirsky 1982: 83) Gosplan operates under the close supervision of the Politburo, which is the ultimate decisionmaker. Guided by the Politburo's priorities, Gosplan draws up the national economic plans—both the five-year plans, which get most of the publicity, and annual plans. A plan, as produced by Gosplan, is a list of targets or control figures for the goods that the economy is to produce. This may appear simple enough, but in fact Gosplan has a staggering task. It is attempting to make all the thousands of decisions that are made in the West by the automatic mechanism of the market. Every economic choice creates new decisions. For example, if the regime wants to increase the production of automobiles, then Gosplan must adjust the target for steel production either by increasing steel output or by shifting steel from other sectors. If its seeks to increase steel output, then it must raise the targets for iron ore and coal, and so on.

The entire planning operation is supervised by the Central Committee apparatus. Each of the economic departments of the party apparatus supervises one sector of Gosplan and must approve Gosplan's major decisions. The apparatus departments themselves are subjected to conflicting demands, but they operate within the Politburo's priorities, just as Gosplan does (Kushnirsky 1982: 83–84).

Once the general plan is approved, the control figures are transmitted to the ministries. Each ministry draws up its own plan, developing specific production targets for each enterprise in its system. Through negotiation between the ministries and Gosplan, minor adjustments may be made in the targets. The ministry then transmits the control figures to the enterprises. Gosplan is not only responsible for drawing up the plan, but also for monitoring compliance. As a consequence Gosplan has grown into an enormous bureaucracy that has overall responsibility for the management of the economy.

Such is the simple outline of the Soviet system of industrial management and planning. As Alec Nove (1980: 95) pointed out, the result of this command economy is to increase the power of the government and minimize the influence of the consumer or citizen. The system was designed for an underdeveloped economy and a government determined to industrialize as rapidly as possible. It allowed the government to make the basic economic decisions, and the government gave highest

TABLE 10.1
Soviet Economic Growth
(annual rate of growth
for recent five-year plans)

Plan	Years	Growth Rate (%)
8	1966-1970	7.5
9	1971-1975	5.8
10	1976-1980	3.8
11*	1981-1985	2.5

Source: T. I. Zaslavskaia, O neobkhodimosti
bolee uglublennogo izucheniia v SSSR sotsi-
alnogo mekhanizma razvitiia ekonomiki, AS
no. 5042, 1983.

*For eleventh five-year plan, table reports
only first year.

priority to the development of heavy industry. The result was an economy that was very strong in those sectors that had priority: the steel industry, engineering industries, and armaments. Since the government could to a considerable extent ignore consumer preferences, the economy also was barely able to meet the basic needs of the population and confronted continuing shortages of food, housing, and other consumer goods.

As the Soviet economy has become more developed, the planning system developed under Stalin has become obsolete. The Soviet consumer has become choosier, and goods that are poorly made or unattractive sometimes pile up in the stores. Some factories find, in a common Soviet expression, that they are producing "for the warehouse" and not for the consumer. Furthermore, setting output levels as high as possible is no longer an efficient way to stimulate economic growth. In the early five-year plans, the whole system seemed geared to production for production's sake. The system poured its resources, both labor resources and raw materials, into the factories, and the result was rapid economic growth. In the modern Soviet economy, growth depends on other factors— the development of new technology, better management of resources, and an increase in the productivity of both workers and machines.

One indicator of the economic problem in the USSR is the steady decline in the rate of economic growth, as shown in Table 10.1. The problem, however, is more than just a slowdown in the growth rate. The system does not encourage technological innovation, and in high-technology industries the USSR lags far behind the Western industrial countries.

The system no doubt is economically inefficient. Enterprises can fulfill their production targets only by economically irrational behavior. The system requires an enormous and costly bureaucracy to develop the plan, transmit the instructions, and monitor compliance. The plant manager's goal is to fulfill the production quota at almost any cost. No strong incentive exists to hold down costs, introduce new technology, or raise productivity (Kushnirsky 1982: 45). Because the managers face continual shortages of materials, they accumulate stocks of supplies and sometimes bribe suppliers. The party leadership constantly insists that untapped reserves exist at the enterprise level that could be used to raise production. These reserves are present because the managers are hoarders. However, the system usually overlooks illegal operations by the enterprise manager if the production goals are satisfied.

One example of irrational behavior is created by the system of success indicators (Nove 1977: 93). The production quotas, like the control figures in the national economic plan, are expressed in physical units rather than ruble values. How the enterprise behaves may depend on how the production quotas are measured. For example, if a factory producing nails was given a quota in terms of units of output (x thousands of nails), then the factory manager would produce only small nails so that the production could overfulfill the plan. On the other hand, if the target was set in terms of the weight of output (x tons of nails), the factory manager would turn out large nails to drive up the tonnage even though a shortage of small nails would be created. Examples of such behavior abound.

To prevent this behavior, the factory is given other targets to meet in addition to gross output. The product mix is often specified in detail, and planning restrictions are placed on the wage bill and other factors. Thus enterprise directors are judged not by one success indicator but by many. They are under great pressure to produce and at the same time subjected to a large number of administrative controls from the center.

The success indicators are the standards by which enterprise performance is judged. But do they really indicate success? From the viewpoint of the enterprise director, the answer is yes. However, from the viewpoint of Gosplan, the success indicators are not useful tools of analysis. In a sense, Gosplan functions like a central investment bank, allocating resources among sectors of the economy. Unlike an investment bank, however, Gosplan is not seeking to maximize the monetary return on its investment. Like the factory manager, Gosplan apparently aims at maximizing output. However, since the indicators measure output in physical units, Gosplan cannot compare the performance of different branches of industry. Investment bankers can compare the return on their capital from very different industries, since they use a single monetary unit. But how can the planners in Moscow compare the performance of the steel industry (measured in millions of tons) with the performance of the electric power industry (measured in millions of kilowatt hours)? Soviet economists have grappled with this problem and have sometimes suggested an integrated indicator that could be used to compare the results from all sectors of the economy. So far these efforts at economic reform have not solved the problem.

Economic Reform

Since the death of Stalin economic reform has been the subject of an ongoing discussion. The most common complaint of the reformers is that the regime relies too much on administrative measures, and too little on economic levers. Administrative measures is a codeword for orders from the top. By economic levers the reformers mean more use of incentives instead of orders and perhaps some reliance on market mechanisms. In general, the proposals advanced by Soviet economists take two forms. First, various proposals have been set forth to reorganize the system that manages the economy through some process of decentralization. The argument in favor of decentralization is that the enterprise managers are closer to the production process and should be given more authority. But authority to do what? They might be given more control over the enterprise fund, so that they can make decisions about investing in new technology and thus raising productivity. But raising productivity can also be accomplished by laying off unskilled or surplus workers. This issue is sensitive in Soviet society and is rarely discussed even by the professional economists. Second, various proposals have been made for reducing the system of political and bureaucratic controls. Some economists have proposed a third kind of reform: a limited legalization of the second economy that would stimulate the output of consumer goods and services.

Khrushchev undertook a sweeping reorganization in 1957 with the aim of decentralization. Most of the economic ministries were abolished, and regional agencies were created to supervise the enterprises. From the point of view of the enterprise, this radical reorganization simply substituted one boss (the regional agency) for another (the ministry). The 1957 reform did not lead to significant change in managerial behavior and was abandoned after Khrushchev left office. A reform introduced in 1965 was somewhat more imaginative. It brought back the ministries and so was a move toward recentralization. The idea behind the 1965 reform was that the individual enterprises were to be given more decisionmaking power, the number of success indicators was to be reduced, and the manager was to have more control over the use of resources. This reform, however, was never really carried through. The ministerial bureaucracies continued to maintain close supervision over the enterprises.

The first solution that Andropov chose was a crackdown on corruption and an increase in labor discipline (*Pravda*, Dec. 11, 1982). In Andropov's first months in office, a strident public campaign was conducted against shirkers, absenteeism, and drunkenness on the job. This campaign, however, did not last long enough to have any visible economic effect. The labor discipline campaign was probably a political mistake (Medvedev 1983: 132). The second economy provides much of the incentive for the Soviet worker, which is why Brezhnev tolerated it. The anticorruption campaign, if carried on seriously, would weaken these incentives. Thus the effect of the campaign would be the opposite of what was intended: It would reduce worker productivity (Beichman and Bernstam 1983: 202).

The Andropov administration also announced an economic experiment in which five industrial ministries were to be reorganized and their enterprises given greater authority. The experiment was continued under Chernenko. In this experiment, the manager has greater scope to make decisions, but the enterprise still operates according to a plan and its goal is still expressed in terms of production targets.

The Zaslavskaia Memorandum

A different approach to the problem of reform has been taken by T. I. Zaslavskaia, a member of the Academy of Sciences and one of the country's leading economists. She emphasized the human factor in the economy. The country's economic problems, she argued, result from a lack of incentive to work hard. The lack of incentive, in turn, can be blamed on the constant shortage of consumer goods and services. Thus she argued for a series of measures that would put more goods on the shelves (Zaslavskaia 1980).

Zaslavskaia put her recommendation into a confidential report prepared in 1983 for a conference in Moscow. This conference was an example of bureaucratic consultation, where the participants were free to express their ideas, but the reports were not intended for publication. Somehow a copy of her statement reached the West and was published (Zaslavskaia 1983).

Zaslavskaia's basic argument is that the development of the economic system has not kept pace with the evolution of Soviet society, and consequently the economy does not make effective use of the great human resources of the country. The command economy evolved in a period in which most workers had recently left the village and were unskilled and untrained. Contemporary Soviet workers are well educated, critical of the existing order, and more aware of their own interests, and in the right environment they could be much more productive. The time has come to move from centralized control to greater reliance on an automatic mechanism based on the market system and also to greater reliance on individual initiative. The usual administrative methods of control are generally counterproductive. The system must learn, she said, that "behavior can be controlled only indirectly, through the use of incentives that take account of the economic and social needs of the workers."

Although her ideas have been expressed before, Zaslavskaia's analysis is unusual in that she asks why previous efforts at decentralization failed and what strategy of reform would be successful in the future. Her answers are that any economic reform affects the interests of certain social groups that may out of self-interest sabotage the reform. A successful reform can only be undertaken through a planned strategy that appeals to the interests of different groups and blocks those groups likely to be hostile. The earlier attempts at reform ignored this fact and failed.

The basic impediment to reform, according to her analysis, is the inflated bureaucracy at the middle (ministerial) level of the system. Officials at this level feel most threatened because a genuine reform will reduce their responsibilities: "It also promises to reduce their rights and their economic influence, and furthermore it promises to reduce the size of their apparatus by liquidating the many agencies, directorates, trusts, departments, etc., which have sprung up like mushrooms in recent years. It is natural that this prospect is not a pleasant one to officials who occupy so many 'comfortable places' with vague responsibilities but a good salary" (1983: 19–20). A reform should appeal to the interests of managers at the enterprise level because they have most to gain. But here, too, Zaslavskaia warns that many managers have become satisfied with the existing system, which they have learned to live with, and are not interested in a shift to more economic methods.

Like other recent advocates of reform, Zaslavskaia calls for a partial legalization of the second economy. (Although she praises Andropov's demand for labor discipline, the concept runs counter to her basic argument.)

In the light of what has been said, we need to recognize that the social mechanism for the development of the economy which now exists in the USSR will not assure satisfactory results. The type of worker that is produced by this mechanism does not meet either the strategic goals of a developed socialist society, nor the technological needs of modern production. The common characteristics of many workers whose personality was formed in the recent period include a low level of discipline, indifference to work, a low quality of work, social inertia, low self-esteem, a consumer orientation, and a low level of morality. We have only to recall the so-called "pilferers" [*nesuny*], the spread of various "shady" dealings at the public expense, the development of production "on the left," false reporting, and padding work reports so that salary does not correspond to the work done. (1983: 29–30)

The political leadership has not responded to this criticism. Although Gorbachev has acknowledged that the country's main problem is to increase the rate of economic growth (*Pravda*, April 24, 1985), he has not offered any new solutions. He seemed to rely on the traditional method of exhortation to do better, to uncover hidden reserves in the economy, to work harder, and to raise productivity.

Managers and the Political System

Stalin showed great favor to the managers toward the end of his regime. Apparently he was grooming some of the younger managers for political positions, but this approach was interrupted by his death. Evidence indicates that the industrial managers developed a strong sense of their own interests in the struggle for succession (Azrael 1966: 122). The managers certainly were a factor in the political struggles of the Khrushchev period; yet they were unable to prevent the 1957 reorganization. In general, the Khrushchev years witnessed a slow erosion of managerial influence and prestige. Although the managers no doubt were glad to see Khrushchev go, no evidence shows that they played any role as a group in the political maneuvering that led to his departure.

No single institution has been set up except for the party itself where the interests of the managerial group can be aggregated. The marshals may be able to resolve their internal differences within the Ministry of Defense and to present a united front to the Politburo. The interests of the scientists are represented in the Academy of Sciences. But industry is represented by forty ministries in Moscow, which have different responsibilities and conflicting interests. The interests of the factory managers are not identical with those of the ministries, and the managers have no organized way of articulating their interests. The Soviets have no counterpart to the National Association of Manufacturers in the United States or the Federation of British Industries. In addition to the ministries, other agencies have a voice in industrial affairs. Within the central apparatus, ten different departments are responsible for various sectors of the economy. These structural differences among groups suggest that the Politburo devotes more time to industrial questions and priorities than to military affairs.

THE MILITARY AND THE POLITICAL SYSTEM

The Soviet state has always been committed to the goal of catching up with and overtaking the advanced industrial countries of the West. Since World War II this goal has become more specific: catching up with the United States and achieving parity with the other superpower. Despite the country's enormous efforts, the goal has proved impossible to achieve, and by most economic indicators the Soviet Union still lags far behind. This discrepancy is particularly true for the high-technology industries that hold the key to future economic advance. However, in one field the USSR has caught up with the United States. The Soviet claim to be a superpower does not rest on economic performance, or technological advancement, or cultural influence; it rests on military strength. This fact accounts for the unique place that the Soviet military occupies in the political order.

A certain mystique surrounds the Soviet military. This aura is partly the result of the victory of World War II, which for many Soviet citizens is the greatest achievement of the regime. The mystique sets the Soviet military establishment apart from Soviet society. The armed forces are thought to be a well-organized, disciplined institution, able to cope with the world of high technology. This image is summed up in the title of a novel by Arkadii Perventsev (1977) that glorifies the nuclear submarine force, *Island of Hope.*

Defense Establishment

Military affairs are almost entirely in the hands of the professionals. For much of the postwar period, the minister of defense has been a career officer. Outside interference in the internal affairs of the ministry is minimal. The Supreme Soviet has no committees for military affairs, and the Central Committee apparatus has no department for military or national security policy. The minister appears to have more authority than his counterparts in the civilian agencies of the government and in recent years has been entitled to a place on the Politburo. The chief of the general staff is the second-ranking official after the minister of defense and is the operating chief of all the armed forces. Despite this domination of the ministry by professional officers, the Soviet regime has maintained the principle of civilian control over the armed forces. The minister is appointed (and can be removed) by the Presidium of the Supreme Soviet. The supreme authority in military affairs is the Defense Council (*Sovet oborony*), which may be composed entirely of civilians. The council coordinates all military affairs (Lunev 1979: 36). Little is known about the council except that it is appointed by the Presidium of the Supreme Soviet (constitution, art. 121), and the general secretary is always the chairman. This position seems to make the general secretary the civilian commander-in-chief. The Defense Council may be a committee of the Politburo with special responsibility for national security, or it may include non-Politburo members (such as the chief of staff). The council does not appear to have a special staff to support its work, and this lack would tend to make it dependent on the General Staff for information and advice. In wartime, control over the military would rest with the Supreme High Command and its headquarters (*stavka*) (Lunev 1979: 21). The Defense Council may in fact be the peacetime equivalent of the Supreme High Command.

Military Spending

Over the past twenty years the ministry has benefited from a massive military buildup. As David Holloway (1984: 367) has suggested, the buildup can be explained by the failure of Khrushchev's policies. Khrushchev's program aimed at a significant shift in priorities, including a reduction in military spending. He attempted to justify the policy by a new military doctrine, which emphasized strategic weapons rather than the conventional ground forces and thus supported a cut in manpower. In 1960 he announced a program of large-scale demobilization that was to send more than a million people from the armed forces into the civilian economy.

The Khrushchev program collapsed as a result of the Cuban missile crisis of 1962, although other foreign policy failures contributed. In an effort to achieve quick strategic parity, the USSR put medium-range missiles with nuclear warheads in Cuba, where they could be aimed at the United States. President John F. Kennedy responded by blockading Cuba, demanding that the missiles be removed, and threatening war if the demands were not met. Khrushchev gave in to U.S. demands, and the missiles were withdrawn. The decisions to install the missiles and then to remove them were political choices for which Khrushchev had to take responsibility. Some evidence indicates, in fact, that Khrushchev's military advisers were opposed to the initial decision. Yet the missile crisis seems to have had a traumatic impact on both the civilian leadership and the military. The military buildup seems designed to ensure that the Soviet Union will not be humiliated in a similar way again.

Kenneth Currie suggested that "as a party leader meddling in military doctrine, Khrushchev was the last of a line" (1984: 33). Since he left office, the military has enjoyed a monopoly in doctrine. Brezhnev was particularly deferential to the military and did not meddle in doctrine.

One Soviet source (Lunev 1979: 20) described military doctrine as only an expression of the political line of the party, but this interpretation does not deny that the military leadership develops the general strategic plans without much interference from the civilian leadership.

The military buildup of the post-Khrushchev period has been enormously expensive. According to U.S. estimates, military spending has regularly consumed about 12 to 13 percent of the gross national product (GNP) of the USSR. (The comparable figure for the United States is about 7 percent, although this amount comes from a much larger GNP.) It has used up resources that could otherwise have gone for investment, and thus the slowdown in economic growth can be attributed partly to military spending. It has also taken resources that could have been used for further improvement in the standard of living. Yet the consensus in Soviet society about the need for a strong national defense apears to be widespread. As Holloway pointed out (1984: 375) even Soviet dissidents have not voiced strong opposition to the arms building. Roy Medvedev, for example, pointed to the economic costs of the military program and yet suggested that it was necessary to match that of the United States (1975: 15).

To the outsider, the military professionals would appear to have no real cause for dissatisfaction with the regime they serve. The emphasis on the development of heavy industry—the foundation of Soviet economic policy—allows a high level of production of military hardware to continue. The political leadership relies on the military to protect national security, but except for the Cuban adventure it has not shown any propensity to take unnecessary risks. Finally, the climate of opinion in the country ought to encourage high military morale. Although public opinion has never been militaristic, neither has it been antimilitary. The army or navy officer occupies a respected place in Soviet society, and the pay and other rewards of a military career attract competent personnel.

Despite the military's favored position in Soviet society, policy differences have arisen between the high command and the political leadership—conflicts over the authority of the military to manage its own affairs (the issue of professional autonomy) as well as over the larger issues of national policy. A former Soviet diplomat has reported that the military leadership was at one point prepared to use nuclear weapons against China. The foreign ministry opposed an attack on China, and the Politburo ruled it out. In this case the action of the political leadership was decisive. He also said that Defense Minister Grechko tried to stall disarmament talks with the United States (Shevchenko 1985: 162, 202). These cases are probably unusual. Kolkowicz described the relationship between the military high command and the civilian leadership in the following way.

As an interest group the military tends to be highly self-centered, competing with other groups for status, resources, and influence. The military employs a variety of ways of influencing policy and social planning, both of a "direct" and an "indirect" kind. Although it possesses substantial potential and inherent political power, it rarely chooses to challenge the party head-on, even when its basic interests are denied. It may nonetheless present its case publicly through speeches and articles, often in a somewhat veiled and esoteric way. It often, however, tends to resort to a form of "passive resistance" acting as a modifier or spoiler of policy by means of institutional inertia, [or] bureaucratic obstructionism. (1971: 144)

Political Organs

The loyalty and political reliability of the armed forces have always been matters of concern to the party. Less than one-fourth of the personnel in the military establishment belongs to the party, although most officers are members of either the party or the Komsomol. The lower ranks of the army, however, contain a mass of young and inexperienced soldiers, armed and subject to military discipline. Most of them are draftees, and their political rather than military training concerns the party.

Long before the revolution, P. L. Lavrov (1875) warned that the socialist state would need an army to defend itself, but the army could not be trusted to be loyal. Therefore, he proposed appointing political observers in the army who would watch over the loyalty of the officer corps. The observers were to be reliable members of the party. A system like this was instituted when the Red Army was formed in 1918. Political commissars were assigned to military units to watch over the officers, nearly all of whom had served in the Tsarist army. The idea was supported by People's Commissar of War Trotskii, who recognized that the Soviet regime could not survive without the help of experienced (but unreliable) officers from the Tsarist army. The political commissars had two functions: to watch over the commanders and to inspire the troops with the rightness of the Communist cause. At one time, all the commander's operational orders had to be countersigned by the political commissar.

The system has undergone many changes, and the commissar has now become the deputy commander for political affairs (*zampolit*). The new title emphasizes the subordinate role of the position: Like any other officer the zampolit is subject to the orders of the commander, and the commander is certain to be a party member. More attention is now given to indoctrinating the troops than to the function of watching over the commander (Kolkowicz 1967: 93). Thus the zampolit is primarily responsible for political education. He may in fact be in charge of most of the nonmilitary activities of a unit, which makes him a recreation officer as well. He supervises the sports program and the club, and if the unit has a newspaper, it is the zampolit's responsibility, too.

The system of political officers functions under the supervision of the Main Political Directorate of the armed forces, which has the status of a department of the Central Committee. Most political officers make a career of service in the MPD system of political organs, and they make up a large organization. Timothy Colton (1979: 15) estimated the total number of political officers at 40,000. The MPD organization has its own training school (the Lenin Military-Political Academy) and its own publication (*Kommunist vooruzhenykh sil*). Some Western analysts have seen the MPD organization as a divisive force, with the professional military officers resentful of the party's intrusion into their sphere. However, Colton (1979) has argued that the MPD is not an effective monitoring organization and that in fact it fulfills a different function. Nonetheless the MPD remains a monument to the party's original distrust of the military.

In addition to the MPD system, there are regular party organizations in the armed forces. A primary organization (usually at the level of the regiment or on a ship in the navy) includes all party members assigned to that unit. As in civilian life, the primary organization elects a bureau and a secretary. In a military organization, the secretary, an elected official, appears to be subordinate to the political officers appointed from above. Moreover, the military party organization is an exception to the territorial-production principle. In the military, the primary organization at the unit level does not come under the jurisdiction of the local or regional secretary.

The primary responsibility for watching over the political reliability of the armed forces belongs to the KGB and its counterintelligence directorate. The KGB maintains a secret network of special departments (*osobye otdely*), staffed by KGB operatives in military uniform.

Military Role

No evidence indicates that the Soviet military leaders have ever plotted to take power. The military tradition in Russia before and after 1917 has been characterized by deference to the established political authority, and no Soviet marshal has emerged as a serious contender for power. The USSR has had neither a Dwight D. Eisenhower nor a Douglas MacArthur. During the purges of the 1930s, the high command was accused of conspiring against Stalin. The commander in chief, Marshal Tukhachevskii, was executed along with several other generals, and a sweeping purge was conducted in the officer corps. After 1953, however,

Tukhachevskii and all the others were cleared of the charges against them and added to the honored list of Stalin's victims.

The only direct involvement of a Soviet marshal in leadership politics came with the Zhukov affair of 1957. G. K. Zhukov, the most famous commander of World War II, became minister of defense in 1955. In 1957 he was promoted to the Politburo, and he apparently sided with Khrushchev during the anti-party affair of that year. In October, Zhukov was suddenly removed from political leadership and dismissed from the ministry. He was charged with having tried to undermine the political organs in the armed forces. He was also accused of adventurism; this charge could mean that he advocated a more aggressive foreign policy. Later he was accused of bonapartism as well. Colton (1979) examined the charges against Zhukov and concluded that for the most part they were exaggerated. Still the political leadership perceived Zhukov as a threat and moved to oust him. Later Zhukov was rehabilitated, although he never again held a position of responsibility.

Since the fall of Marshal Zhukov, the military and political leaders have been careful to avoid an open confrontation. Disagreements over minor issues have sometimes been detected by kremlinologists, and they may reflect conflict over more substantive political questions. In September 1984 the chief of the general staff, Marshal Ogarkov, was removed without explanation (*Pravda*, Sept. 7). Ogarkov had impressed Westerners as knowledgeable and competent and also as a vigorous defender of military interests. He was generally regarded as the most likely candidate to succeed Ustinov as minister (Ustinov was already ill and died three months later). Ogarkov may have been removed so that he would not be in line to move up to the minister's chair.

THE SCIENTIFIC ESTABLISHMENT

Both economic growth and national defense depend on scientific research and on the development of new technology, as past Soviet leaders have recognized. Gorbachev's call for introducing advanced technology into industry is hardly a new idea. The success of the idea depends on his answers to two questions: (1) How is the new technology to be acquired? (2) How will the regime cope with the social and political questions raised by the introduction of new technology?

The management of basic scientific research is the responsibility of the USSR Academy of Sciences. Its jurisdiction is quite broad and covers not only the natural sciences but also the social sciences, philosophy, the humanities, and law. The academy is organized along the lines of a union-republic ministry, and it supervises the academies of sciences in the union republics. Its work is carried on in a number of highly specialized research institutes—most located in Moscow but some found in other cities. Over the past twenty years, the Siberian department, located in Novosibirsk, has become almost an independent institution and has acquired a reputation for liberalism in the social sciences. Zaslavskaia is on the staff of the Siberian department.

The State Committee for Science and Technology is responsible for applied research (research and development). Most applied research is done in institutes attached to the industrial ministries, which are loosely coordinated by the committee. The universities and other vuzes also sponsor research, but their primary function is education. Some Soviet scientists have criticized the sharp distinction between teaching and research, a distinction formalized by the administrative separation of the academy and the universities. The separation, however, has the support of long-standing tradition. In addition to the Academy of Sciences, there are also specialized academies, such as the Academy of Agricultural Sciences and the Academy of Medical Sciences.

Membership in the Academy of Sciences is a high honor generally reserved for persons who have genuinely distinguished themselves in their research. A full member has the title of academician (*akademik*) and belongs to one of the most privileged groups in the Soviet society. Just a rank below is the corresponding member of the academy. Although some party officials have been elected to the academy, the title of academician is jealously guarded and must be earned. The reluctance to elect Trapeznikov to the academy was a reassertion of this traditional independence.

The Stalinist economic system profited from the advantage of backwardness: It built up basic industries with existing technology and was not crucially dependent on research and development. Stalin did encourage research in areas of high priority, and under his regime Soviet scientists built the atomic bomb and carried on the development of rocket technology that led to the first artificial satellite in 1957. Some research was actually carried on by scientists incarcerated in Stalin's prisons, as Solzhenitsyn recounted in *First Circle*. Under Stalin biological science came under the control of a charlatan, Trofim Lysenko. Lysenko was a plant breeder who made fantastic claims about his ability to produce hardy new grains. The party appeared to side with Lysenko, and in the late 1930s some prominent geneticists who disputed his claims were denounced and even imprisoned. Lysenko rose to become president of the Academy of Agricultural Sciences, although the Academy of Sciences resisted his influence (Joravsky 1970: 45). The party apparatus was not united on the Lysenko question. The agricultural specialists were eager to try his new methods, but the science department supported the anti-Lysenko scientists (Joravsky 1970: 109). Eventually, Lysenko won a complete victory over the scientists. Pro-Lysenko people took control of biological research even in the Academy of Sciences.

Several factors caused the Lysenko affair: Lysenko's own remarkable capacity for publicizing himself and avoiding scientific criticism; the regime's desire to find quick and practical solutions to the problems of agriculture; and the ideological belief that "there are no fortresses that Bolsheviks cannot take." Furthermore, there was the belief that all activity should follow the rule of *partiinost*, although Lysenko himself never belonged to the party. Eventually Lysenko was repudiated, and biologists were able to engage in research without fear of the political consequences. Nonetheless the shadow of Lysenko hangs over all Soviet science.

Throughout the Brezhnev period debate was taking place about the priority that should be given to technological innovation, and this policy debate has been studied by Bruce Parrott (1983). The crucial issue was the acquisition of Western technology. Some party leaders wanted a kind of technological autarky and insisted that the Soviet Union had no need for scientific ideas from the West. Their argument was supported with the traditional claim that the Soviet socialist order was inherently superior to any Western society. Philip Hanson (1981) called this attitude "technological chauvinism." Their real concerns seem to have been different. First, acquiring Western technology meant increasing contact with the West, with all the political danger this represented. A real fear exists about the spillover effect of technology transfer: Acquiring Western technology might lead to acquiring Western ideas. On this point the opponents of technology transfer were undoubtedly right. Making the best use of Western technology would require great changes in the outlook of Soviet managers and in the managerial system itself. Second, concern arose in the Academy of Sciences bureaucracy that buying Western technology would reduce the resources available to Soviet scientists.

Those who favored technology transfer assumed that the Soviet Union really had no choice: Either it must acquire the advanced technology of the Western world or stagnate economically. This argument was persuasive with Brezhnev, and in the 1960s the regime began a program of buying industrial technology from the West. One of the more spectacular results of this policy was that the Fiat company contracted to design and build a modern automobile plant and train Soviet engineers to run it. The Soviet Fiat (Zhiguli) became the most popular passenger car in the country.

Many scientists (as distinguished from the managers of science) favored the policy because the scientists had long sought greater contact with the West. However, opposition continued from various sources: Some bureaucratic interests preferred to avoid any contact that would lead to comparison (likely to be unfavorable) between Soviet and Western technology; and the police were in principle against any policy that might open the country to Western visitors or increase the number of Soviet travelers in the West (Parrott 1983: 207, 223, 291.)

Parrott concluded that even though some scientists oppose the bureaucratic system that manages Soviet science, many have become reconciled to the system. It provides professional security, and in many fields it gives scientists freedom to define their own research. The regime clearly tends to distrust the scientists. One reason is that a disproportionate number of dissidents have come from the scientific community—not only academician Sakharov, but Igor Shafarevich (a mathematician and corresponding member of the academy), Iurii Orlov, and Anatolii Shcharanskii. In his first dissident article, Sakharov wrote: "The views of the author were formed in the milieu of the scientific and scientific-technical intelligentsia, which manifests much anxiety over the principles and specific aspects of foreign and domestic policy . . ." (1974: 56).

Are the military and the scientific and industrial complex associated with the military an "island of hope" in Soviet society? Sakharov (1975: 31) would deny it: "All the great scientific and technological discoveries of recent times" were made in the West, and not in the USSR. Along with other dissidents, he has insisted that there is an "actual and growing disparity, on a wide front, of the scientific and technical level of our country and that of the developed countries of the West." Instead of catching up, the USSR is falling further behind (Sakharov 1974: 120). Mikhail Agursky has also argued that the efficiency of the Soviet military-industrial complex is greatly exaggerated in the West. Although scientists and managers working in this field are often better off in terms of equipment, working conditions, and pay, according to Agursky's testimony they remain inefficient and backward because of unnecessary secrecy, compartmentalization, and extensive bureaucratic control (Agursky 1980; Agursky and Adomeit 1979).

REFERENCES

Agursky, Mikhail. 1980. *The Soviet Military-Industrial Complex*. Hebrew University of Jerusalem, Jerusalem Papers on Peace Problems, 31. Jerusalem: Magnes Press.

Agursky, Mikhail, and Hannes Adomeit. 1979. The Soviet Military-Industrial Complex. *Survey* 24, no. 2: 106–124.

Azrael, Jeremy R. 1966. *Managerial Power and Soviet Politics*. Cambridge: Harvard University Press.

Beichman, Arnold, and Mikhail S. Bernstam. 1983. *Andropov: New Challenge to the West.* New York: Stein and Day.

Colton, Timothy. 1979. *Commissars, Commanders, and Civilian Authority.* Cambridge: Harvard University Press.

——. 1981. The Impact of the Military on Soviet Society. In *The Domestic Context of Soviet Foreign Policy*, edited by Seweryn Bialer. Boulder, Colo.: Westview Press, pp. 119–138.

Currie, Kenneth. 1984. The Soviet General Staff's New Role. *Problems of Communism* 33 (March-April): 32–40.

Hanson, Philip. 1981. *Trade and Technology in Soviet-Western Relations.* New York: Columbia University Press.

Holloway, David. 1984. War, Militarism, and the Soviet State. In *The Soviet Polity in the Modern Era*, edited by Erik P. Hoffman and Robbin F. Laird. New York: Aldine, pp. 359–391.

Joravsky, David. 1970. *The Lysenko Affair.* Cambridge: Harvard University Press.

Kolkowicz, Roman. 1967. *The Soviet Military and the Communist Party.* Princeton, N.J.: Princeton University Press.

——. 1971. The Military. In *Interest Groups in Soviet Politics*, edited by H. Gordon Skilling and Franklyn Griffiths. Princeton: Princeton University Press, pp. 131–169.

Kushnirsky, Fyodor I. 1982. *Soviet Economic Planning, 1965–1980.* Boulder, Colo.: Westview Press.

Lavrov, P. L. 1875. *Gosudarstevennyi element v budushchem obshchestve.* In *Sobranie sochinenii*, vol. 7. Petrograd: "Kolos," 1920.

Lenin, V. I. 1918. *State and Revolution.* In *Selected Works*, vol. 2, pt. 1. Moscow: Foreign Languages Publishing House, 1952, pp. 199–325.

Lunev, A. E., A. S. Bakhov, B. M. Beznadezhnykh et al. 1979. *Sovetskoe administrativnoe pravo—upravlenie v oblasti administrativno-politicheskoi deiatelnosti.* Moscow: Iuridicheskaia literatura.

Medvedev, Roy. 1975. *On Socialist Democracy.* New York: Knopf.

Medvedev, Zhores A. 1983. *Andropov.* New York: Norton.

Niskanen, William A., Jr. 1971. *Bureaucracy and Representative Government.* Chicago: Aldine, Atheron.

Nove, Alec. 1977. *The Soviet Economic System.* London: Allen & Unwin.

——. 1980. Socialism, Centralised Planning and the One-Party State. In *Authority, Power, and Policy in the USSR*, edited by T. H. Rigby, Archie Brown, and Peter Reddaway. New York: St. Martin's Press, pp. 77–97.

Parrott, Bruce. 1983. *Politics and Technology in the Soviet Union.* Cambridge, Mass.: MIT Press.

Perventsev, Arkadii. 1977. *Ostrov nadezhdy.* In *Sobranie sochinenii*, vol. 5. Moscow: Khudozhestvennaia literatura.

Sakharov, Andrei. 1974. *Sakharov Speaks.* New York: Random House.

——. 1975. *My Country and the World.* New York: Random House.

Shevchenko, Arkady. 1985. *Breaking with Moscow.* New York: Knopf.

Singireva, I. O., and L. S. Iavich. 1967. *Gosudarstvo i profsoiuzy.* Moscow: Profizdat.

Stalin, Joseph. 1953. *Problems of Leninism.* 11th ed. Moscow: Foreign Languages
Publishing House.
Zaslavskaia, T. I. 1980. Ekonomicheskoe povedenie i ekonomicheskoe razvitie.
Ekonomika i organizatsiia promyshlennogo predpriiatie 3: 15–33.
———. 1983. O neobkhodimosti bolee uglublennogo izucheniia v SSSR sot-
sialnogo mekhanizma razvitiia ekonomiki. AS no. 5042. *Materialy Samizdata*
35/85, August 26.

11
Public Policy
and the Welfare State

As described earlier, some features of the Soviet system find widespread acceptance not only among Soviet citizens but even among emigrés who have left the country. The welfare state is one aspect of the system that enjoys this general support. Alex Inkeles and Raymond Bauer (1959: 236ff.) found that almost all the former Soviet citizens they interviewed expected the state to provide for their welfare, including such services as job security, free education, and medical care. Even those respondents who showed hostility to the Soviet system wanted to retain the welfare state. Interviews conducted more recently among former Soviet citizens confirm this finding: They generally wanted the state to play an active role in providing social and cultural services (White 1979: 100).

Lenin assumed that with the development of socialism more and more services would be provided without charge until eventually money disappeared altogether. In the lower, or first, phase of socialist society, workers are paid in accordance with their work, but even in this phase the state provides extensive services for which the citizens do not have to pay. Those unable to work are supported by society. Because in this first phase society is affluent and productivity is high, plenty exists for everyone except those who shirk their duties. Out of what society produces a reserve fund is deducted, which is used for investment in new industrial equipment. A fund is also deducted for social consumption, which pays the costs of such services as schools, hospitals, and homes for the aged (Lenin 1918a: 294). The rest of society's product is distributed among individuals "in accordance with their work." Lenin described socialist society as follows.

The means of production are no longer the private property of individuals. The means of production belong to the whole of society. Every member of society, performing a certain part of the socially necessary work, receives a certificate from society to the effect that he has done such and such an amount of work. And with this certificate he receives from the public store of articles of consumption a corresponding quantity of products. After a deduction is made of the amount of labor which goes to the public fund, every worker, therefore, receives from society as much as he has given to it. (1918a: 295)

The state and its bureaucracy still exist in this phase of development. The state makes the decision about how much of society's product goes into the public fund and how much individual workers receive for their labor. In the higher stage of development, workers are paid according to the principle "from each according to his ability, to each according to his needs" (Lenin 1918a: 299, 303). Also during this phase the state and the bureaucracy withered away.

In 1984, in his last published article General Secretary Chernenko made a significant pronouncement about this theory, which could be interpreted as a revision of Lenin's original teaching. He warned against overoptimism, against seeking goals impossible to reach, even though attractive. Then he said that the "fundamental principle of socialism" was the rule "to each according to his work" (1984: 14–15). In this statement the general secretary drew no distinction between lower and higher phases of socialism and implied that the rule "to each according to his work" was a permanent principle of socialist society.

Lenin acknowledged that the higher stage still lay in the future. Before the promise of the higher stage could be realized, extensive social development would have to take place. Universal literacy (which, he admitted, already existed in the advanced capitalist countries) would have to be achieved. Training and discipline were needed for the mass of workers, to prepare them to live in this new society. In a famous remark, Lenin admitted that the Russian worker was a "bad" worker compared with the workers of capitalist countries (1918b: 470). Above all, the government needed to raise the productivity of labor, and to do this, it needed to lift the educational and cultural level of the masses. In a frequently quoted passage, Lenin described the new values that must be instilled in the worker: "Keep regular and honest accounts of money, manage economically, do not steal, observe the strictest labor discipline" (1918b: 458).

The Soviet regime has given the highest priority to economic growth. In the first five-year plans, tremendous sacrifices were demanded so that all available resources could be channeled into the development of industry. On the other hand, the regime has always recognized that economic growth requires investment in human resources to create a trained and healthy work force. Furthermore, the workers must be housed, clothed, and entertained and given an incentive to work hard and efficiently. Expenditures on social and cultural services should raise the productivity of labor and therefore can be justified as part of the cost of continued economic development. Gosplan plans the output of "young specialists" from higher education, just as it plans investment in the steel industry. Chernenko repeated the familiar idea that to live well, one must work hard, but he added that "the opposite formula is no less true: in order to work better, one must live better" (1984: 14).

SOCIAL SERVICES

What Lenin called social consumption provides the theoretical basis for the Soviet welfare state. Most of the goods and services provided to the population come from the government. The exceptions to this general rule include the collective farm markets where the peasants are allowed to sell their produce directly to the consumer, small and individually operated businesses, such as a shoe-repair stall or a photographic studio, and illegal operations in the second economy. Small businesses are an insignificant part of the economy. The collective farm markets, however, provide a large part of the food supply for Soviet consumers. Although the size of the second economy cannot be estimated, expenditures for its services seem to be a significant part of the family budget, especially for middle- and upper-income people.

The state distributes goods and services according to two principles, which correspond to the public and private sectors in a Western society. Some state-owned enterprises function according to the commercial (*khozraschet*) principle, and they are expected to pay their operating costs out of the revenue they receive. In these enterprises, the consumer pays directly for goods or services received. Some enterprises receive a government subsidy so the consumer may pay less than actual cost, but these are still khozraschet enterprises. Such subsidized enterprises include the opera and ballet theaters and the public transportation system.

Benefits Without Charges

Other, non-khozraschet agencies of the state distribute benefits without charging for them, and the costs are covered out of the government budget. The major benefits provided without a user's charge include health services and education. Although health services are in principle free, there are also paying clinics that charge for their services.

The resources that pay for social and cultural services are referred to in the budget as "social consumption funds" (*obshchestvennye fondy potrebleniia*) (Zverev 1970: 215). The Soviet workers' disposable incomes, paid in rubles, form only part of the stream of benefits that they receive from the government. Goods and services purchased out of disposable income are individual consumption. In addition, society at large consumes a variety of goods and services that are paid for out of social consumption funds. Thus Robert Osborn (1970: 20) referred to social consumption funds as the "social wage." Even though this is not Soviet terminology, Osborn's term is a good description of Soviet theory.

The real income of the Soviet citizen (goods and services) can be divided as follows.

Earned income: Paid in rubles and used for personal consumption.
Social consumption:
  • Monetary payments (transfer payments): student aid, pensions for retirees (social security), assistance to the disabled (social insurance), maternity and family payments.
  • Services: medical care, education, prepaid vacations.
  • Subsidies: housing and food products.

As C. R. Nechemias (1980: 174) pointed out, the Soviet government has a dual system of funding social and cultural services, and social consumption funds come from two sources. Most of these funds come from the state budget and provide for services which in theory are available to all citizens on the basis of need. In practice the funds in the national budget are distributed to local governments, which are responsible for delivery of services. But some funds are allocated to employers through the planning process. Thus some social and cultural services are provided by employers from the enterprise fund, and in general these services are available only to the employees. This system of allocating social consumption funds results in a kind of rationing of services. As A. G. Zverev (1970: 216) acknowledged, the employers' social consumption funds provide a source of material incentive to the worker.

Concentrating resources on social consumption relieves the individual from the burden of paying directly for health, education, and similar services. It does not mean that more of these services are available. In the USSR, expenditures for housing, education, and health are significantly lower than in other industrialized countries. A U.S. study (Schroeder and Edwards 1981) found that overall consumption in the USSR, measured on a per capita basis, was about one-third the level of that in the United States. This overall estimate included both individual and social consumption. Of the major categories of social consumption, the study found that the level of spending in the USSR was only a fraction of that in the United States: housing, 14 percent; education, 77 percent; and health care, 33 percent.

Why not take the funds to be used for social consumption and distribute them in the form of disposable income so that the Soviet consumer would have a choice among goods and services? This question has been asked by some thoughtful Soviet citizens too. One newspaper published a letter with this statement: "Instead of paying a worker 100 rubles, for example, and then giving him handouts in the form of public consumption funds, it is better to increase his wages and make him pay for day-care centers, education and so on." Another Soviet letter writer remarked that nothing is free, and social consumption is just a system of distribution: "You write that our education is free, as is medical care, and the state pays for day-care centers. But where does it get the money for all these benefits? Can it be that we live at the expense of the state . . . ?" (*Sovetskaia Rossiia*, quoted in Osborn 1970: 46)

There are two answers to these questions. First, the social consumption concept makes economic planning easier. Since the state is paying for education, health care, and other benefits, the planners know how much funding will be available and approximately what the demand will be for these services. Second, the regime can rest assured that the citizen will make use of the benefits available, since no payment is necessary. If Soviet citizens had to pay directly for health and education, they might exercise consumers' choice and spend their money in other ways, ways that would be socially less desirable.

In Lenin's vision of the future, as society moves toward the higher phase of development the range of social services should increase. The khozraschet enterprises should gradually be phased out, and eventually no consumer should have to pay a direct charge for any of the benefits provided by the state. In fact this is not happening. Transfer payments have been growing at a faster rate than the direct delivery of services. Alastair McAuley (1979: 264) pointed out that these payments are increasing as a percentage of total expenditures for social consumption. Such a tendency, of course, is the opposite of what Lenin predicted. Soviet economists recognize this tendency in the distribution of social benefits (Rimashevskaia and Shatalin 1977), although they offer no explanation for it.

Educational Policy and Administration

The development of a system of universal education has been one of the most significant social achievements of the Soviet regime. Before the revolution, access to education was extremely limited: The educated were a minority in Russian society, and most of the population was illiterate. To achieve its economic goals, the regime would have to overcome illiteracy and create an educated population, and this task presented the Soviet government with one of its greatest challenges. Many years of effort were required to train new teachers and build new schools, and (as discussed in Chapter 3) educational opportunity still varies markedly particularly between cities and villages. The continuing effort to equalize educational opportunity has been one of the most controversial issues in Soviet society.

To understand the issue, we need to review briefly the structure of the educational system. The basic educational program, which provides ten years of primary and secondary schooling, is highly academic in orientation and seems designed primarily to prepare students for higher education (the vuzes). Priority is given to science, mathematics, and foreign languages. Only a minority of Soviet teenagers manage to complete the ten-year academic program. Even so, far more students compete for admission to higher education than the vuzes can accommodate.

For students who do not complete the ten-year program these are the other educational opportunities.

1. The *tekhnikum.* The tekhnikum is a technical-training school for educating technicians and semiprofessionals. Normally students enter the tekhnikum after eight years of secondary school and receive two or three years of training. The tekhnikums train the country's librarians, nurses, printers, bookkeepers, and computer operators.
2. Vocational school (PTU). Vocational schools provide minimal training, much of it on the job, for unskilled and some semiskilled workers.
3. Schools of working youth. Night or parttime schools are provided for young people who left school and entered the labor force but wish to continue their general education.

The general schools are managed by the USSR Ministry of Education and the tekhnikums by the Ministry of Higher and Secondary Specialized Education (MHE). Vocational education is supervised by a state committee, although the actual training may be provided by industrial ministries or their enterprises. The tekhnikum and the PTU are regarded as educational dead ends. Young people who finish these schools are expected to enter the work force, and their prospect for further education is limited to the schools of working youth.

The universities and the other vuzes are highly specialized institutions where students are trained for specific professions. The MHE actually controls only about one-half of the vuzes. The remainder are under the supervision of other ministries: Teacher training schools come under the

Ministry of Education, the conservatories under the Ministry of Culture, medical schools under the Ministry of Health. Thus no single government agency has overall responsibility for educational policy. This fact undoubtedly increases the authority of the party apparatus in educational policy (see Matthews 1982: 111).

The Soviet social tradition places a high value on advanced education, which accounts in part for the great pressure on the vuzes. Soviet parents expend considerable effort to get their children qualified for higher education, and the second economy plays a role in this process. That role is both legal (hiring a tutor to prepare a student for entrance examinations) and illegal (bribing the examiners). So intensive is the competition that the competition of students is sometimes transformed into a competition of parents. Obviously the system favors the urban white-collar class. Government policy aims at more equal educational opportunity and at reducing the pressure on higher education. The policy causes resentment among parents with white-collar positions because they fear that their children will be denied an advanced education and forced to take blue-collar jobs.

Khrushchev forced through a general reform of education, beginning in the late 1950s (Schwartz and Keech 1969; Kelley 1972). The aim of the reform was to increase training for productive labor. In principle, all students (including those headed toward the universities) were required to have some job-oriented training as part of their education. Khrushchev's educational reforms were designed to provide more equal educational opportunity and also to give each child some experience with productive labor. However, Khrushchev's reforms also had a practical aspect: The economy faced a critical labor shortage, and some means had to be found to channel more young people into factory work.

No other social program of the Khrushchev era generated as much opposition and resentment as the educational reform. It was opposed by both professional educators (who saw their own academic values under threat) and white-collar parents (who saw their children threatened with the life of a factory worker). Sakharov, who was still a respected member of the scientific community, was among those who opposed the reform (Sakharov 1974: 10–11). The whole reform plan was eventually abandoned (Stewart 1969: 47).

The problem was not only the organization of the school system but social attitudes. Too many school children, encouraged by their parents, wanted to go on to higher education—more than higher education could accommodate and more than the economy could spare. Surveys in the 1960s and 1970s show that these expectations had not changed. The overwhelming majority of school children wanted to continue their education in the vuzes.

The shortage of labor, especially skilled workers, is still a critical problem (Avis 1983: 228). It is a problem that will certainly increase the pressure to channel more young people into job-related training. In 1984 the Andropov administration announced plans for a reform of the school system that resembled, in its stated objectives, the discredited program of Khrushchev. This time, however, there was much less fanfare, and the reform was to be introduced only gradually over a period of several years. Furthermore, as part of the reform plan the government promised a pay raise to teachers.

According to the guidelines published in 1984, the government's aim is to provide universal vocational training for young people. The school-entering age will eventually be lowered to six, so that most children will have eleven years instead of ten before leaving school. The long-range goal is to combine the traditional academic school and the PTU into one "secondary, general-education and vocational school." Like the reform of 1958, this program is dictated by labor needs. On completing school, young people may still go on directly to higher education, if qualified; however, their fate will basically be determined "in accordance with the needs of the economy" (Supreme Soviet Decree, April 12, 1984).

Probably as much opposition will develop to these guidelines as to the reform of 1958 and for the same reasons. The regime has tried to forestall some criticism by phasing in the new system only gradually. The reform will not be completed before 1990.

Health Care

The USSR actually maintains three different systems for delivering health services to the population. First, there is the public health service of the Ministry of Health. The ministry maintains a network of polyclinics and hospitals where health services are provided free of charge. The city or district polyclinics are part of this system. Second, some employers provide medical services, and in some cases they have an extensive medical administration. Both the Ministry of Railroads and the Ministry of Civil Aviation, for example, have medical directorates in their central apparatus (Dorokhova 1980: 265). Several agencies in Moscow maintain hospitals for their employees, including the Ministry of Railroads, the Academy of Sciences, the KGB, and the *Pravda* publishing house. The fourth directorate of the Ministry of Health maintains hospitals and clinics that provide for the needs of high-level officials.

Third, the ministry also operates a network of paying clinics that operate on a commercial basis and serve the dental and the medical needs of those willing to pay for service. The existence of these paying clinics indicates that at least some Soviet citizens are dissatisfied with public health care. The second economy also plays a role in the provision of health care. A very small number of doctors engage in private practice. The government discourages private practice, and doctors are required to pay a high tax on their private income. There is also a large private practice that is concealed to evade the tax. This medical component of the second economy is so widespread that Kaser (1976: 66) maintained that it can scarcely be called illegal.

The quality of health care is difficult to evaluate because of the lack of statistical information (Kaser 1976: 48). By one indicator, however, it has been declining in recent years. Life expectancy for Soviet males is lower, and the figure for women has not improved. The trend is particularly marked in the infant mortality rate, which rose by more than one-third between 1971 and 1976. Two Western demographers who reported on this rise in infant mortality (Davis and Feshbach 1980) drew no firm conclusions as to the cause. But this must be of concern to the managers of the health care system.

Housing

Housing remains a critical social problem, and one of the main concerns of the average Soviet citizen. During the period of rapid industrialization, housing was given a low priority. The government took control of the distribution of housing, but it provided little new housing. As a result, millions were forced into communal apartments where several families shared the bathroom and kitchen. Single workers typically lived in dormitories where conditions were even more crowded. Years ago the government set a norm for living space: nine square meters per person, which is a space about ten feet square. Many Soviet families still live in housing that, even by this modest norm, is substandard.

On the other hand, many families have housing that is better than the norm: This situation results because a large amount of the housing stock is owned by employers and is used as incentives. Not uncommonly a worker may change jobs just to get a better apartment. Furthermore managerial personnel generally have better housing (provided by the employer) than do workers.

The housing subsidy listed under social consumption takes two forms. First, most housing is constructed with government funds. Second, part of the cost of maintaining housing is paid from the government budget (channeled through local government or employers). The result of this subsidy is that housing cost is a small part of the typical family budget— as little as 4 or 5 percent.

The Khrushchev administration launched a crash program of housing construction in hopes of solving the problem. Although it did improve the situation (especially in the city of Moscow), the problem is hardly solved. About 20 percent of Soviet families still live in communal apartments. Moreover, since the Khrushchev period government investment in housing construction has dropped (Nechemias 1980: 188). Another problem is that much of the housing built during the Khrushchev era was not well constructed, and for the current government maintenance costs are quite high.

An administrative reform discussed in recent years is a proposal to take housing out of the control of employers and give overall responsibility to local government (Morton 1983: 196–197). This is unlikely to happen. Employers are generally opposed because they value housing as a method of attracting workers. Furthermore, those who are now comfortably housed (by Soviet standards) fear that they would not do as well at the hands of local government. For their part, the cities are reluctant to take control of the apartment houses now owned by employers because they do not have the resources to maintain them.

THE DEMOGRAPHIC PROBLEM

The census figures in Table 7.1 reveal a crucial fact about the contemporary Soviet population: the rapid growth of the traditional Islamic peoples in Central Asia compared with the slow growth of the Slavic (including Russian) peoples. Each postwar census has seen a slow decline in the proportion of ethnic Russians in the country. The Russians are still a majority but only by a slender margin. If present trends continue, the Russians will one day be a minority within the USSR, and that will be a significant development, if only because of its psychological effect. Does this prospect represent a threat to the stability of the political system or to the survival of the Soviet multinational state? Probably the Islamic threat has been exaggerated. The census figures do not mean that the Islamic peoples will compose a majority of the Soviet population. The prospect is that the USSR will become a society of minorities where the Russians will be the largest ethnic group—but a majority no longer.

The reasons for this demographic trend are not hard to discern. The Islamic peoples live in a more rural and traditional culture, where a high value is put on large families. In the Russian regions of the USSR, as in every Western country, urbanization and industrialization have brought a lower birth rate, a higher rate of divorce, and smaller families. This same trend can be seen in the Baltic republics.

Officially, the regime's long-standing policy has been to encourage a high birth rate among all peoples of the USSR. This policy has been manifested in social programs: supplementary payments to large families,

TABLE 11.1
Comparative Figures for Population Growth

	Death Rate	Birth Rate	Crude Rate of Natural Increase
Tadzhik SSR	6.0	36.0	30.0
Turkmen SSR	7.0	37.2	30.2
Pskov oblast	11.3	11.9	0.6
Kalinin oblast	10.4	11.8	1.4

Source: K. Voronov, Demograficheskie problemy Rossii, Grani 98: 256–257.

beginning with the third child, maternity leave, and glorification of women with large families, who are awarded the title of Mother Heroine of the USSR. But these policies have not led to a high birth rate among the European (including Russian) nationalities.

Published Soviet sources reveal the concern of some ethnic Russians about the demographic problem: (1) The Soviet budget favors the minority nationalities, so that the smaller republics receive a larger share of the resources of the country at the expense of the Russian republic (RSFSR); (2) the agricultural regions of Central Asia are better provided for than those of the RSFSR; (3) family policy should aim at achieving a uniform birth rate throughout the USSR and change a situation where the Central Asian population is growing much faster than the Russian population (Litvinova and Urlanis 1982). Russians tended to argue for a differentiated policy that would encourage a higher birth rate among the Slavic population. They also argued that support for families should begin with the first child.

In contrast, a Kazakh demographer has argued that different population growth rates are not necessarily undesirable, especially if balanced out by mobility of the labor force. Attempts at implementing a deliberate policy of changing the birth rate will not work: "Every violation of freedom of choice in the reproductive behavior of individuals is bound to fail." Instead, he advocated a neutral policy, so that the birth rate would evolve naturally. All nationalities would gradually achieve a reduction in the birth rate without the intervention of the policymakers (Tatimov 1978: 78).

A samizdat article (Voronov 1975) calculated the natural population growth (difference between death rate and birth rate) for certain oblasts of the Russian republic and compared the data with those for the two Islamic republics. The results are shown in Table 11.1. In terms of demography, Pskov can be taken as a model of the RSFSR minus the autonomous (non-Russian) republics. K. Voronov disagreed with the view that the difference in birth rate could be attributed to modernization and development: "Some scholars—demographers and economists—assert that the sharp decline in the birth rate is explained by an increase in the material and cultural level of the people. . . . If that is so, then the Russian population of the country has already achieved the height of well-being, and the greatest of these heights is in Pskov oblast" (1975: 261). Voronov then gives data to show that Pskov oblast is one of the culturally and economically deprived regions of the country.

This debate clearly presented the regime with a dilemma. The leadership seemed reluctant to accept a differentiated policy, since such a policy would be seen as discrimination against the ethnic minorities and a radical revision of the established policy on nationalities. Furthermore, if the regime were successful in encouraging a higher birth rate in the European areas of the country, then women would be leaving the work force (even if only temporarily), which would create a serious labor shortage. Finally, expenditures to raise the birth rate have a multiplier effect: More children mean more demand for daycare facilities, housing, and other services that the government would have to provide (Weber and Goodman 1981: 280).

The debate was resolved in 1981. Under a new and more generous policy, the government was to make one-time grants of 50 rubles for the first child and 100 rubles per child for other children. Plans were also announced to extend the period of maternity leave. This policy was partially differentiated because it was to take effect in three stages (USSR Council of Ministers decree, Sept. 2, 1981):

1. In certain regions of the RSFSR with a low birth rate (including Pskov oblast) the new policy would take effect almost immediately.
2. In the rest of the RSFSR—and in the Ukraine, Belorussia, Moldavia, and the Baltic republics—implementation would be delayed by one year.
3. In the Caucasus and Central Asia, implementation would be delayed by two years.

COPING WITH ALCOHOL ABUSE

In May 1985 the government announced a stringent new policy to curb excessive drinking. This decision was important not only because alcoholism is a major social problem but because of what the policy reveals about the political style of Gorbachev.

Alcohol abuse is one of the major causes of the health problems—such as the increasing death rate—already mentioned. Heavy drinking is also one of the causes of the country's low labor productivity. At midday, stores that sell liquor are filled with workers on lunch break. Although many Soviet sources make reference to the problem, alcohol abuse does not seem to have been a major concern of the government. All legally produced alcoholic beverages come from state-owned distilleries, so at least in theory the government has had the power to cut down on production. (Alcohol distilled at home, *samogon*, is also a significant part of total consumption, though obviously much more difficult to control.) Yet although the government's economic priorities have caused critical shortages in most consumer goods, there has always been vodka to drink.

V. G. Treml (1982) published statistics showing the magnitude of the problem. Per capita consumption of alcohol has risen sharply in the last twenty-five years, growing at an annual rate of 7.2 percent (for consumption of state-produced beverages). Significant differences exist between regions, with consumption highest in the Russian republic and lowest in the traditionally Islamic regions. Treml also found that expenditures for alcohol were a significant part of the consumer's budget. In 1977 it accounted for 15.0 percent of household expenditures.

These Western estimates are confirmed by a samizdat document that appears to be a summary of a report prepared by researchers in the Academy of Sciences. The report says that the primary cause of the country's health problems is alcoholism, and it also blames the sharp increase in the birth of retarded children on alcohol. It shows a deep concern about the effect of alcoholism on the Russian nationality, which is faced with a "progressive degeneration." "To encounter a sober male in a village in the evening, is about as common as encountering a Martian." On the other hand: "In the Central Asian villages, where there is almost no drinking, there are well-kept houses, autos, motorcycles. This makes it even more heart-rending to look at the dying Russian village." The report adds that most violent crimes can be attributed to alcohol abuse (Pravda ob alkogolizme v SSSR 1985).

In an effort to cope with the problem, the government has announced stringent measures: No liquor is to be sold before 2 P.M. on working days, alcohol production is to be cut down, and the legal drinking age is to be raised from eighteen to twenty-one (*Izvestiia*, May 17, 1985). The government has chosen to rely primarily on administrative measures, but it has not completely ignored Zaslavskaia's advice that an indirect policy would be more effective in regulating behavior. The announcement of the new anti-alcohol campaign also called for improved opportunities for leisure-time activities, such as the construction of more movie theaters, clubs, and sport facilities.

There is reason to doubt that these new policies will be effective in solving the problem. In the first place, a substantial amount of liquor is already produced as samogon, and such illegal distilling is likely to increase as the state cuts down on production. Second, the second economy will probably expand to meet the demand for strong drink, as it has met other forms of consumer demand.

MANAGING SOVIET CULTURE

One of the aims of the revolution was to bring culture to the people. In the early years of the Soviet regime, culture had a simple meaning: mass education and an end to illiteracy. But the revolutionary leaders also wanted to make culture, in the highest sense of the word, accessible to the masses. After the revolution, the Winter Palace was opened to the public, and the imperial family's collection of art and treasure was put on exhibit. The classic works of Russian literature were reprinted in large and inexpensive editions, and as literacy increased, so did the readership of Pushkin, Dostoevskii, and Tolstoi.

The Bolsheviks brought about a political and social revolution, but changes in the cultural tradition of Tsarist Russia were saved for the future. When they talked of bringing culture to the masses, they meant the literature, art, and music of the old society. This approach explains the curious fact that in the Soviet revolutionary society, artistic experimentation has not been welcomed. Writers, composers, and painters who continued the accepted cultural tradition were honored and subsidized by the Soviet state. But Russians in the avant-garde of modern music and modern art went into exile. Until very recently, Stravinskii, Chagall, and Kandinskii were unknown names in their own homeland.

In the current Soviet usage culture involves a wide array of human activities, including the creative activity of Soviet artists and much of the approved leisure-time activity of the citizenry. More specifically, culture is defined to include art (painting, drama, music), cultural-enlightenment work (libraries, clubs, and museums), the cinema, television and radio, and the publishing industry.

As in the case of education, no single government agency is responsible for the management of culture. When the USSR Ministry of Culture was created in 1953, it enjoyed a near monopoly: It controlled higher education, the arts, the publishing industry, and radio and television, and it also supervised Glavlit. Over the next several years it was stripped of most of its responsibilities, and several agencies became responsible for various cultural services: (1) Gosteleradio, the State Committee for Television and Radio; (2) Goskino, the State Committee for Cinematography, which manages the film industry; and (3) Goskomizdat, the

State Committee for Publishing Houses, Printing, and the Book Trade. The functions of the Ministry of Culture fall into two categories. First, the ministry manages culture in the traditional sense of the word: painting, sculpture, and the performing arts. This latter category ranges from symphony orchestras and the opera to the circus and popular music groups. Second, the ministry manages cultural enlightenment work (see Figure 11.1). The ministry has an important educational function because it controls the training of young artists in the con- servatories and in the ballet and theater schools. The ministry also functions as a theater censor. Every theatrical production must be seen and approved by the ministry's representatives before public perfor- mances can be given.

Goskomizdat is not responsible for censorship. This state committee does, however, enjoy broad control over the printing industry, in addition to the publishing houses under its direct supervision. No ministry or other agency can operate a printing plant without the committee's approval, and all publishing houses are required to submit an annual plan of projected publications, which the committee must approve.

In addition to these governmental agencies, the unions of creative artists play a significant role in the management of culture. Six of these "creative unions" have been formed—for writers, composers, artists, cinematographers, journalists, and architects (Iampolskaia 1970). The unions are organized on a pattern that by now should be familiar. A national congress, which theoretically meets every four years, represents the entire profession. The congress elects an executive board (*pravlenie*) empowered to manage the union's affairs, but the board usually meets only once or twice a year. The real authority is a secretariat, which is formally elected by the executive board. The creative unions are subsidized by the state and seem to possess ample resources. They provide important services to their members. The writers' union, for example, can help a struggling young author get published, provided that the writing is ideologically acceptable. The union has its own publishing house, a newspaper (*Literaturnaia gazeta*), and the country's most prestigious literary journal (*Novy mir*). The writers' union can also provide grants, travel, and vacations in its own facilities. Established authors like Pasternak and Solzhenitsyn, who have been expelled from the union, have no hope of getting their work published in the USSR.

Some Western writers have regarded the creative unions primarily as control agencies that do the party's bidding. However, as already described, many bureaucratic organizations created by the party develop their own values and interests. The writers' union does not openly oppose party policy in cultural affairs, and in particular, it is not likely to ask for an end to literary censorship. But the union does serve its

220

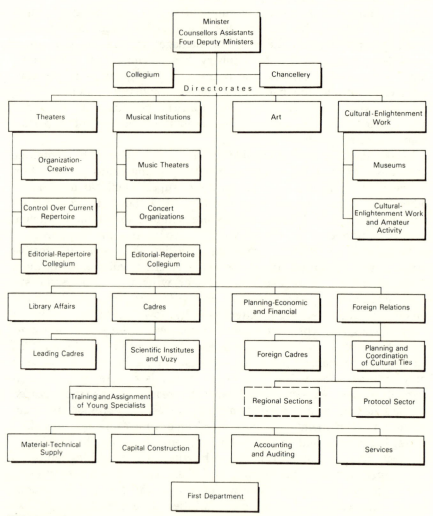

FIGURE 11.1
USSR Ministry of Culture

Reprinted with permission from Darrell P. Hammer, Inside the Ministry of Culture: Cultural Policy in the Soviet Union, in *Public Policy and Administration in the Soviet Union,* edited by Gordon B. Smith (New York: Praeger, 1980), pp. 53–78. © 1980 by the American Society for Public Administration.

members' material interests, and in this sense it is a representative organization, seeking a share of society's resources for the literary profession.

Boris Schwarz, in a careful study of the musical world, concluded that the composers' union "is the power behind all musical decisions of the Soviet Government." The union influences the award of Lenin Prizes in music, the repertoire of orchestras and opera companies, and, above all, the creative activity of young composers (Schwarz 1972: 398–399). Ideological conformity is demanded of composers, as it is of all artists. But, according to Schwarz, the union has a significant voice in determining what is acceptable and what is not: It is not simply a passive instrument of the party's will.

The Soviet trade unions are also dispensers of culture. The trade union organization manages most of the palaces of culture found in every Soviet city that provide leisure-time activities for Soviet workers. A typical palace of culture includes a theater, a library, and meeting rooms for clubs and other workers' organizations.

The activities of all these public organizations and government agencies are supervised by the Department of Culture of the Central Committee. The party (through party groups or primary party organizations) monitors the activities of all these organizations (Iampolskaia 1970: 34).

Socialist Realism

As culture is supposed to educate, it is thought to be a part of the ideological work of the party (Dorokhova 1980: 230). The function of culture is to develop the right kind of thinking in the population. A Soviet scholar put it this way: "Education, the sciences and culture are an important tool in the ideological education of the people, in the formation of a Communist consciousness. . . " (Shabailov 1974: 13). In keeping with this approach, all creative artists are supposed to conform to the ideal of socialist realism, the official doctrine for literature and art. Socialist realism is not easy to explain because it is not realism in the usual sense of the word; it is the application of ideological conformity to the world of art. According to socialist realism, the creative artist's task is to depict the world as the official doctrine sees it. This interpretation is based on the belief that future Communist society is somehow more real than the society of today. The present-day society, after all, is quite imperfect (even in the USSR) and still in a process of development.

The future Communist society has been compared to a building under construction: It is a noble edifice of grander design than anything now existing, but it is still unfinished. Socialist realism teaches that the artists or writers should depict the building in its ultimate glory. They should not show the scaffolding, the missing roof, or the debris around the construction site. Artistic works produced in the spirit of socialist realism should inspire people to work harder to bring this higher reality into being.

Another important principle of Soviet literature is *partiinost*—the principle that the arts should conform to the party line. *Dostupnost* (accessibility) is just as important: Culture must be understood by the mass audience, or it does not serve its ideological and educational function. Abstract art and modern music have a limited audience and are therefore disapproved of. Another important factor is the bureaucratization of culture. The writers' union and the similar institutions that manage art and music are under the control of older and more established figures who remain loyal to the traditions of the past and are prepared to use their administrative authority to preserve these traditions.

In culture as in other fields, the Brezhnev regime proved to be more tolerant than its predecessor without appearing to be so. The best known cultural events in the Brezhnev era were the trial of Siniavskii and Daniel (1966) and the expulsion of Solzhenitsyn from the USSR (1974). (Siniavskii and Daniel were two writers who had published abroad under pseudonyms and were tried and imprisoned under article 70.) These incidents hardly seem evidence of tolerance. Yet under Brezhnev, several writers whose works had been suppressed were quietly published again; among them were Anna Akhkmatova, Boris Pilniak, and Josip Mandelshtam. The Brezhnev period also saw the development of a major new school in Russian literature—the village writers such as Valentin Rasputin and Fedor Abramov. These writers concentrate on themes related to village life, but even this choice of a theme implies criticism of Soviet reality—of urbanization, forced social change, and the cult of technology. During the last weeks of the Brezhnev administration some signs suggested a tightening of cultural policy.

At a June 1983 Central Committee meeting devoted to ideological questions, Chernenko addressed the problems of culture. He implicitly criticized the village writers and explicitly chastised the Culture Department of the Central Committee, apparently, for being overly tolerant. Had Chernenko remained in power longer, he might have presided over a general crackdown on culture. Certainly his expressed attitude was quite orthodox: Since the regime pays the bills, it has a right to set the line in literature and in the other arts. In a speech to the writers' union, Chernenko put it this way:

> Our party and state create the conditions which allow talent to develop to the fullest, to be creative for the people. We absolutely reject petty

tutelage over the creative individual. Creativity is creativity precisely because it is free. . . .

However, creative freedom is not a privilege for the select few. The party is solicitous of talent, because it perceives something of great value to society. But no one and nothing can free the individual from the demands and the laws of society, which are binding on all. It is naive to think that one can blacken the moral and political foundations of our system, and still expect its blessing and its recognition. (*Pravda*, Sept. 26, 1984)

REFERENCES

Avis, George. 1983. Access to Higher Education in the Soviet Union. *Soviet Education in the 1980s*, edited by J. J. Tomiak. New York: St. Martin's Press, pp. 199–239.

Chernenko, K. 1984. Na uroven trebovanii razvitogo sotsializma. *Kommunist* 18: 3–21.

Cristostomo, Rosemarie. 1982. *The Demographic Dilemma of the Soviet Union.* U.S. Bureau of the Census, Center for International Research, Doc. no. 10. Washington, D.C.: Bureau of the Census.

Davis, Christopher, and Murray Feshbach. 1980. *Rising Infant Mortality in the U.S.S.R. in the 1970's.* U.S. Department of Commerce, Bureau of the Census, International Population Reports Series P-95, no. 74.

Dorokhova, G. A., I. L. Davitnidze, T. I. Kozyreva et al. 1980. *Sovetskoe administrativnoe pravo: upravlenie sotsialno-kulturnym stroitelstvom.* Moscow: Iuridicheskaia literatura.

Hammer, Darrell P. 1980. Inside the Ministry of Culture: Cultural Policy in the Soviet Union. In *Public Policy and Administration in the Soviet Union*, edited by Gordon B. Smith. New York: Praeger, pp. 53–78.

Iampolskaia, Ts. A., A. I. Schiglak, Iu. Ia. Lvovich et al. 1970. *Tvorcheskie soiuzy v SSSR.* Moscow: Iuridicheskaia literatura.

Inkeles, Alex, and Raymond Bauer. 1959. *The Soviet Citizen.* Cambridge: Harvard University Press.

Kaser, Michael. 1976. *Health Care in the Soviet Union and Eastern Europe.* Boulder, Colo.: Westview Press.

Kelley, D. R. 1972. Interest Groups in the USSR: The Impact of Political Sensitivity on Group Influence. *Journal of Politics* 34: 860–888.

Kerblay, Basile. 1983. *Modern Soviet Society*, translated by Rupert Sawyer. New York: Pantheon Books.

Lenin, V. I. 1918a. *State and Revolution.* In *Selected Works*, vol. 2, pt. 1. Moscow: Foreign Languages Publishing House, pp. 199–325.

———. 1918b. *The Immediate Tasks of the Soviet Government.* In *Selected Works*, vol. 2, pt. 1, pp. 448–491.

Litvinova, G. I., and B. Ts. Urlanis. 1982. Demograficheskaia politika Sovetskogo Soiuza. *Sovetskoe gosudarstvo i pravo* 3: 38–46.

McAuley, Alastair. 1979. *Economic Welfare in the Soviet Union: Poverty, Living Standards, and Inequality.* Madison: University of Wisconsin Press.

Madison, Bernice. 1968. *Social Welfare in the Soviet Union.* Stanford, CA: Stanford University Press.

Matthews, Mervyn. 1982. *Education in the Soviet Union: Politics and Institutions Since Stalin.* London: Allen & Unwin.

Morton, Henry W. 1983. Local Soviets and the Attempt to Rationalize the Delivery of Urban Services: The Case of Housing. In *Soviet Local Government and Politics,* edited by Everett M. Jacobs. London: Allen & Unwin, pp. 186–202.

Nechemais, Carol R. 1980. Welfare in the Soviet Union: Health Care, Housing, and Personal Consumption. In *Public Policy and Administration in the Soviet Union,* edited by Gordon B. Smith. New York: Praeger, pp. 172–206.

Osborn, Robert J. 1970. *Soviet Social Policies: Welfare, Equality, and Community.* Homewood, Ill.: Dorsey Press.

Pravda ob alkogolizme v SSSR. 1985. *Russkaia mysl,* Feb. 7.

Rimashevskaia, N., and S. Shatalin. 1977. Struktura lichnogo i obshchestvennogo potrebleniia v sotsialisticheskikh stranakh. *Voprosy ekonomiki* 12: 95–105.

Sakharov, A. D. 1974. *Sakharov Speaks.* New York: Random House.

Schroeder, Gertrude E., and Imogene Edwards. 1981. *Consumption in the USSR: An International Comparison.* Study prepared for the Joint Economic Committee of the U.S. Congress. Washington, D.C.: Government Printing Office.

Schwartz, J. J., and W. R. Keech. 1969. Group Influence and the Policy Process in the Soviet Union. In *Communist Studies and the Social Sciences,* edited by Frederic J. Fleron, Jr. Chicago: Rand McNally, pp. 298–317.

Schwarz, Boris. 1972. *Music and Musical Life in Soviet Russia 1917–1970.* New York: Norton.

Shabailov, V. I. 1974. *Upravlenie sotsialno-kulturnym stroitelstvom v soiuznoi respublike.* Minsk: Nauka i tekhnika.

Stewart, P. D. 1969. Soviet Interest Groups and the Policy Process: The Repeal of Production Education. *World Politics* 22 (October): 29–50.

Tatimov, M. B. 1978. *Razvitie narodonaseleniia i demograficheskaia politika.* Alma-Ata: Izdatelstvo Nauka Kazakhskoi SSR.

Treml, Vladimir G. 1982. *Alcohol in the USSR: A Statistical Study.* Duke Press Policy Studies. Durham, N.C.: Duke University Press.

USSR Council of Ministers Decree. Sept. 2, 1981. *Sobranie postanovlenii pravitelstva SSSR* 24, item 141.

USSR Supreme Soviet Decree on Guidelines for the Reform of General Educational and Vocational Schools. April 12, 1984. *Vedomosti verkhovnogo soveta SSSR* 16, item 237.

Voronov, K [pseudonym]. 1975. Demograficheskie problemy Rossii. *Grani* 98: 255–276.

Weber, Cynthia, and Ann Goodman. 1981. The Demographic Policy Debate in the USSR. *Population and Development Review* 7, no. 2: 279–295.

White, Stephen. 1979. *Political Culture and Soviet Politics.* New York: St. Martin's Press.

Zverev, A. G. 1970. *Natsionalnyi dokhod i finansy SSSR.* 2d ed. Moscow: Izdatelstvo Finansy.

12
Bureaucratic Pluralism

The development of a professional bureaucracy certainly violates Lenin's vision of a simplified administrative system that could be managed by any literate person. Today, Soviet social theory frankly admits that the administrative system will survive even after the state has withered away. On this point no less an authority than Viktor Afanasyev, chief editor of *Pravda*, has said that the state will disappear in the future classless society, but administrative relations will survive. In contrast to Lenin, Afanasyev has argued that under socialism the problems of administration become much more complicated. The people, therefore, have no choice but to set up a system of organizations to control the administration. However, in those organizations control by the people will be indirect; "direct control is the job of a large group of professional managers" (Afanasyev 1971: 109, 120, 142).

Afanasyev's argument can be summed up in the following way: Administration will still be needed even after the state has withered away; administration requires control, and control requires organization, including a large staff of professional managers. Thus administration and the organizations that control administration will not wither away in the higher phase of socialism. F. M. Burlatskii put it even more directly:

> Some people have the impression that the withering of the state must lead to the withering of all administration. Here life in a Communist society is imagined as a kind of automatic mechanism, set once and for all and put into action, and therefore not requiring any additional adjustment or regulation. This is a primitive idea, which takes no account of the real needs of the future society. It can hardly be doubted, for example, that Communism will need a planned economy and the activity of production. The development of a socialist society demonstrates the growth in importance of the planning principle. . . . *This means that under Communism, administration will survive.* (Emphasis added.) (1970: 411)

In the preceding chapters, the political institutions and the political culture of Soviet society were discussed, as were particular problems of policymaking. In this chapter, we will take a more theoretical approach to the Soviet system, paying particular attention to the role of the bureaucracy in the decisionmaking process. This role must not be exaggerated. Although ultimately the party leadership in the Politburo makes decisions about Soviet policy, the bureaucracy plays a crucial role in the process: It provides information and advice to the decisionmakers, and it carries out policy after it is made. (These two points will be discussed later in the chapter.) Finally, it may sometimes formulate policy by default, as will now be discussed.

In the classic model of bureaucracy, the government makes policy and the bureaucracy carries it out: By this division, the government is a rule-making body, and a bureaucracy is a rule-implementing organization. In practice, the relationship is not quite so simple. The government may fail to formulate a policy for several reasons: The members of the government are unable to agree on a policy, or an issue may be regarded as too trivial for their attention. Existing policy statements may be contradictory so that the bureaucracy must choose which rule to implement. The bureaucracy may interpret a rule in a manner different from that which the government intended (the phenomenon called authority leakage).

Bureaucracy was defined in Chapter 1 as a large professional organization that provides goods or services to a group of clients. These benefits are not sold in the marketplace but are distributed in a process of bureaucratic allocation. The role of government in this process is to determine what the bureaucracy will produce, to lay down the rules for allocation among clients, and to provide the resources to cover the costs of the bureaucracy's operations. Bureaucracies ordinarily do not have to compete for clients. The Soviet health service, for example, offers its services free of charge, so it does not have to advertise for patients. However, bureaucracies do have to compete for resources.

The government is served by many different bureaucratic organizations, which produce different benefits and serve different groups of clients. The resources of the government include rubles, paid out to bureaucratic organizations in accordance with the government's budget. However, the resources are not only money. In the Soviet planning system, as described in Chapter 10, Gosplan allocates raw materials among various sectors of the economy. The government also is directly responsible for allocating human resources, at least at the entry level. Graduates from vuzes are assigned to different jobs on the basis of quotas determined by Gosplan. In fact, some competition develops among organizations for the young doctors, engineers, and other specialists coming out of the higher education system.

TOTALITARIANISM VERSUS PLURALISM

In recent years, analysis of the Soviet political system has followed two schools of thought. One group of scholars has attempted to update the totalitarian theory by careful reexamination of the original premises of the model. The revised version, which generally avoids the word totalitarian, has abandoned some of the concepts of the model. Less emphasis is given to terror and usually less to ideology. Scholars of this school generally agree that the society is dominated by a small ruling group so that the political structure is an oligarchy rather than a dictatorship. However, the system is still viewed as highly centralized and despotic. The essential characteristics of the political system are command and control. The society is seen as hierarchical in structure, with political power tightly concentrated at the top level. This system can be called the directed society model (Hough and Fainsod 1979: 523).

The second school of thought emphasizes conflict and disagreement over policy issues and the influence of various groups in the policymaking process. This group can be called the pluralist school, although many Western scholars who agree with the approach reject the term. The pluralist school does not argue that the Soviet system is a liberal democratic society or that it shares the characteristics of Western pluralism. Its approach differs from the directed society model because it emphasizes organizational conflict and looks on the policymaking process as much more complex and as involving more participants and more diverse interests. The approach is pluralist in the sense that power is seen as divided among conflicting organizations, with no one group exercising supreme and unlimited authority.

Both the directed society school and the pluralists regard the Soviet system as highly bureaucratic, but they draw different conclusions from this fact. In the directed society model, the bureaucracy is a weapon in the hands of the one-party regime. Every bureaucratic organization, according to this model, is penetrated and dominated by the Communist party and serves the party's interests. On the other hand, the pluralist approach generally looks on the bureaucracy as a constraint on the regime. This school would argue that as the system becomes more bureaucratized, the regime will find that it has fewer options in the decisionmaking process.

PLURALIST APPROACH

No standard pluralist text has been written that is comparable with the classic work of C. J. Friedrich and Z. K. Brzezinski (1965) on totalitarianism. The major works that employ a pluralist approach in the study of the Soviet political system (Skilling and Griffiths 1971; Meissner and Brunner 1975) are collections of case studies that examine the influence of specific groups in the policy process. For this reason, several pluralist approaches have been used rather than one pluralist model. The approaches have been given different names: institutional pluralism (J. F. Hough), pluralism of elites (H. G. Skilling), centralized pluralism (Alec Nove), or bureaucratic pluralism (D. P. Hammer). All these approaches have a common framework but differ in important ways.

The most systematic model of pluralism, developed by British economist Alec Nove, focuses on the process of resource allocation and on the role that the ministries play in this process. Nove's model of centralized pluralism applies to both economic and political decisionmaking. In theory, Gosplan makes decisions about priorities and the economic ministries carry them out, but in practice the system does not quite work this way. The planners simply do not have the information-processing capacity to make all the required decisions. So the theory is disregarded, and many decisions devolve upon lower-level organizations or on local authorities, who have access to information.

In centralized pluralism the ministries are not just servants of the central planners. In fact, the ministries become interest groups that make a variety of demands on the center. Some demands are the result of bureaucratic empire building, but Gosplan is not always able to separate the real needs of the ministries from other demands. "Ministerial empires, and upward pressures originating with them, are facts of economic and political life, and it is this which could be called 'centralized pluralism.'" (Nove 1977: 63). Thus the centralized economy becomes divided into a number of quasi-autonomous units, each of which has interests, needs, and demands of its own.

Nove commented that the information-processing capacity of the system is a constraint on the decisionmakers. As shown throughout this study, the Soviet regime is engaged in a constant effort to obtain information, and a main function of the party apparatus is providing it. Yet the regime never has all the information that it needs, limiting its capacity to manage the political system.

The autocracy also is limited in its ability to oversee the execution of policy decisions. George Kennan, writing in 1945 from the U.S. Embassy in Moscow, concluded that even Stalin did not and could not exercise continuous control over the Soviet government. Stalin was a dictator; however, Kennan went on, in many matters calling for governmental decision Stalin could not even be consulted. Kennan concluded that Stalin "is evidently not in a position to follow through with the detailed execution of the orders he gives" (1968: 481). What happened in those areas of policymaking in which Stalin could not be consulted? We have to conclude that in these instances the responsible bureaucracy was left on its own, not necessarily to make new policy, but probably to carry on in a routine way the established policies.

The pioneering work in the study of Soviet interest groups was done by H. Gordon Skilling (1966, 1971a). His purpose was to develop a set of tentative hypotheses and not to apply some Western version of interest group theory to the USSR. Skilling's work has generated a number of studies of policy formation, some of which we have already examined. By his definition political interest groups in the USSR are not formal organizations but usually "loose groupings of like-minded" individuals. Such "nonassociational groups" are important in the USSR because organized groups (Skilling gave the Writers' Union as an example) do not represent the interests of their members. In fact Skilling wrote: "Political groups in the Soviet Union are seldom organized, and if organized, are dominated by functionaries who are usually not elected and not responsive to the wishes of their constituents" (1971b: 382). This concept of interest group behavior is quite different from Nove's centralized pluralism. For Skilling, the important groups are those based on special interests, which lack permanent organization. Interest groups, almost by definition, are seen as oppositional elements within the political system.

Like Skilling, J. F. Hough perceived the Soviet system as somewhere between totalitarianism and classical pluralism—but as moving slowly and tentatively toward the latter form. Different interests coexist, and the political process can be understood as the "accommodation of demands of some groups," usually at the expense of others. The function of the political leadership is to serve as "brokers" in this process of accommodation (Hough 1977: 23).

The problem with the pluralist approach is political scientists do not agree on what the principal interest groups are. Skilling did not consider bureaucratic organizations as true interest groups because he assumed that they represent only the interests of the ruling group within the organization. On the other hand, Hough argued that bureaucratic organizations may represent the interests of a larger constituency, serving as a communications channel for the articulation of interests (1977: 105–106). In any case, some instances must arise where the interests of the bureaucratic leadership correspond to the interests of the group that the bureaucracy supervises Later in this chapter we give an example of the Writers' Union acting in the interests of the writers.

In the case studies, the influential interest groups are coalitions of representatives from different organizations. In his study of the education issue P. D. Stewart (1969) found that sometimes groupings were formed within a single bureaucratic organization and sometimes they cut across organizational lines. John Löwenhardt (1981: 25) called these groups policy coalitions. Most writers of the pluralist school assume, along with Skilling, that such policy coalitions are more influential than bureaucratic organizations. This assumption may be a product of the case study method where influence is measured in terms of the ability to affect one particular policy outcome. Over the long term and measured across a series of policy issues, informal groups might appear to be much less influential.

Some evidence indicates that informal groupings exist within the party apparatus, although diligent searching is needed to find them. J. Valenta has published a detailed analysis of the 1968 decision to intervene in Czechoslovakia that was explicitly based on a bureaucratic politics model. He interpreted the decision as the outcome of a tug of war among various bureaucratic organizations, each with its own idea of where the national interest lay. Valenta concluded that the International Department of the Central Committee tended to oppose intervention because it would complicate the department's mission. On the other hand, the Ukrainian party apparatus favored intervention because it perceived the "Prague spring" as a more immediate threat, especially to the Western regions of the republic. Thus various bureaucratic interests had different perceptions of the threat from Czechoslovakia. According to Valenta's account (1979), the bureaucracies were engaged in complex maneuvering designed to arrive at a decision beneficial to their own interest and perhaps the interest of their constituencies.

General agreement exists that associational interest groups do not play a significant role in the policy process, even though a large number of membership associations have been formed in the USSR. The best-known of these are the trade unions and unions of creative intellectuals already discussed. More specialized organizations include the Society of the Blind, the All-Russian Theater Society, and the Soviet Chess Federation. Some organizations attract a large voluntary membership. For example, the Znanie Society has 2.5 million enrolled members (Iampolskaia 1976: 87). The All-Russian Society for the Preservation of Cultural Monuments is even larger and lobbies openly for the restoration of old buildings. All these organizations may have some influence on the course of government policy in their special area of interest.

ARGUMENT AGAINST PLURALISM

The most frequent objection to the pluralist approach is that it represents a naive attempt to apply Western (mainly U.S.) interest group theory to a system where it is not appropriate (Odom 1976: 544; Janos 1970: 437; Ploss 1973: 35). Skilling explicitly denied that he was applying this Western theory, and most proponents of the pluralist approach would also deny it. Some of the discussion and controversy over the pluralist approach is in fact a problem in semantics: The assertion that pluralist elements are present in the Soviet system is sometimes equated with the argument that the system is becoming more liberal or even democratic. Since Western scholars are unwilling to attribute any democratic qualities to the system, there is a general reluctance to use the term pluralism.

Most of the critics of the pluralist approach would accept a bureaucratic model of the political process. G. Brunner (1977: 159), for example, explicitly rejects the concept of pluralism, and yet he acknowledges that group interests may well develop in connection with bureaucratically organized institutions. Similarly, W. E. Odom (1976: 545) suggested that a bureaucratic model would be better than the group concept in explaining the process. R. K. Furtak (1974: 785) objected to the word interest group in the Soviet context, although he recognized that certain organizations, in trying to influence decisionmaking, may exercise a function equivalent to that of an interest group.

The most important objection to the pluralist approach is that it overlooks an axiom in the Soviet system: that the society is dominated by the Communist party and that no other organization could significantly influence policymaking against the will of the party (Unger 1974: 62–63). Odom insisted that the key members of any organization are party agents first and organization members second and that these key members can always be counted on to put the party's interest above the interest of the organization. He would object to "identifying the bureaucracies as interest groups because with a large portion of party members in the upper reaches of the key bureaucracies, the distinction between the party and the bureaucracy tends to become academic" (Odom 1976: 550).

The political role of the party is thus the central issue between the directed society model and the pluralist approach. All the versions of the directed society model assume that a single, authoritarian party completely dominates the bureaucracy and, through it, the total society. To the pluralists, the party in some sense shares power with other organizations. The party is no longer committed to the transformation of society according to the precepts of a revolutionary ideology. Not all the pluralists would agree with Hough that there is no single dominating interest and that the function of political leadership is to broker diverse and conflicting interests. But all the pluralists seem to agree with the premise that some interests are independent of the party.

CONFLICTS OF INTEREST

Not only do conflicts of interest occur within the Soviet bureaucratic system, but Soviet writers on administration and social theory show increasing acceptance of this fact. They frequently refer to departmentalism (*vedomstvennost*) and localism (*mestnichestvo*), or putting the interests of one's agency or region ahead of the general interest. Brezhnev (8: 474) acknowledged this fact, while calling on the center to make the basic decisions and to resist both departmental and local tendencies. At the same time Brezhnev accepted Nove's point: The center cannot decide everything; many questions can only be resolved at the operating level.

A. P. Butenko (1982) acknowledged that the productive capacity of the country is not yet sufficient to allow complete satisfaction of all individual needs. Society must set some priorities, using some of its resources for investment and returning the rest to individuals, according to the famous principle "From each according to his ability, to each according to his work." Inevitably this system of resource allocation leads to a conflict between personal and social interests. Of course, Butenko wrote, social interests are simply the aggregate of all individual interests, but this fact does not eliminate the conflict. Butenko concluded that the political stability of the system depends on society's ability to resolve these conflicts.

Butenko's analysis is one of the most interesting to come from a Soviet writer. He could, however, have said much more. In the first place, investment and consumption are not the only claimants. The military, which he did not mention, also receives some of society's resources. Furthermore, setting aside funds for investment is only the beginning of a long and complex process in which the ministries compete for their share of funds. The ministries, too, represent conflicting interests.

The interests include not only those of the individual and of society as a whole, discussed by Butenko, but also those of class, social group, collectives, and nationalities. Trade unions, cooperatives, and cultural societies may also possess interests. The political leadership has the task of integrating the general interest with the interest of various groups or organizations. B. M. Lazarev classified interests by the institution or group they represented: (1) the state, in general, (2) republics or lower administrative units, (3) particular branches of the economy, (4) particular economic organizations or enterprises, and (5) individuals. "In practice we frequently observe contradictions of interests of various branches of the economy, between the interests of each branch of the economy and general interests, between the general interests of the state and local interests" (Lazarev 1971: 86).

Other Soviet writers have argued that under socialism the role of interests is not diminished but should be expected to increase (Vishnevskii 1967: 181; Tikhomirov 1972: 53). In the past, Soviet social theory assumed a unity of interests (*edinstvo interesov*) or a community of interests (*obshchnost interesov*). More recently, theorists such as Butenko write about the reconciliation of interests (*sochetanie interesov*). Reconciliation is the task of the government: Brezhnev once acknowledged that the function of the party is to combine or coordinate the interests of diverse groups (3: 274).

PARTY AND BUREAUCRACY

Are the ministries, as Nove contended, interest groups in the Soviet Union? Or was Odom correct in his statement that the bureaucracy and the Communist party are so fused that the difference between them is academic? Most writers of the pluralist school would say that the ministries are not really interest groups. By concentrating on policy coalitions and other groupings of this type, the pluralist writers have tended to treat interest group activity as fragmented and episodic. However, if an interest group is defined as any organization that tries to influence policymaking, then the ministries certainly qualify. In fact Nove's approach, in which established organizations become interest groups in the course of carrying out their bureaucratic functions, is more consistent with contemporary group theory.

Even in Western and democratic systems, groups are rarely organized for the specific purpose of articulating interests. Mancur Olson has pointed out that the most powerful interest groups in the United States were generally created for some other purpose. Their interest-articulation or lobbying activity developed as a byproduct of the original organization (Olson 1965). The same argument can be made in the Soviet case. The bureaucratic organizations that manage Soviet society were not created for the purpose of representing interests. Inevitably, however, these bureaucracies have developed their own attitudes, values, and procedures. The bureaucracy's own perception of its interest does not necessarily conform to the views of the party leadership. No doubt the bureaucracy perceives no conflict between its interest and its perception of the national interest. Bureaucracies rarely do. They do appear to develop specific interests of their own and gradually acquire experience in articulating these interests. Such a development is quite consistent with Olson's analysis.

The leading officials in most bureaucratic organizations are also members of the Communist party. This fact should not prevent them from pressing their own views. Furthermore, the perceived identity of interest between the party and a bureaucratic organization does not mean that no possible conflict of interest can arise between the bureaucracy and the party apparatus. On the contrary, such a conflict of interest must be a continuing feature of Soviet political life.

In addition to its other functions, the apparatus is a monitoring agency, whose job is to report on the activities of an operating bureaucracy. A monitoring agency has three characteristics: (1) It is administratively separate and has a different personnel structure, (2) its basic task is reporting, though it may have other communications functions (e.g., transmitting orders down the chain of command), and (3) at its top level it is integrated into some major bureaucracy or political structure (Downs 1967: 148). The central apparatus of the Communist Party of the Soviet Union (CPSU) conforms to this description. The party apparatus is integrated into the top-level political leadership in the sense that the central secretariat (a part of the leadership) heads the apparatus.

The apparatus of the party has access to a constant flow of information about the activities of each ministry. Much of the information originates in the primary party organizations within the ministry itself. This flow of information is consistent with the apparatus's function as a monitoring agency. A clear administrative separation, as well as a differentiation of functions, divides the party apparatus and ministerial bureaucracy. Because of the difference in functions, the bureaucracy cannot be regarded as virtually identical with the party.

A fundamental conflict of interest is inherent between the party apparatus as a monitoring agency and the operating agencies. This conflict is not the outcome of any presumed ideological antagonism between the bureaucracy and the party apparatus. It is sometimes suggested that the officials who staff the bureaucracies are better educated, less ideological, and more pragmatic in their outlook than the apparatchiks. However, as evinced in our examination of the party, the officials who serve in the apparatus have had the same technical training and often the same early career experience as those who staff the bureaucracies.

The conflict of interest is a direct result of the different functions performed by the apparatus and the bureaucracies and it will not diminish if more pragmatic or better educated officials are recruited into the apparatus. Like all bureaucracies, the party apparatus has an instinct for survival. It therefore has a vested interest in uncovering problems within the operating bureaucracy, just as the bureaucracy has an interest in seeing such problems kept to a minimum. The conflict between the apparatus and the bureaucracies is not a struggle for power. The leading officials of the bureaucracies are committed to the prevailing political system, including the system of party monitoring, and to supporting the existing regime. They have no wish for fundamental political change, so they will not attack the system of one-party rule.

POLICY PROCESS

Many policy decisions are made by committees representing different interests. The ministry collegium is just one example of an advisory committee in which interested groups or organizations are formally consulted. Within these committees, bureaucratic officials often have an advantage because they have the knowledge and the access to information. Ellen Jones (1984: 187) studied the patterns of committee decisionmaking and found that there was a "broad representation of institutional interests." However, she also concluded that the procedures used by committees tended to maximize the influence of fulltime bureaucratic officials.

Bureaucratic politics is a struggle for resources. Every bureaucratic organization in the USSR finds itself in such a struggle to acquire personnel, equipment, and authority. Even when the organization honestly strives to carry out its functions in the optimal way, there is room for disagreement over resource allocation. The political leadership must make its decisions in the face of competing claims from various organizations and on the basis of incomplete and imperfect information. The function of the party apparatus (and other monitoring agencies) is to overcome the problem of imperfect information, but the apparatus must be given the means to carry out that function, which creates additional claims on the resources available to the regime.

The functions that a bureaucratic organization carries out are valuable, perhaps even indispensable, to the regime. Consequently the leadership cannot turn a deaf ear to the demand for resources. The claims of informal or nonassociational interest groups can sometimes just be ignored. But the regime needs to listen to and try to accommodate the claims of bureaucratic interests. The political leadership might try a direct attack on a recalcitrant or unresponsive bureaucracy through structural reorganization or the radical reassignment of functions. That approach apparently was used by the Khrushchev regime in dealing with the problems of industrial management in 1957 or the regional party apparatus in 1962. But in the long run that strategy failed, and the lesson cannot have been lost on Khrushchev's successors. Much of the criticism of Khrushchev seems to be a thinly disguised charge that he did not give due attention to bureaucratic interests in making policy decisions.

Bureaucratic interests can influence the making and implementation of policy in at least three ways: policy consultation, policy initiation, and policy implementation.

Policy Consultation. The process of policy consultation begins when the political leadership considers changes in policy or the formulation of new policy. Organizations knowledgeable about a subject can make recommendations on specific policy issues, getting them before the leadership and perhaps before the public. The process occurs in two forums: Most of the consultation takes place in secret, without open public discussion of the issues, but on some issues discussion takes place in public sources.

Consultation, although it is a form of lobbying, is not necessarily the most powerful technique available to a bureaucratic organization. Furthermore when using that technique the organization, in pressing its own case, may have to compete with others that have ideas of their own. On many issues, the regime deliberately consults with as wide a circle of people and interests as possible to receive recommendations from outside the closed circle of the bureaucracy. The bureaucracy thus may have to compete with policy coalitions on certain issues.

Expert opinion is always available within the bureaucracy, but the political leadership may want to hear the views of an impartial expert. T. Kirstein pointed out that the system of outside consultation is highly institutionalized in the Soviet policymaking process. Outside experts are frequently consulted but usually secretly, both by the party apparatus and by the government. In her view this institutionalized process of outside consultation is a substitute—but not a perfect one—for the unhampered articulation of group interests which takes place in Western states (Kirstein 1975: 75). Afanasyev also noted the importance of getting an independent judgment on important issues (1975: 162).

Policy Initiation. In the consultative process, the bureaucracy is reacting to proposals put forward by the political leadership for discussion and decision. By using available channels of information, a bureaucratic organization may also take the initiative and raise issues of its own. If the Soviet political process (including the articulation of interests) is viewed as continuous, then this information flow may be just as important to a bureaucracy as consultation.

Policy initiation by the bureaucracies does not occur on the big issues of Soviet politics in which the political leadership seems to enjoy a monopoly on making the first move. But on many issues highly important to the bureaucracy, the initiative may come from below. For example, for some time the Writers' Union had been seeking to increase the income of its members. The writers had two complaints against the government: New works by Soviet writers appeared in editions that were too small, and the royalty rate was too low. These issues seem to have been the subject of continuous discussion between the union and the government, without getting into the press. In 1979, the government went a long way toward satisfying the writers' demands: It raised the royalty rate by an average of 10 percent (which increased the cost of publication), and it ordered a review of the process by which publishers decided how large an edition to print (RSFSR Council of Ministers Decree, May 8, 1979).

Policy Implementation. Policy, as discussed and decided upon, may not be the same thing as policy carried out. A characteristic that distinguishes bureaucratic interests from other interest groups is that a bureaucracy not only makes recommendations but has to carry out policy. It thus has an opportunity to determine policy output as well as input.

Authority leakage has many causes, and it is not always the result of a deliberate effort by a bureaucracy to thwart the will of the government. Nove pointed out that Gosplan has no choice but to delegate some responsibility downward, so that the ministries and enterprises are left with the task of making certain decisions without close supervision. Delegation of responsibility applies to noneconomic decisionmaking as well.

Soviet writers are quite aware of the problems of information flow within bureaucracies. Afanasev (1975: 138) pointed out that as information flows up the hierarchy, not only does the information increase in quantity but many opportunities arise for the distortion (*iskazhenie*) of information. The same situation is true for orders and policy decisions as they flow downward in the bureaucratic hierarchy.

Even when authority is not deliberately delegated, subordinate agencies within any bureaucratic structure must have some discretion in translating policy, made at a higher level, into action. In some cases, policy may be misunderstood or priorities unclear, and subordinate officials use their own judgment to interpret the intentions of higher authority. A bureaucratic agency may pursue its own course of action in the sincere belief that it is acting in accord with the wishes of the political leadership. So authority leakage may just be the result of inadequate information flow.

In any complex organization, the leakage of authority (intentional or not) tends to be cumulative. The regime makes a policy pronouncement, usually in general terms, and the operating head of the bureaucratic organization must translate it into specific instructions. As these instructions filter down the bureaucratic hierarchy, more specific and more detailed orders may be issued, but at each step officials of the bureaucracy have an opportunity to inject their own interpretation.

The opportunity for authority leakage is probably increased within the Soviet bureaucracy because of the nature of the party-state relationship. Many Politburo decisions are transmitted orally to the government, usually through the central party apparatus, and no written record exists of precisely what the decision was or when it was transmitted. Unless the apparatus officials conduct a deliberate follow-up, this method of transmitting orders creates opportunities for authority leakage.

CONCLUSION

The development of bureaucratic pluralism has not changed the authoritarian character of the political system (Perlmutter 1981: 69). The bureaucracies that manage the system are not opposition groups, even though they may try to change or otherwise influence government policy.

The articulation of interests appears to be an integral part of bureaucratic politics in the Soviet Union. Of course not all interests are bureaucratic, but those that the regime seems most anxious to accommodate certainly fall into this category. The model of bureaucratic pluralism is not really an interest group theory. The model is based on the fact of a plurality of bureaucracies and not a plurality of social interests.

Bureaucratic politics, it has been suggested, is not a struggle for power but a struggle for resources. This kind of politics is not episodic but continuous. Every bureaucratic organization must reconcile itself to the reality that sometimes it will win, sometimes it will lose, and more often it will compromise. The Soviet leadership is faced with its own problems in coping with bureaucratic politics. The leadership has the recurring problem of deciding about the allocation of resources in the face of conflicting claims and incomplete information. The regime's effort to control the bureaucracies through the mechanism of the party apparatus has not been entirely successful.

Within the Soviet system the bureaucratic character of organizations gives them power and influence in the process of making and carrying out policy. Policy coalitions can try to influence policy, but they appear to concentrate on a single policy issue and they do not survive for long. Bureaucratic organizations and bureaucratic interests, on the other hand, are permanent features of the political landscape in Moscow.

REFERENCES

Afanasyev, V. G. 1971. *The Scientific Management of Society*, translated by L. Ilitskaya. Moscow: Progress.

———— [Afanasev, V. G.]. 1975. *Sotsialnaia informatsiia i upravlenie obshchestvom.* Moscow: Politizdat.

Brezhnev, L. I. 1970–1981. *Leninskim kursom.* 8 vols. Moscow: Politicheskaia literatura.

Brown, A. H. 1983. Pluralism, Power and the Soviet Political System: A Comparative Perspective. In *Pluralism in the Soviet Union. Essays in Honour of H. Gordon Skilling,* edited by Susan Gross Solomon. New York: St. Martin's Press, pp. 61–107.

Brunner, G. 1977. *Politische Soziologie der UdSSR,* vol. 2. Wiesbaden: Akademische Verlagsgesellschaft.

Burlatskii, F. M. 1970. *Lenin, gosudarstvo, politika.* Moscow: Nauka.

Butenko, A. P. 1982. Protivorechiia razvitiia sotsializma kak obshchestvennogo stroia. *Voprosy filosofii* 10: 16–29.

Downs, A. 1967. *Inside Bureaucracy.* Boston: Little, Brown.

Friedrich, C. J., and Z. K. Brzezinski. 1965. *Totalitarian Dictatorship and Autocracy.* 2d ed. New York: Praeger.

Furtak, R. K. 1974. Interessenpluralismus in den politischen Systemen Osteuropas. *Osteuropa* 24, no. 11-12 (December): 779–792.

Hammer, Darrell P. 1974. *USSR: The Politics of Oligarchy.* New York: Praeger/ HRW.

Hough, J. F. 1977. *The Soviet Union and Social Science Theory.* Cambridge: Harvard University Press.

Hough, J. F., and M. Fainsod. 1979. *How the Soviet Union Is Governed.* Cambridge: Harvard University Press.

Iampolskaia, Ts. A., ed. 1976. *Dobrovolnye obshchestva pri sotsializme.* Moscow: Nauka.

Janos, A. C. 1970. Group Politics in Communist Society: A Second Look at the Pluralistic Model. In *Authoritarian Politics in Modern Society: The Dynamics of Established One-Party Systems,* edited by S. P. Huntington and C. H. Moore. New York: Basic Books, pp. 437–450.

Jones, Ellen. 1984. Committee Decision Making in the Soviet Union. *World Politics* 34: 165–188.

Kennan, George F. 1968. Excerpts from a Draft Letter Written at Some Time During the First Months of 1945. *Slavic Review* 27: 481.

Kirstein, T. 1975. Die Konsultation "Aussenstehender" durch die politischen Entscheidungsgremien in der Sowjetunion. In *Gruppeninteressen und Entscheidungsprozess in der Sowjetunion,* edited by Boris Meissner and Georg Brunner. Koln: Verlag Wissenschaft u. Politik, pp. 61–78.

Lazarev, B. M. 1971. Sotsialnye interesy i kompetentsiia organov upravleniia. *Sovetskoe gosudarstvo i pravo* 10: 86–94.

Lewytzkyj, B. 1978. Grundzuge des sowjetischen bürokratischen Herrschaftsmodells. *Osteuropa* 28 (September): 761–779.

Löwenhardt, John. 1981. *Decision Making in Soviet Politics.* New York: St. Martin's Press.

Meissner, B. 1975. Der Entscheidungsprozess in der Kreml-Führung unter Stalin und seinen Nachfolgern und die Rolle der Parteibürakratie. In *Gruppeninteressen und Entscheidungsprozess in der Sowjetunion,* pp. 21–60.

Meissner, B., and Georg Brunner. 1975. Gruppeninteressen und Entscheidungsprozess in der Sowjetunion. Koln: Verlag Wissenschaft u. Politik.

Nove, Alec. 1977. *The Soviet Economic System.* London: Allen & Unwin.

Odom, W. E. 1976. A Dissenting View on the Group Approach to Soviet Politics.
World Politics 28: 542–567.

Olson, Mancur. 1965. *The Logic of Collective Action: Public Goods and the Theory
of Groups.* Cambridge: Harvard University Press.

Perlmutter, Amos. 1981. *Modern Authoritarianism.* New Haven, Conn.: Yale
University Press.

Ploss, S. 1973. New Politics in Russia? *Survey* 19: 23–35.

RSFSR Council of Ministers Decree, May 8, 1979. On Further Improvements
in the Conditions of Payment for the Creative Work of Soviet Writers. *Sobranie
postanovlenii pravitelstva RSFSR,* no. 14, item 90.

Skilling, H. G. 1966. Interest Groups and Communist Politics. *World Politics* 18
(April): 435–451.

———. 1971a. Interest Groups and Communist Politics: An Introduction. In
Interest Groups in Soviet Politics, edited by H. G. Skilling and F. Griffiths.
Princeton, N.J.: Princeton University Press, pp. 3–18.

———. 1971b. Group Conflict in Soviet Politics: Some Conclusions. In *Interest
Groups in Soviet Politics,* pp. 379–416.

———. 1983. Interest Groups and Communist Politics Revisited. *World Politics*
34: 1–27.

Skilling, H. G., and F. Griffiths. 1971. *Interest Groups in Soviet Politics.* Princeton,
N.J.: Princeton University Press.

Stewart, P. D. 1969. Soviet Interest Groups and the Policy Process: The Repeal
of Production Education. *World Politics* 22 (October): 29–50.

Tikhomirov, Iu. A. 1972. *Upravlencheskoe reshenie.* Moscow: Nauka.

Unger, A. L. 1974. *The Totalitarian Party.* Cambridge: Cambridge University
Press.

Valenta, J. 1979. The Bureaucratic Politics Paradigm and the Soviet Invasion of
Czechoslovakia. *Political Science Quarterly* 94: 55–76.

Vishnevskii, S. S. 1967. Interesy i upravlenie obshchestvennymi protessami. In
Nauchnoe upravlenie obshchestvom, edited by V. G. Afanasev. Moscow: Mysl,
vypusk 1, pp. 173–217.

Afterword:
The 27th Party Congress

The 27th Congress of the CPSU, which was held from February 25 to March 6, 1986, produced no surprises. The congress was a media event, staged to provide a ceremonial setting for the Gorbachev regime to publicize its program. The most important policies discussed at the congress had been announced three months earlier, when the press published the new party program, the revised Party Statute, and the guidelines for the five-year plan. The changes in the national party leadership that were announced at the end of the congress continued the process of consolidation of power that was discussed in Chapter 8.

Acceleration of the social and economic development of the country was the theme of the Gorbachev program, tirelessly repeated during the congress. This slogan was widely understood as a promise to "get the country going again" and thus as a criticism of the Brezhnev regime. Indeed, in the speech that opened the congress, Gorbachev attacked the inertia and bureaucratism of the preceding era, without mentioning Brezhnev by name. According to Gorbachev, that period was one in which a "strange psychology" gripped the party, a belief that matters could be improved without actually changing anything (*Pravda*, Feb. 26, 1986). But Gorbachev was quite vague about his own proposals for reform, even while calling for "radical changes" in the economy.

The new program introduces no significant changes in the official Marxist-Leninist ideology. Like the old party program, it describes the USSR as a socialist country making a transition to communism. The old program, a product of the Khrushchev era, promised that, in the main, communism would be achieved by 1980 and that the "present generation of Soviet citizens" would live under communism (Triska 1962: 70–71, 129). The new program is much less optimistic. It admits

241

that there had been "unfavorable tendencies" in the 1970s and early 1980s that had prevented the achievement of the Khrushchev promises. (This formula for criticizing Brezhnev was another ritualistic phrase at the congress.) The new program gives no timetable for reaching the Communist stage of development and provides no details on what communism would be like. On the contrary, we read in the program that "it is not the task of the CPSU to anticipate in detail the features of full communism" (*Pravda*, March 7, 1986).

The most significant political developments took place prior to the congress, which merely ratified decisions that had already been made. The most important development was the emergence of Egor Ligachev as the party's second-ranking secretary. Ligachev, whose earlier career was described briefly in Chapter 8, had been put in charge of cadres by Andropov; he then rose rapidly to become a party secretary and a full member of the Politburo. His activities in 1985 indicate that he had acquired general responsibility for internal party affairs and was also supervising ideology (Ligachev 1985a, 1985b). Ligachev thus appears to have assumed the position once held by M. A. Suslov. Like Suslov, Ligachev is not a likely candidate for the succession to the post of general secretary (he is ten years older than Gorbachev). Unlike Suslov, Ligachev worked within the regional apparatus for a long period of time, waiting for promotion. He was first secretary in Tomsk, in Siberia, for eighteen years and knows that his career was held back by Brezhnev's policy of "stability" in cadres. So although Ligachev seems to be a spokesman for conservative interests within the leadership, it is not surprising that he criticizes Brezhnev's cadres policy, charging that it led to "immobility" (*nepodvizhnost*) in the party (*Pravda*, Feb. 28, 1986).

A second significant political change was the dismissal of Viktor Grishin as first secretary for the city of Moscow (*Pravda*, Dec. 25, 1985). Grishin, who is seventy-one years of age, had been the Moscow secretary since 1967 and was a senior member of the Politburo. His replacement was Boris Eltsin, a man of Gorbachev's generation. Like Gorbachev, Eltsin is a product of the territorial apparatus. He served for nine years as first secretary in Sverdlovsk, a major industrial region in the Urals.

Grishin's dismissal was accompanied by published reports of extensive corruption in the capital. The continuing campaign against corruption may account for the unusual Central Committee meeting held just a week prior to the congress. At that meeting Grishin was expelled from the Politburo and Eltsin was elected a candidate member (*Pravda*, Feb. 19, 1986). It was unprecedented for the party to make such leadership changes prior to a congress; in any case, it seemed certain that Grishin would be quietly dropped from the Politburo when the congress adjourned. Some political controversy must have forced the leadership to take action at that time. The dispute may have been over how far to carry the public campaign against official corruption and how to deal with the related issue of special privilege and social justice.

These issues were the subject of extended discussions in the period preceding the congress. The reform-minded economist Tatiana Zaslavskaia wrote that the worker will lose the incentive to work hard if there is a widespread sense of injustice (Zaslavskaia, 1986). The head of the procuracy published an authoritative article promising a vigorous struggle against "protectionism," abuse of privilege, and other "undesirable tendencies" of the 1970s and early 1980s. In addition to the Rostov oblast and the Uzbek republic, which had already been accused of official corruption (see p. 176), the procurator singled out the Azerbaidzhan republic. This was a surprising charge because G. A. Aliev, the current vice-premier and a Politburo member, had been first secretary of Azerbaidzhan during the period in question. The reference to Azerbaidzhan must have been approved at the highest level. Finally, the procurator criticized certain party organs for trying to protect party members from the law, saying that "every citizen, whether non-party or a member of the party, must be accountable under the law for any criminal action" (Rekunkov 1986: 50–51).

In keeping with this principle the party leadership proposed a significant change in the statutes. Under the old Party Statute (art. 12), a party member accused of a crime first would have to be expelled from the party and only then could be brought to trial. The new version of article 12 adopted by the congress called for "dual responsibility" for party members—responsibility to the state and responsibility to the party. Presumably the procuracy can now indict party members without having to wait for the party's own bureaucratic procedures to run their course.

Under the heading "Advancing to the XXVII Congress" *Pravda* published some surprising criticism of social policy and special privilege. One reader wrote that a useless party-administrative stratum stood between the party leadership and the working class. According to the reader, this stratum is not interested in serious reform but expects only a continuation of its special privileges: "There are some persons who carry a party card, but long ago ceased to be Communists."

Under the same heading, *Pravda* published a criticism of the "special" stores that serve party and government officials:

> In discussing social justice, we cannot close our eyes to the fact that party, government, labor union, economic and even Komsomol leaders often contribute objectively to a deepening of social inequality, by making use of all kinds of special eating places, special stores, special hospitals

and so on. Yes, we have socialism, and everyone should be paid in accordance with his work. Let it be just this way, without leveling [*uravnilovka*]: the director gets a higher salary, in money. But privilege should be abolished. Let the leader go along with everyone else to an ordinary store and stand in line—perhaps the lines, which everyone is tired of, would then disappear. But these "users of special goods" are hardly going to give up their privileges. What is needed is law and a thorough purge of the apparatus. (*Pravda*, Feb. 13, 1986)

Eltsin, the new candidate member of the Politburo, delivered an outspoken speech on this subject on the second day of the congress.

Why from congress to congress do we raise the same series of problems? Why has our party vocabulary acquired the alien word "stagnation"? Why, for so many years, have we been unable to eliminate from our life the roots of bureaucratism, social injustice, abuses? Why, even now, does the demand for radical changes get stuck in the inert stratum of time-servers with a party card? (*Pravda*, Feb. 27, 1986)

Ligachev, who spoke the next day, called for a halt to the discussion of social justice. Criticizing "those who spoke yesterday" (obviously a reference to Eltsin), Ligachev asserted that after Gorbachev's lengthy speech, nothing more needed to be said. Ligachev also criticized *Pravda*, probably with the February 13 article in mind (*Pravda*, Feb. 28, 1986).

Although there was general agreement on the need for a review of social policy, there were two different views within the leadership on what the term *social policy* meant. Ligachev appeared to agree with Chernenko: To work harder, one must live better (see p. 207). Indeed he acknowledged that the political stability of Soviet society depended on the party's social policy. For Ligachev, the correct policy was the established line: to provide more social and cultural services and to raise the material standard of living without touching on the sensitive issue of special privileges for officials. The more radical view, for which Eltsin emerged as the spokesman, called for "social justice" rather than a "correct social policy," and seemed willing to reexamine the system of privilege.

On the final day of the congress delegates elected new central organs, and the new Central Committee then elected the Politburo and secretariat. These elections were largely determined by the political changes of the precongress period. As was pointed out in Chapter 5, membership in the Central Committee is mainly determined by the office an individual holds. In the months preceding the congress, the leadership made some significant changes in both the government and the party in which about one hundred younger men were moved into positions that entitled them to Central Committee membership. The process of generational change, which had been slowed by Brezhnev's policy of "stability," was speeded up under Gorbachev. However, there is no evidence that Gorbachev was using the precongress elections to install a clique of his own followers in high office. With one or two exceptions, the men rising to top-level positions in the party and the government had no history of career connections with Gorbachev.

Two examples illustrate the process of political change that was taking place. In 1983, when G. V. Romanov moved into the central secretariat, he was replaced as first secretary in Moscow by L. N. Zaikov, the mayor of Leningrad. Vladimir Khodyrev, who succeeded Zaikov as mayor, was an experienced apparatchik who had spent most of his career in the Leningrad party organization, rising eventually to the post of second secretary. Khodyrev's new post as mayor entitled him to Central Committee membership, and he was duly elected by the congress.

In 1984 the minister of shipbuilding, M. V. Egorov, was quietly retired at the age of seventy-six. His successor was Igor Belousov (age fifty-five), who had spent his entire career in the shipbuilding industry and for fifteen years had been deputy minister or first deputy minister under Egorov. Belousov, too, was elected to the Central Committee by the congress.

Khodyrev and Belousov are typical of the new men coming into the Soviet political elite. Like Ligachev, they have good reason to dislike Brezhnev's policy of stability. They owe their new status to Gorbachev, and they are probably prepared to carry out a modest program of economic reform. But like the men they are replacing, the members of the new elite are products of the Soviet bureaucratic system. They are not likely to favor any overarching reform of the system in which they have made their own careers. In particular, they can be expected to obstruct any serious change in the established practice of special privileges for officials, even in the name of social justice.

The elections that concluded the congress appear to have strengthened the influence of the professional party apparatus. Of the twelve current Politburo members, nine have spent a significant part of their careers in the apparatus. Most of the candidate members are also experienced apparatchiks.

The most radical changes took place in the national secretariat, where several somewhat surprising appointments were made. Aside from Gorbachev, the only holdovers from the Brezhnev era are Dolgikh and Zimianin. Of the senior secretaries, Zaikov probably supervises industry, and Nikonov, who was appointed in 1985, is in charge of agriculture. Five new secretaries were appointed:

TABLE A.1
Soviet Leadership in March 1986

Name*	Year of Birth	Year Elected	Position
Members of Politburo			
M. S. Gorbachev	1931	1980	General secretary
G. A. Aliev	1923	1982	Vice premier
V. I. Vorotnikov	1926	1983	RSFSR premier
A. A. Gromyko	1909	1973	President
L. N. Zaikov	1923	1986	Central Committee secretary
D. A. Kunaev	1912	1971	First secretary, Kazakh republic
E. K. Ligachev	1920	1985	Central Committee secretary
N. I. Ryzhkov	1929	1985	Premier
M. S. Solomentsev	1913	1983	Chairman, Party Control Committee
V. M. Chebrikov	1923	1985	Chairman of KGB
E. A. Shevardnadze	1928	1985	Minister of foreign affairs
V. V. Shcherbitskii	1918	1971	First secretary, Ukrainian republic
Candidate Members of Politburo			
P. N. Demichev	1918	1964	Minister of culture
V. I. Dolgikh	1924	1982	Central Committee secretary
B. N. Eltsin	1931	1986	First secretary, city of Moscow
N. N. Sliunkov	1929	1986	First secretary, Belorussian republic
S. L. Sokolov	1911	1985	Minister of defense
Iu. F. Solovev	1925	1986	First secretary, Leningrad oblast
N. V. Talyzin	1929	1985	Chairman of Gosplan
Other Members of Central Committee Secretariat			
A. P. Biriukova	1929	1986	
A. F. Dobrynin	1919	1986	
M. V. Zimianin	1914	1976	
V. A. Medvedev	1929	1986	
V. P. Nikonov	1929	1985	
G. P. Razumovskii	1936	1986	
A. N. Iakovlev	1923	1986	

Source: Pravda, March 7, 1986.

*Except for Gorbachev, listed in Russian alphabetical order within
each category.

Aleksandra Biriukova began her career in the textile industry but since 1968 has been an official of the trade union apparatus. Presumably she will have responsibility for the unions, social policy, and perhaps women's issues.

Anatoly Dobryin, a career diplomat who served for more than twenty years as ambassador to Washington, apparently will take over responsibility for international affairs from Boris Ponomarev, who is now retired.

Vadim Medvedev, director of the Central Committee's department of science and education institutions, presumably will continue to supervise science and education.

Georgii Razumovskii, a product of the party apparatus in Krasnodar, who replaced Ligachev as director of the department of party and organizational work, will probably supervise cadres policy.

Aleksandr Iakovlev served for twenty years in the central apparatus, rising to the post of first deputy director of the propaganda department. In 1973, apparently after arousing Brezhnev's ire over an ideological issue, he was exiled to the post of ambassador to Canada. He seems to have made a strong impression on Gorbachev during the latter's visit to Canada in 1983 and returned to Moscow to direct an Academy of Sciences think tank on world politics. He accompanied Gorbachev on his widely publicized visit to England in December 1984, and was later promoted to director of the Central Committee propaganda department. As a party secretary he will have general responsibility for ideology.

Perhaps the most important outcome of the congress was this reinvigoration of the party secretariat. Gorbachev now has in place a staff of experienced officials who could supervise a major reform of the Soviet system. We do not yet know, however, just how far or how fast Gorbachev will move in carrying out his "radical changes." Although Gorbachev's stand on the new issue of social justice is not clear, the questions this issue raises will not go away.

REFERENCES

Ligachev, E. 1985a. Gotovias k partiinomu sezdu. *Kommunist* 12: 8–12.

————. 1985b. Sovetuias s parteie, s narodom. *Kommunist* 16: 77–92.

Rekunkov, A. 1986. Na strazhe pravoporiadka i sotsialnoi spravedlivosti. *Kommunist* 1: 42–51.

Triska, Jan F., ed. 1962. *Soviet Communism—Programs and Rules*. San Francisco: Chandler Publishing Company.

Zaslavskaia, T. 1986. Chelovecheskii faktor i sotsialnaia spravedlivost. *Sovetskaia kultura*, Jan. 23.

Index

Abramov, Fedor, 222
Academy of Agricultural Sciences, 200
Academy of Medical Sciences, 200
Academy of Sciences, 86, 95, 96, 112, 199–200, 201, 212, 217, 247
Administrative Organs, Department of (CPSU), 93, 94, 170, 172
Adventurism, 199
Afanasyev, Viktor, 225, 236, 237
Agitprop (agitation and propaganda) program, 31, 53, 54
  anti-, 178, 180
Agriculture, 215. *See also* Collective farms; Food, production; Peasants
Agriculture Department (CPSU), 107
Agursky, Mikhail, 202
Akhkmatova, Anna, 222
Alcoholism, 216–218
Aleksandrov-Agentov, Aleksandr, 148
Alexander II (emperor of Russia), 16
Alexander III (emperor of Russia), 16
Aliev, Gaidar A., 138, 149(table), 156, 158(table), 160(table), 243, 246(table)
Allen, William S., 8
Allocation of resources, 185, 186, 189, 226, 228, 232, 235, 238
"All Power to the Soviets!" 20
All-Russian Congress of Soviets (1917), 19, 20, 21, 25
All-Russian Society for the Preservation of Cultural Monuments, 230
All-Russian Theater Society, 230
All-Union Communist League of Youth. *See* Komsomol
All-Union government. *See* State government
All-union ministries, 113. *See also* Council of Ministers
Alphabet, 42
Amalrik, Andrei, 70, 74
Ambassadors, 156, 247
  in CPSU, 86
  and Supreme Soviet, 104, 107
Anarchists, 17, 21
Anarchy, 73–74
Andropov, Iurii V., 94, 109, 111, 151, 153, 162
  and corruption, 176
  and CPSU, 95

death (1984), 156, 157
  General Secretary (1982–1984), 3(table), 91, 96, 99, 108, 154–156, 157, 159, 242
  KGB chairman (1967), 116, 147, 149(table)
  and nationalities, 140
  President (1982–1984), 3(table), 104, 108
  reforms, 191, 212
Anti-party affair (1957), 86, 145–146, 199
Antireligious campaigns, 43, 44
AO. *See* Oblast, autonomous
Apolitical character, 61
Appointments. *See* Nomenklatura
April theses (Lenin) (1917), 20
Arabic, 133
Armaments, 188
Armed forces, 52. *See also* Military; Soviet Army
Armenia, 130, 141
Armenians, 42, 44, 129(table), 130, 155
  in CPSU, 78(table), 132(table)
Art, 218, 219, 221, 222
Assembly, 131
Assimilation, 125
ASSR (autonomous Soviet socialist republic). *See* Republics, autonomous
Austro-Hungary, 125
Authoritarian system, 7, 8, 33, 36, 71, 73, 74, 80, 231, 238
Authority leakage, 11, 83, 237–238
Autocracy, 2, 7, 15, 16, 32–33, 60, 61, 64, 85, 165, 228
"Autocracy, orthodoxy, nationalism," 33
Automobile Industry, Ministry of the, 113
Automobiles, 201
Autonomous Soviet socialist republic (ASSR). *See* Republics, autonomous
Awards and titles, 107
Azerbaidzhan, 121, 130(table), 139, 141, 243
  CPSU apparatus structure, 97
Azeri, 42, 129(table)
  in CPSU, 78(table), 132(table), 156

Ballet, 207, 219
Baltic region, 42, 214, 216
Baptists, 44
Bashkir ASSR, 127
Bashkirs, 129(table)
Bauer, Raymond, 46, 54, 55, 59, 205

Bauman Technical School, 51
Belorussia, 130(table), 216, 246(table)
Belorussians, 42, 44, 129
  in CPSU, 78(table), 132(table)
Belousov, Igor, 245
Berdyaev, Nicolas, 60
Beria, Lavrentii, 166
Bialer, Seweryn, 148
Bicameral legislature. *See* Supreme Soviet
Biriukova, Aleksandra, 245–247
Birth rates, 214, 215–216
Black market, 175
Bolsheviks, 18, 19, 20–21, 22–23, 27, 28, 62,
  63, 65, 66, 67, 69, 123, 134, 164, 165,
  218
Bonapartism, 199
Border Guards, 167
Border Patrol (U.S.), 167
Boris the Gypsy, 154
Brest-Litovsk treaty (1918), 21, 22, 23
Brezhnev, Leonid I., 93, 109, 153–154, 156
  and corruption, 176, 191
  and CPSU, 96, 146, 147, 232, 233, 242,
    247
  and CPSU membership, 80, 245
  and culture, 222
  daughter, 154
  death (1982), 154, 156
  education, 198
  First Secretary (1964–1966), 3(table), 91,
    146, 147, 148
  General Secretary (1966–1982), 3(table),
    117, 147–148, 149(table), 150, 151, 241,
    242
  and military, 195
  and nationalities, 140, 141, 153
  President (1977–1982), 3(table), 92, 108,
    149(table)
  reforms, 35–36
  and technology, 201
Bribery, 176, 211
Brinton, Crane, 20
Brunner, Georg, 231
Brusilov, Aleksei, 22
Brzezinski, Z. K., 58, 228
Budget system, 137
Bukharin, Nikolai, 27, 28
Bureaucracy, 4, 8–12, 13, 38, 66–67, 70, 77,
  83, 103, 118, 135, 183, 186, 187, 202,
  225–238
  centralized, 4
  characteristics, 9–10, 185
  in CPSU, 86, 87, 89, 234
  defined, 226
  function, 234–235
  personnel, 40, 41, 50, 116
  priorities, 12, 233
  reform, 35, 235
  See also Economic planning; *under* Military
Bureaucratic pluralism, 228, 235–238
Bureaucrats in CPSU, 78, 79
Burlatskii, F. M., 225
Buro, 80, 81, 83–84, 93, 131, 138
Butenko, A. P., 232, 233

Cadres, 92, 139, 147–148, 161, 242, 247
Cadres Abroad, Department for (CPSU), 95
Calendar, 21
Canada, 247
Capitalism, 5, 15, 28, 64, 67. *See also*
  Marxism, and capitalism; State capitalism
Capitalist society, 4, 5
Catholics. *See* Roman Catholics
Caucasian Christian peoples, 42
Caucasus, 42, 216
CC. *See* Central Committee
Censorship, 174, 178–179
  tsarist, 16, 17
  See also Glavlit
Central Asia, 42, 43, 45, 134, 135, 214, 215,
  216, 217
Central Auditing Commission. *See under*
  Communist Party of the Soviet Union
Central Committee (CC), 66. *See also under*
  Communist Party of the Soviet Union;
  Republics
Central Intelligence Agency (CIA) (U.S.), 167
Centralism, 7
Centralized pluralism, 228
Chagall, Marc, 218
Chebrikov, Viktor, 116, 156, 158(table), 159,
  160(table), 246(table)
Cheka (secret police), 164–165, 166
Chernenko, Konstantin U., 90, 109, 148,
  149(table), 153, 154, 206, 207
  and corruption, 176–177, 244
  and culture, 222–223
  death (1985), 156, 158
  education, 55
  General Secretary (1984–1985), 3(table), 91,
    99, 108, 155, 158, 159
  President (1984–1985), 3(table), 104, 108
  reforms, 191
Chicherin, Boris, 16
Child upbringing, 48–49, 50
China, 196
Christian Committee for Believers' Rights, 180
Chronicle of the Lithuanian Catholic Church,
  140
Chukchi, 128
Churbanova, Galina, 154
Church and state, 21, 174, 179–180. *See also*
  Religion
Chuvash, 129(table)
CIA. *See* Central Intelligence Agency
Circus, 219
Citizen complaints, 108
City
  committee, 84
  first secretary, 88, 98, 242
  government, 126, 137, 138
Civil Aviation, Ministry of, 212
Civil law, 167. *See also* Procuracy
Civil war (1918–1921), 22–23, 24
Classless society, 4, 39, 63, 73
Class struggle, 2, 3
Clergy, 79, 180
Coal Industry, Ministry of the, 187
Coast Guard, U.S., 167

Cohen, Stephen F., 35
Collective farms, 30, 47–48, 82, 83, 171
  markets, 207
Collectivism, 61
Collectivization, 30–31, 38, 47–48, 49, 50
Collegium, 113, 235
Colton, Timothy J., 147, 198, 199
Command economy, 186, 187, 191
Commercial principle, 207, 209, 212
Committee, 80, 83, 84
Commune, 46, 47, 61
Communications security, 167
Communism, 60, 70
  building toward, 2, 59, 67, 221, 241–242
  scientific, 73
Communist leaders. *See* Political leaders
Communist Party of the Soviet Union (CPSU)
  (1918), 1, 21, 122, 184
  age group in, 79–80, 148–150, 156, 159–
    161, 246(table)
  apparatus, 88–98, 99, 116–117, 152, 234–
    235, 238, 242, 244, 245
  Central Auditing Commission, 85
  Central Committee (CC), 1, 2, 7, 25, 85–
    87, 88, 89, 91, 92, 94, 99, 102, 104, 105,
    106, 107, 111, 116, 117, 118, 138, 144,
    145, 148, 149(table), 157, 158, 169, 177,
    185, 187, 194, 198, 221, 222, 230, 242,
    244–245, 247
  Congresses (all-union), 25, 31, 35, 84–85,
    87, 91, 118, 146, 148, 151, 161, 241, 244,
    247
  crisis (1964), 146, 147
  departments, 87, 92, 93–96, 97(fig.), 107,
    157, 186, 198, 221, 247. *See also
    individual names*
  as dominant, 6, 7, 24, 29, 74, 117, 184, 231
  educational level in, 79–80, 95, 96
  general secretary, 2, 3(table), 27, 28, 55,
    56(table), 85, 88, 90–92, 110, 143, 144–
    145, 152–153, 195. *See also* Second
    secretaries
  and ideology, 92, 95–96, 152, 221, 241, 247
  immobility, 242
  Left, 23, 27, 28, 29, 31
  membership, 40, 41, 45–46, 52, 56, 73, 77–
    80, 81, 82, 87, 93, 131, 132(table), 134
  membership as part of total population, 77
  official organ. *See Pravda*
  opposition to, 25
  organizational structure, 80–98
  Party Control Committee, 85, 246(table)
  Politburo, 1, 2, 6, 7, 11, 85, 86, 87–88, 89,
    90, 91, 92, 93, 94, 102, 107, 110, 111,
    117, 118, 138, 143, 144–145, 147,
    149(table), 152, 155, 156, 159, 160(table),
    161, 165, 183, 185, 186, 187, 194, 196,
    226, 238, 242, 244, 245, 246(table)
  and public support, 77
  Right, 28, 29
  schools, 99, 198
  Secretariat, 85, 87, 88, 89–90, 91, 94, 143,
    149(table), 151, 159, 160(table), 244, 245–
    247

Statute, 80–81, 82, 90, 92, 161, 241, 243
succession process, 144–150, 152–158, 162
  See also Bureaucracy; Cadres; Political
    leaders; Primary party organization; State
    government
Communist society, 3, 4, 5
Composers' union, 221
Conference level, 80, 83
Conflicts of interests, 232–233, 234
Conformity, 72, 80, 82
Conservatories, 211, 219
Constitution
  amendments, 108
  1936, 39, 108
  1977, 102, 103, 105, 108, 111, 117, 122,
    127, 141, 168, 177–180
  See also under Republics
Consumer goods, 29, 35, 136, 188. *See also*
  Second economy
Corruption, 175–177, 191, 242, 243
Council for Religious Affairs, 180
Council of Ministers, 86, 102, 104, 107, 110–
  117, 167
  and CPSU, 110, 114
  departments, 114
  directorates, 114
  Presidium, 112
  system, 114, 116–117
  See also specific ministry names
Council of People's Commissars, 21
Council of Workers' Deputies (St. Petersburg),
  18–19
Counterrevolutionary crimes, 174
Courts, 94, 136, 163, 164, 167, 168, 172, 173
CPSU. *See* Communist Party of the Soviet
  Union
Creative unions, 219, 221, 230
Crime, 163, 217
Crimean War (1853–1856), 14
Criminal law, 109, 136, 164, 167, 173–177,
  178. *See also* Procuracy
Criminal police, 171
Cuban missile crisis (1962), 195
Cultural elite, 41, 86, 104
Cultural services, 136, 218–221
Culture, Department of (CPSU), 221, 222
Culture, Ministry of, 93, 211, 218, 219,
  220(fig.)
  minister, 116, 246(table)
Currie, Kenneth, 195
Czechoslovakia, 230

Dagestan peoples, 129(table)
Dalstroi (Far Eastern Construction Trust), 166
Daniel, Iulii, 222
Daniels, Robert, 68
Dead Souls (Gogol), 46
Death penalty, 173, 174, 175, 176
Death rate, 215. *See also* Alcoholism
Decentralization, 190, 192
Decisionmaking. *See* Bureaucracy; Communist
  Party of the Soviet Union, Politburo;
  Interest groups
Decrees, 111–112, 168

Defense, Ministry of, 161, 195
  minister, 87, 88, 116, 159, 194, 196,
    246(table)
  newspaper. *See Red Star*
  See also Main Political Directorate
Defense Council, 194–195
Defense policy, 183
Demichev, Petr N., 87, 149(table), 158(table),
    160(table), 246(table)
Democracy, 63, 64, 71, 72
Democratic centralism, 81, 113
Denisov (literary character), 84
Departmentalism, 232
Departments. *See individual names*
Deputy commander for political affairs
    (*zampolit*), 197–198
De-Stalinization, 35
Detente. *See* United States, and Soviet Union
Dictatorship, 4, 5, 35, 62, 63, 65, 66, 163,
    164. *See also* Autocracy
Dictatorship of the proletariat, 1, 21, 67, 163
Directed society model, 227, 231
Directorate of Services (CPSU), 96
Disposable income, 207–208, 209
Dissidents, 69–72, 175, 178, 180, 196, 202
Districts, 126, 167
  autonomous, 128
Divorce, 21, 49, 214
Djilas, Milovan, 41
Dobrynin, Anatoly F., 246(table), 247
Doctrine. *See* Socialist realism; *under*
    Marxism-Leninism; Military
Dolgikh, V. I., 90, 149(table), 153, 158(table),
    160(table), 161, 245, 246(table)
Dostoevskii, Feodor, 218
Dostupnost (accessibility), 222
Downs, Anthony, 9, 11, 185
Drawing together of nations, 123, 125, 141
Dual subordination, 113–114, 115(fig.), 132,
    135, 171
Duma, 17
Dzhugashvili, Josif. *See* Stalin, Josif V.

Eastern Slavic peoples, 42
Economic crimes, 171, 173, 175–176, 177
Economic departments, 94, 186
Economic exploitation, 2–3
Economic growth, 188–190, 193, 206
Economic planning, 8, 11, 23, 74, 110, 139,
    187, 209
  centralized, 136, 190, 191
  policy, 183, 186, 241
  See also Collectivization; Gosplan; New
    Economic Policy; State capitalism
Economic production, 11, 139, 187, 189, 193
Economic reform, 9, 190–193, 243
Economic rights, 177
Edict, 109–110
Education, 21, 37, 38, 50, 137, 207, 208, 209–
    212
  childcare centers, 49, 209
  and CPSU, 211, 221
  and entering age, 212
  higher, 50–51, 96, 210, 211

legislation, 109
  political. *See* Komsomol
  priorities, 210
  and productive labor, 211, 212
  and social class, 50, 51, 56, 211
  See also under Republics
Education, Ministry of, 210, 211
Egalitarianism, 38–39
Egorov, M. V., 245
Elections, 105, 144, 167
Element of the State in the Future Society, The
    (Lavrov), 63
Elite, 40–42, 50, 143, 228. *See also* Oligarchy;
    Political leaders
Eltsin, B. N., 159, 160(table), 242, 244,
    246(table)
Embezzlement, 176
Engels, Friedrich, 62
Engineering industries, 188
Esenin, Sergei, 69
Esenin-Volpin, Alexander, 69–70
Estonia, 103, 126, 127, 130(table)
Estonians, 42, 44, 129(table)
  in CPSU, 78(table), 132(table)
Ethnic groups. *See* Nationality
Executive and administrative body. *See*
    Council of Ministers
Executive board. *See* Buro
Expert opinion, 236
Extraordinary Commission for Struggle with
    Counterrevolution and Sabotage. *See*
    Cheka

Faibishenko (black marketeer), 175
Family, 49–50
  law, 109
  payments, 208, 214, 216
  size, 214
Far Eastern Construction Trust. *See* Dalstroi
FBI. *See* Federal Bureau of Investigation
Federal Bureau of Investigation (FBI) (U.S.),
    167
Federal principle, 122, 126, 134, 140–141
Fedorchuk, Vitalii, 116, 153, 156, 177
Fiat company, 201
Fifth main directorate, 166–167
Finance, Ministry of, 113, 114, 115(fig.), 116,
    137
Fire protection, 171
First Circle (Solzhenitsyn), 200
First main directorate. *See* Secret intelligence
    service
First secretaries, 138, 242, 245, 246(table). *See
    also under* Republics
Five-Year Plans, 54, 92, 187, 188, 206, 241
  First (1928–1932), 30, 33
  Second, 34
  Eight through Eleven (1966–1985),
    188(table)
Fixed prices, 47–48
Food
  prices, 47–48
  production, 23, 24, 25, 30, 47
  shortages, 188

subsidies, 208
supply, 207
Foreign Affairs, Ministry of, 93, 95, 111
  minister, 111, 246(table)
Foreign exchange, 29
Foreign investment capital, 28
France, 22, 28
Freedom of conscience, 177, 179–180
Freedom of expression, 178–179
Friedgut, Theodore H., 108
Friedrich, C. J., 58, 228
Führerprinzip, 33
"Fundamental Principles of Criminal Law of
  the USSR and the Union Republics"
  (1958), 109
Furniture industry, 136
Furtak, R. K., 231

GAI. *See* State traffic police
General Department (CPSU), 96
General Staff, 195, 199
Generational change, 148–150
Georgia, 130(table), 133, 134–135, 139, 140,
  155, 176
Georgian (language), 140–141
Georgians, 42, 44, 129(table)
  in CPSU, 78(table), 132(table), 134
Germans (in Soviet Union), 43, 128,
  129(table), 130
Germany. *See* Nazi Germany; World War I
Glavlit (censorship agency), 112, 179, 218
Glebov (literary character), 81–82
GNP. *See* Gross national product
Goal displacement, 11–12
Gogol, Nikolai, 46
Gorbachev, Mikhail Sergeevich, 150, 153
  appointments of, 159
  Central Committee secretary, 149(table), 151
  and CPSU, 150, 157, 241, 245, 247
  and economy, 193, 241
  education, 150
  General Secretary (1985–), 3(table), 90,
    100, 108, 111, 122, 151–152, 158–159,
    160(table), 161–162, 246(table)
  and Komsomol, 150
  party secretary, 84, 104
  Politburo member, 151
  political standing (1984–1985), 158
  Presidium member, 108, 151
  Supreme Soviet deputy, 106–107
  and technology, 199
Gorkii, 70, 175
Gorkom. *See* City, committee
Goskino (State Committee for
  Cinematography), 218
Goskomizdat (State Committee for Publishing
  Houses, Printing, and the Book Trade),
  218–219
Gosplan (State Planning Committee), 111,
  112, 159, 187, 189–190, 207, 226, 228,
  237, 246(table)
Gosteleradio (State Committee for Television
  and Radio), 218
GPU (State Political Directorate), 165

Grain shortage (1928), 30
Grand Duchy of Moscow. *See* Muscovy
Great Britain, 143, 247
Grechko, A. A., 147, 196
Grishin, V. V., 149(table), 158(table),
  160(table), 242
Gromyko, Andrei A., 108, 116, 147,
  149(table), 158, 160(table), 161, 246(table)
Gross national product (GNP)
  military share of, 196
GULAG (Main Directorate of Camps), 171

Hammer, Darrell P., 228
Hanson, Philip, 201
Health, Ministry of, 211, 212
Health care, 207, 208, 212–213
  legislation, 109
Herzen, Aleksandr, 61–62
Higher and Secondary Specialized Education,
  Ministry of (MHE), 210
Higher Diplomatic School, 95
Higher Party School (Moscow), 99
Historical Letters (Lavrov), 63
Hitler, Adolf, 7, 33
Holloway, David, 195, 196
Homosexual acts, 174
Hospitals, 212
Hough, Jerry F., 79, 153, 228, 229, 232
Housing, 136, 137, 188, 208, 213–214

Iakovlev, Aleksandr N., 246(table), 247
Iakunin, Gleb, 180
"Ideological determinism," 59
Ideology. *See* Primary party organization;
  under Communist Party of the Soviet
  Union; Marxism-Leninism
Imperialism, 69
Inakomysliashchii. See Dissidents
Inauri, A. N., 134
Incentive, 38, 190, 191–192, 208
Indirect election, 80
Individualism, 61
Individual rights, 177–180
Indoctrination, 6, 38, 48, 52, 54, 81, 197
"Industrial and technical intelligentsia," 39
Industrialization, 5, 15, 28, 29, 33–34, 37–38,
  55, 187–188, 200, 213
  opposition to, 61
  See also Five-Year Plans
Industrial managers, 193
Industrial production, 23, 24, 25–26, 30. *See
  also* Economic production
Industry, 136, 137
Infant mortality, 213
Information distortion, 10–11, 237
Inkeles, Alex, 40, 46, 54, 55, 59, 205
Institute for Foreign Relations, 95
Institutional pluralism, 228
Intellectuals, 26, 27, 40, 63, 86, 95, 96
Intelligentsia, 16, 39, 40–41, 103
Interest groups
  associational, 183–184, 230, 231
  coalitions, 230
  institutional, 183, 184–186, 193, 228, 233
  nonassociational, 229

See also Bureaucratic pluralism; Conflicts of
    interests
Internal Affairs, Ministry of (MVD), 114, 166,
    171, 172, 177
Internal exile, 174, 175
Internal passports, 171
International Department (CPSU), 87, 94–95,
    230
International Information, Department for
    (CPSU), 95
International socialist revolution, 28
Islamic peoples, 42–43, 44–45, 121, 133, 214,
    215
Island of Hope (Perventsev), 194
Ispolkom (regional executive committee), 136,
    138
Izvestiia (newspaper), 53

Jacobs, Everett M., 135
Jails, 170
Jews, 43, 129(table), 130
    AO, 127–128
Jones, Ellen, 235
Judges, 167, 168–169
Jury, 168
Juvenile delinquency, 49

Kalinin oblast, 215(table)
Kamenev, Lev, 27, 28
Kandinskii, Wassily, 218
Kapitonov, Ivan V., 80, 81, 149(table), 157,
    158(table), 160(table)
Karlov, V. A., 107
Kaser, Michael, 213
Kassof, Allen, 52
Kazakhs, 129(table), 130
    in CPSU, 78(table), 132(table)
Kazakhstan, 130, 246(table)
Kennan, George F., 228, 229
Kennedy, John F., 195
Kerenskii, Aleksandr, 19
KGB (security police), 83, 94, 112, 114, 116,
    137, 153, 156, 166–167, 170, 171, 172,
    177, 212, 246(table)
    in CPSU, 86, 87, 88, 93, 161
    in military, 198
    republic, 134, 167
    See also GPU; NKVD; OGPU
Khakassian oblast, 127
Khodyrev, Vladimir, 245
Khozraschet. *See* Commercial principle
Khrushchev, Nikita S.
    and CPSU, 86, 93, 193, 199
    and CPSU membership, 77, 80, 86, 87, 88
    First Secretary (1953–1964), 3(table), 91,
        145, 147
    and housing, 213–214
    and military, 195
    and nationalities, 125, 153
    Premier (1958–1964), 3(table), 91, 110, 111,
        146, 147, 242
    reforms, 35, 36, 164, 190, 211, 235
    and religion, 44
Kirgiz, 129(table)

    in CPSU, 78(table), 132(table)
Kirgizistan, 130(table)
Kirichenko, A. I., 146
Kirilenko, A. P., 149(table), 153, 154
Kirov, Sergei, 31
Kirstein, T., 236
Kiselev, T. Ia., 149(table)
Knowledge Society. *See* Znanie Society
Kolkhoz. *See* Collective farms
Kolkowicz, Roman, 196
Kollarz, Walter, 44
Kommunist vooruzhenykh sil (MPD
    publication), 198
Komsomol, 51–52, 82, 86, 93, 98, 99, 133,
    150, 152, 184, 197
    newspaper. *See* Komsomolskaia pravda
Komsomolskaia pravda (Komsomol), 53
Kontrol. See Monitoring
Korean Air Lines plane shooting (1983), 154–
    155
Kosygin, Alexei N., 110, 111, 148
Kozlov, F. R., 146
Krai, 126, 150
Krasnaia zvezda. See Red Star
Krasnodar, 176, 177, 247
Kremlinology, 143–144, 154, 157, 161, 199
Kulakov, Fedor, 150, 151
Kunaev, D. A., 149, 158(table), 160(table),
    246(table)
Kuznetsov, V. V., 109, 149(table), 158(table),
    160(table)

Labor camps, 166, 170
Labor discipline, 206
    campaign, 191, 192
Labor shortage, 211, 212, 216
Lampert, Nick, 176, 177
Land redistribution, 21, 23, 26
Lane, David, 50
Language, 123, 124, 125, 126, 129, 130–131,
    140–141
Lapidus, Gail Warshofsky, 41
Latvia, 130(table)
Latvians, 42, 44, 129(table)
    in CPSU, 78(table), 132(table)
Lavrov, Petr L., 62–63, 65, 66, 67, 197
Laws, 107–108, 111, 116, 164, 168, 173–174.
    See also Supreme Soviet, legislative
    process
Lazarev, B. M., 232
League of the Militant Godless, 43, 44
Lenin, Vladimir I., 1, 2–7, 26, 27, 35, 38, 39,
    65, 73, 102, 163, 164, 183
    and Bolsheviks, 18, 20, 21
    and bureaucracy, 225
    death (1924), 2, 25
    and the family, 49
    and leadership, 59
    and Marxism, 2–3, 64–65, 66, 68
    and nationalities, 123, 125, 140
    opposition to, 18, 19, 21, 22, 23, 25
    and political party, 65–66, 72, 77, 117–118
    Premier (1917–1924), 3(table), 20, 21, 23,
        90, 110

and procuracy, 169
programs, 21–22. *See also* New Economic Policy
and welfare state, 205–206, 207, 209
Leningrad, 27, 121, 137, 245, 246(table)
"Leningrad affair," 111
Leningrad Polytechnical, 51
Leningrad University, 51
Leninism, 65–67, 70, 73, 164. *See also* Marxism-Leninism
Lenin Military-Political Academy, 198
Lenin prize, 154, 221
Letter to the Soviet Leaders (Solzhenitsyn), 70, 71, 72
Lewin, Moshe, 47, 67
Liberal democracy, 28
Liberals, 70, 71
Liberation of Labor group (1883), 64
Libraries, 179, 221
Life expectancy, 213
Ligachev, Egor K., 106(table), 156, 157, 158(table), 159, 160(table), 161, 242, 244, 245, 246(table), 247
Linz, Juan J., 7–8
Literacy, 206, 218
Literature, 218, 219, 221–222
Literaturnaia gazeta (Union of Soviet Writers), 219
Lithuania, 121, 130(table)
Lithuanians, 42, 44, 129(table), 140
in CPSU, 78(table), 132(table)
Localism, 232
Löwenhardt, John, 230
Lutherans, 42, 44
Lvov, Georgii, 19
Lysenko, Trofim, 200–201

McAuley, Alastair, 209
Madison, James, 72
Main Directorate for the Protection of State Secrets. *See* Glavlit
Main Directorate of Camps. *See* GULAG
Main Political Directorate (MPD), 96, 198
Malenkov, G. M., 145
Managerial elite, 41, 83, 213
in CPSU, 78, 88
Mandelshtam, Josip, 222
Market economy, 28
Marriage, 21, 46
Marx, Karl, 3, 39, 63, 68
Marxism, 1, 2–3, 6, 17, 29, 60, 68
and capitalism, 64, 73
creative, 72–73
as economic theory, 63–64
and revolution, 64
See also under Lenin, Vladimir I.
Marxism-Leninism, 6, 33
and dissent, 69
doctrine, 58, 59–60, 64–69, 72
ideology, 58, 59–60, 72–75, 241
Marxist parties (in Western countries), 65, 66
Marxists, 17, 62
Masses, 77
and culture, 218, 222

and political party, 66, 67
and revolution, 63, 73
Mass organizations, 184
Maternity benefits, 208, 215, 216
Mayors, 83, 98, 245
Means of production, 205
Medical training, 50–51, 211
Meditsinskaia gazeta (medical newspaper), 53
Medunov, Sergei, 154, 177
Medvedev, Roy, 196
Medvedev, Vadim, 96, 157, 246(table), 247
Medvedev, Zhores A., 155
Mensheviks, 18, 19, 22, 134
Merging of nations, 123, 124, 125, 141
Meyer, Alfred, 65
MGB. *See* State Security, Ministry of
MHE. *See* Higher and Secondary Specialized Education, Ministry of
Middle class, 70, 74
Military
bureaucracy, 183, 184, 197
counterintelligence, 167, 198
and CPSU, 94, 96, 195, 196–198, 199
in CPSU, 78, 86, 194, 197
demobilization, 195
doctrine, 195–196
high command appointments, 107. *See also* Supreme High Command
spending, 195, 196
strength, 194
in Supreme Soviet, 104
tribunals, 168
Ministries, 186–187, 190, 191, 193, 228, 233. *See also* Council of Ministers; *individual names; under* Republics
Mironov, N. R., 170
Mobilization system, 34, 52
Modernization, 21, 37, 46, 47, 55, 60
Moldavia, 130(table), 216
Moldavians, 42, 44, 129(table)
in CPSU, 78(table), 132(table)
Monarchists, 22
Monitoring, 83, 105–106, 117, 131, 234
Mordovians, 129(table)
Moscow, 13, 121, 137, 242, 245, 246(table)
Moscow Electric Lamp Plant, 81
Moscow University, 51
Moscow-Volga canal, 166
Mother Heroine of the USSR, 215
Movie studios, 11, 133, 218
MPD. *See* Main Political Directorate
Mukhitdinov, N. A., 138
Multinational people (narod), 141
Murmansk, 121
Muscovy, 13
Music, 218, 219, 221, 222
Muslims. *See* Islamic peoples
MVD. *See* Internal Affairs, Ministry of
Mzhavanadze, V. P., 176

Narod, 141
Narodnichestvo (socialist movement), 62, 64
Nationalism, 33, 34, 70, 122, 123, 125, 140
Nationality, 39, 42–43, 122, 128–130

in CPSU, 77, 78(table)
policy, 122–125, 127–128, 130–131, 140–141, 155
population, 214–216
National Security Agency (U.S.), 167
"National self-determination," 123, 124
Nation concept (*natsiia*), 141
"Natural identity of interests," 74
Natural resources, 109
Nazi Germany, 7, 8, 33
Nechemias, Carol R., 208
NEP. *See* New Economic Policy
Neva river, 137
New Economic Policy (NEP), 24–25, 26, 28, 29, 30, 163, 165
News agency. *See* TASS
Newspapers, 53
Nicholas II (tsar of Russia), 16, 17
abdication, 18, 19
Night school, 210
Nikonov, V. P., 159, 160(table), 245, 246(table)
Niskanen, William A., Jr., 185
Nixon, Richard M., 147
NKVD (People's Commissariat of Internal Affairs), 165–166, 170
Nomenklatura, 92, 94, 117, 131, 139, 143, 172, 184
Nonterritorial nationalities, 43
Nove, Alec, 187, 228, 232, 233, 237
Novosibirsk, 200
Novy mir (Union of Soviet Writers), 219

OBKhSS. *See* Economic crimes
Obkom. *See* Regional committee
Oblasts, 83, 126, 127, 135, 137, 138
autonomous (OA), 127–128
courts, 168
See also Regional committee
Occupational groups. *See* Social class
Occupational prestige, 55, 56(table)
Odom, W. E., 231, 233
Ogarkov, Nikolai, 103, 199
OGPU (united GPU), 165
Old Believers, 44
Oligarchy, 1–2, 6, 7, 85, 143, 227
Olson, Mancur, 233, 234
One-man management, 113
Opera, 207, 219
Oral decisions, 238
Order and discipline, 74
Orders, 111
Orlov, Iurii, 202
Osborn, Robert J., 208
Ottoman Empire, 13

Palaces of culture, 221
Parasite law, 164, 174
Pardons and amnesties, 107
Parrott, Bruce, 201, 202
Participation, 138
Partiinost, 72, 201, 222
Partkom, 81, 98
Party and Organizational Work, Department of (CPSU), 93–94, 157, 247
Party group, 82

Party secretaries, 84, 85, 87, 88, 90, 92, 99, 104, 110, 122, 138, 139, 152, 157, 172–173, 242
Pasternak, Boris, 219
Patriotism, 139–140
Peasants, 14, 16, 23, 24, 26, 29, 30, 37, 38, 40, 46–48, 50, 137, 166
in CPSU, 78, 79, 86
in Supreme Soviet, 104
Pelshe, Arvid Ia., 149(table), 156
Pentecostal sects, 180
People's assessors, 167–168
People's commissariat, 113
People's Commissariat of Internal Affairs. *See* NKVD
People's commissars, 21, 32
Permanent revolution, 28
Perventsev, Arkadii, 194
Peters, B. Guy, 11
Peter the Great (emperor of Russia), 13–14, 21, 60
Petrograd, 17, 19, 20, 27
Soviet, 134
Petty tutelage, 118
Philosophical Treatise (Esenin-Volpin), 69
Pilniak, Boris, 222
Plamenatz, John, 5, 65
Plekhanov, Georgii V., 18, 64, 65, 68
Pluralist school, 227–230, 233
arguments against, 231–232
Pobedonostsev, Konstantin P., 16
Poland, 13, 14
Poles (in Soviet Union), 43, 128, 129(table), 130
Police, 94, 167, 171. *See also* KGB; Political police; Secret police
Policy consultation, 236
Policy implementation, 237–238
Policy initiation, 236–237
Political cleavage, 39, 45
Political crimes, 173
Political culture, 58, 60–61, 121
Political dissent, 167. *See also* Dissenters
Political elite, 40–41, 58, 85, 104, 133, 138. *See also* Oligarchy
Political information specialists, 82, 95
Political leaders, 1, 2, 3(table), 5, 6, 26–27, 32, 33, 73, 74, 77, 121–122, 145, 148–150, 160(table), 232, 236, 238, 241, 242, 245–247
and doctrine, 59
education, 55, 98
recruitment, 52, 86–87, 98–99
social class, 55
standings (1984–1985), 158
See also individual names
Political parties, 16, 65, 72. *See also* Communist Party of the Soviet Union; Revolutionary party
Political police, 70, 164, 165, 170–171
in CPSU, 86
power, 35
Political rights, 177, 178
Political socialization, 48–56

Politinformatory. See Political information specialists
Polukarpov, Iurii I., 139
Polyclinics, 212
Ponomarev, Boris N., 87, 90, 94, 95, 106(table), 107, 149(table), 158(table), 160(table), 247
Population, 121, 214–216
Poskrebyshev, Aleksandr, 93
"Prague spring," 230
Pravda (newspaper), 53, 212, 243, 244
Presidium. *See under* Council of Ministers; Supreme Soviet
Press secretary, 95
Primary party organization (CPSU), 80, 81–84, 114, 117, 198, 234
apparatus, 89, 94
and courts, 169
See also Republics, first secretaries
Prisons, 170
Private enterprise, 24, 47, 48, 63, 207, 213
Privilege, 41–42, 50, 200, 243–244
Procedural rights, 177
Procuracy, 136, 167, 169–171, 172, 243
Production principle. *See* Territorial-production system
Productivity, 5, 207, 217
Professional people, 40, 41, 50–51, 55, 56(table)
Profit, 186–187
"Progress, Coexistence, and Intellectual Freedom" (Sakharov), 71
Proletariat, 3–4, 66
Propaganda, 6, 31, 38, 53, 82
Propaganda, Department of (CPSU), 95, 247
Prostitution, 174
Protestants, 180
Protestant work ethic, 38
Protocol, 143, 144, 154
Provisional government (1917), 19–20
Pskov oblast, 215, 216
PTU. *See* Vocational school
Public goods, 136
Public opinion, 54, 176, 196
Publishing industry, 218–219
Purges (1936–1938), 2, 31–32, 33, 198
Pushkin, Aleksandr, 14, 218

Radio, 218
Radio Moscow, 95
Railroads, Ministry of, 212
Rakhmanin, Oleg V., 95, 106(table)
Rakowska-Harmstone, Teresa, 134
Rashidov, Sh. R., 149(table), 176
Rasputin, Valentin, 222
Rasulov, Dzhabar, 138
Razumovskii, Georgii P., 246(table), 247
Real income, 208
Recall power, 105
Recentralization, 190
Red Army (1918), 21, 22, 23, 24, 26, 197. *See also* Soviet Army
Red Star (military newspaper), 53
Reform, 16–17, 35–36, 47

Reform versus conservatism, 35
Regional committee, 83, 84, 90, 92, 96–98, 116. *See also* Ispolkom
Regional government, 121–127, 138–139. *See also* Republics; Soviets
Regional Party Secretary, The (Kochetov), 84
Reign of terror (1934–1938), 31–32
Relations with Communist and Workers' Parties of the Socialist Countries, Department for (CPSU), 95
Religion, 39, 42, 43–45, 121, 140. *See also* Freedom of conscience
Repression, 4, 6
Republics, 43, 122, 130(table), 141
academies of sciences, 133
autonomous (ASSR), 103, 127, 128, 130, 131, 133–135
buros, 93
central committee, 84, 92
constitutions, 140–141
Council of Ministers, 132
CPSU apparatus structure, 96–98, 139
and education, 124, 133, 134, 137
first secretaries, 88, 132, 134, 138–139
government, 124, 126–128, 131–135
KGB, 134, 167
largest, 127
ministries, 113, 114, 115(fig.), 132–133
movie studios, 133
premiers, 86, 112, 132
presidents, 108, 132
presidium, 132
and secession, 127
second secretaries, 145
supreme court, 168, 175
Supreme Soviet, 131, 132
theaters, 133
union, 103, 126, 127, 129(table), 130(table), 131, 133, 167
Research and development, 200–201
Retarded children, 217
Revolution, 4, 62, 63, 72
1905, 16–17, 18
1917, 18–19, 20, 73
Revolution and the State (Tkachev), 62
Revolutionary government, 62–63, 65
Revolutionary party, 62, 63, 65–66
Revolution Betrayed, The (Trotskii), 67
"Revolution from above," 33, 62
Rigby, T. H., 80
Rokotov (black marketeer), 175
Roman Catholics, 42, 44, 60, 121, 140, 180
Romanov, G. V., 149(table), 156, 158(table), 159, 245
Romanov, Peter Alekseevich. *See* Peter the Great
Rossi, Peter H., 55
Rostov oblast, 176, 243
RSDLP. *See* Russian Social Democratic Labor party
RSFSR. *See* Russian Soviet Federative Socialist Republic
Rumanian (language), 42
Rural districts (raiony), 126

Rusakov, K. V., 149(table), 158(table),
    160(table)
Rush, Myron, 145
Russell, Bertrand, 4–5, 33
Russian (language), 130–131, 133, 140
Russian Empire, 13–17
Russianization, 129, 130, 131, 134
Russian Orthodox Church, 42, 43, 44, 61, 70,
    180
Russians, 42, 44, 121, 129(table), 130, 134,
    135, 138, 139, 152, 155
    in CPSU, 78(table), 132(table)
    population, 214, 215–216
Russian Social Democratic Labor party
    (RSDLP) (1898), 17–18
Russian Soviet Federative Socialist Republic
    (RSFSR), 127, 128, 129(table), 130, 131,
    133, 135, 138, 167, 175, 215–216,
    246(table)
Russia on the Eve of the Twentieth Century
    (Chicherin), 16
Russo-Japanese War (1904–1905), 14
Ryzhkov, Nikolai I., 110, 111, 156, 158(table),
    159, 160(table), 161, 246(table)

St. Petersburg, 13, 14, 15, 18. *See also*
    Leningrad; Petrograd
Sakharov, Andrei, 70, 71, 72, 96, 175, 202,
    211
SALT. *See* Strategic Arms Limitation Talks
Samizdat, 69, 70, 140, 178, 215, 217
Samogon, 217, 218
Schapiro, Leonard, 30
Schwarz, Boris, 221
Science and Educational Institutions,
    Department of (CPSU), 95, 96
Science and technology, 71, 199–202
Scientific elite, 41, 86, 95, 104, 201–202
Second economy, 176, 177, 191, 192, 207,
    211, 213, 218
Second main directorate, 166
Second secretaries, 139, 145–146, 162
Secret chancellery, 93
Secret intelligence service, 167
Secret police, 164–167
Secularization, 21
Security police. *See* KGB
Serfdom, 46
Shafarevich, Igor, 202
Sharlet, Robert, 176
Shcharanskii, Anatolii, 202
Shchelokov, Nikolai, 177
Shcherbitskii, V. V., 149(table), 158(table),
    160(table), 246(table)
Shevardnadze, Eduard, 116, 149(table),
    158(table), 159, 160(table), 246(table)
Shevchenko, Arkady N., 111
Shtromas, A., 131
Siberia, 121, 127, 174, 200, 242
Siegler, Robert W., 106
Simis, Konstantin, 176
Siniavskii, Andrei, 222
Skilled labor, 38, 39, 212
Skilling, H. Gordon, 228, 229, 230, 231

Slavic peoples, 214, 215
Slavophiles, 60–61, 62
    neo-, 70–71
Sliunkov, S. L., 246(table)
Smith, Gordon B., 170
Social class, 39, 40–42, 55
    and CPSU, 78–79, 80
Social cleavage, 39–46
Social consumption, 207, 208–209, 213
Social Democrats, 17–18, 21, 65
Social insurance, 208
Socialism, 4, 5, 8, 28, 29, 61, 67, 68, 73,
    205–206, 241, 244
    and Slavophile philosophy, 61, 62
Socialism in One Country (Stalin), 28, 68
Socialist legality, 163–164, 167, 172
Socialist realism, 221–222
Socialist revolution, 3, 17–19, 21, 62, 63, 64.
    See also International socialist revolution
Socialists, 65
Social policy, 244, 247
Social revolutionary party (anti-tsarist), 16
Social Revolutionary party (SR), 17, 19, 22,
    24, 62, 63
Social security, 208
Social stratification, 39
Society of the Blind, 230
Sokolov, Sergei L., 159, 160(table), 246(table)
Solidarity, 6–7
Solomentsev, M. S., 149(table), 158(table),
    160(table), 246(table)
Solovev, Iu. F., 246(table)
Solzhenitsyn, Aleksandr, 70–72, 200, 219
Soviet Army, 32, 130
Soviet Chess Federation, 230
Sovietization, 46, 47–48, 131
Soviet of Nationalities (Supreme Soviet), 103,
    106(table), 141
    Committee on Agriculture, 107
Soviet of the Union (Supreme Soviet), 103,
    106(table)
    Committee on Education, Science and
    Culture, 107
Soviet political system, 1–2, 6–7, 59, 73–75,
    77, 143. *See also* Bureaucracy; Communist
    Party of the Soviet Union; Marxism-
    Leninism; Socialism
Soviets, 1, 19–20, 21, 24, 82, 118
    definition, 18
    regional, 103, 135–138
Soviet socialist republics. *See* Republics
Soviet society, 74–75, 77, 81
Sovkhoz. *See* State farm
Sovnarkom 25
SR. *See* Social Revolutionary party
Ssylka. See Internal exile
Stalin, Josif V., 2, 7, 27, 32, 38, 40, 67, 68–
    69, 134, 164, 228–229
    and CPSU, 85, 86, 89, 92, 93, 132, 184
    death (1953), 2, 33, 35
    and economic planning, 187–188, 193, 200
    and the family, 49
    General Secretary (1922–1953), 3(table), 27,
    90, 110, 145

and military, 198
and nationalities, 122–123, 124–125, 127, 128, 153
opposition to, 31
and police, 165–166, 170, 171, 172
Premier (1941–1953), 3(table), 91, 110
programs, 28, 30–31, 33–34, 37
and religion, 43, 44
and science, 200–201
and Supreme Soviet, 105
See also De-Stalinization
Stalinism, 33–34, 39, 68–69
Standard of living, 30, 35, 196
State and Revolution (Lenin), 3, 5, 6
State bank, 112
State capitalism, 24, 29
State Committee for Science and Technology, 200
State farm, 47
State government
and CPSU, 117–118
elected bodies. *See* Duma; Supreme Soviet
power, 6, 74
premier, 2, 3(table), 85, 88, 104, 107, 110–111, 161, 246(table)
president, 2, 3(table), 88, 104, 108, 110, 161, 246(table)
vice-president, 108, 109
See also Council of Ministers; Regional government
Stateless society, 163, 225
State-owned enterprise, 24, 136, 186, 207, 217. *See also* State farm
State Planning Committee. *See* Gosplan
State Political Directorate. *See* GPU
State Security, Ministry of (MGB), 166
State traffic police (GAI), 171
Statute, 109, 110
Stavropol, 150, 151
Steel industry, 188
Stewart, P. D., 230
Stolypin, Piotr A., 47
Stolypin reforms, 47
Strategic Arms Limitation Talks (SALT), 147
Stravinskii, Igor, 218
Student aid, 208
Subsidies, 208, 213
Subsidized enterprises, 207
Substitution principle, 6, 80, 85
Success indicators, 189, 191
Supreme Court, 168, 171
Supreme High Command, 195, 196, 198
Supreme Soviet, 9, 102–104, 106(table), 138, 169, 194
bulletin, 110
and CPSU, 104–107
elections, 144, 157
legislative process, 109–110
Presidium, 102, 103, 105, 107–109, 110, 111, 112, 194, 195
standing committees, 105–107
Suslov, M. A., 72, 149(table), 151, 152, 153, 156, 242
Sverdlovsk, 242

Sweden, 13, 14

Tadzhikistan, 130(table), 133–134, 135, 138, 139, 172, 215(table)
Tadzhiks, 129(table)
in CPSU, 78(table), 132(table)
Talyzin, Nikolai V., 159, 160(table), 246(table)
Tarakanova, N. Ia., 169
Tashkent, 43
TASS (news agency), 112
Tatar autonomous republic, 103
Tatars, 42, 129(table)
Teachers, 45
Teacher training schools, 210
Technical intelligentsia, 202
in CPSU, 80
Technocrats, 89
"Technological chauvinism," 201
Technological innovation, 188–189, 201
Tekhnikum, 201
Television, 54, 218
Territorial-production system, 81–84, 85, 88, 96–98
Theater, 219, 221, 230
"Third revolution," 30
Third World, 67, 95
Tikhonov, Nikolai A., 104, 110, 111, 148, 149(table), 158, 159
Timasheff, N. S., 33
Tkachev, Petr, 62, 66
Tobacco, 134
Tolstoi, Leo, 218
Tomsk, 242
Totalitarian system, 33, 227, 228
defined, 7–8
Tourism, 202
Trade unions, 82, 83, 93, 221, 230
congress, 184–185
and CPSU, 86, 184
Transportation, 207
Transportation, Ministry of, newspaper. *See Whistle*
Trapeznikov, S. P., 96, 200
Treaty ratification, 107
Treml, Vladimir G., 217
Troika, 27
Trotskii, Lev, 2, 19, 20, 23, 26, 27, 28, 64, 65, 66, 67–68, 179, 197
death (1940), 2
and Marxism, 68
Trotskyism, 67–68
Tsarist government, 4, 15–17, 21, 46–47, 62, 63, 64, 197. *See also* Autocracy
Tsukanov, Georgii, 148
Tucker, Robert C., 59
Tukhachevskii, M. N., 198–199
Turkestan, 42, 215(table)
Turkey, 14
Turkmen, 121, 129(table)
in CPSU, 78(table), 132(table)
Turkmenia, 130(table)

Ukaz. See Edict
Ukraine, 130(table), 216, 246(table)
Ukrainian party, 88, 230

Ukrainians, 42, 44, 129–130, 132(table), 140
Uniate church, 180
Union of Soviet Writers, 86, 219, 221, 222, 229, 230, 236–237
United States, 71, 125, 143, 144, 167, 168, 196, 208
  and Soviet Union, 147, 157, 194, 195, 196
University, 50, 52, 133
  admission, 46, 51
  tuition, 51
  See also Education, higher
University of Tbilisi, 140
Unskilled labor, 38, 39
Upward mobility, 55–56
Uralmash (industrial firm), 111
Ural Polytechnical Institute (Sverdlovsk), 111
Urban districts, 126
Urban population, 40
Urban workers, 29, 37–38, 40, 50, 137
  in CPSU, 77, 78(table), 80, 86
  in Supreme Soviet, 103, 104
Ustinov, Dimitry F., 116, 149(table), 156, 158, 199
Uzbekistan, 130(table), 138, 176, 243
Uzbeks, 129(table)
  in CPSU, 78(table), 132(table)

Vacations, prepaid, 208
Valenta, J., 230
"Vanguard of the working class," 66, 77
Vanneman, Peter, 103
Villages
  administrative level, 126, 138
  elders, 46
  in literature, 222
  sovietization, 46, 47–48
Vocational school (PTU), 210, 212
Volga-German Autonomous Republic, 128
Von Laue, Theodore H., 38
Voronov, K., 216
Vorotnikov, Vitalii, 156, 158(table), 160(table), 246(table)
Voslensky, Michael, 144
Vuzy. See Education, higher

Wallace, Donald Mackenzie, 46
Water pollution, 137
Welfare state, 205–214
Western Allies (World War I), 22, 24
Western Europe, 60

Westernization, 14, 46, 60, 61
Western peoples, 42
What Is to Be Done? (Lenin), 65, 66
Wheeler, Geoffrey, 44
Whistle (railroad newspaper), 53
White, Stephen, 61
White-collar workers, 40, 41, 50, 211
  in CPSU, 78
White forces (anti-Bolshevik), 22, 24
White Sea canal, 166
Winter Palace, 218
Withering away of the state. *See* Stateless society
Women
  and CPSU, 41
  and homosexuality, 174
  Islamic, 43, 45, 135
  life expectancy, 213
  in Soviets, 137–138
  in Supreme Soviet, 103
  workers, 37, 216
Workers. *See* Urban workers; White-collar workers
Workers' and Peasants' Red Army. *See* Red Army
Workers' Opposition, 23, 25, 165
Working class, 64, 68
  mythology, 39
World War I, 14, 15, 17, 18, 19, 21–22
World War II, 42

Young Communist League. *See* Komsomol
Young Pioneers, 51, 52

Zagladin, Vadim V., 95, 106(table)
Zaikov, L. N., 159, 160(table), 245, 246(table)
Zakon. See Statute
Zamiatin, L. M., 95, 106(table)
Zampolit. *See* Deputy commander for political affairs
Zaslavskaia, T. I., 191–192, 200, 217, 243
Zasulich, Vera, 64
Zhdanov, A. A., 110–111, 145
Zhiguli (Soviet Fiat), 201
Zhukov, G. K., 199
Zimianin, M. V., 106(table), 149(table), 158(table), 160(table), 245
Zinoviev, Georgii, 27, 28, 31
Znanie Society, 53–54, 95, 230
Zverev, A. G., 208